Language, Identity, and Study Abroad

Language, Identity, and Study Abroad

Language, Identity, and Study Abroad
Sociocultural Perspectives

Jane Jackson

Published by

UK: Equinox Publishing Ltd., Unit 6, The Village, 101 Amies St.,
London SW11 2JW
USA: DBBC, 28 Main Street, Oakville, CT 06779

www.equinoxpub.com

First published 2008

British Library Cataloguing-in-Publication Data
A catalogue record for this book is available from the British Library.

ISBN   978 184553 141 6   (hardback)
         978 184553 142 3   (paperback)

Library of Congress Cataloging-in-Publication Data

Jackson, Jane, 1954-
  Language, identity, and study abroad : sociocultural perspectives /
Jane Jackson.
       p. cm. -- (Studies in applied linguistics)
  Includes bibliographical references and index.
  ISBN 978-1-84553-141-6 (hb) -- ISBN 978-1-84553-142-3 (pb) 1.
Language and languages--Study and teaching. 2. Foreign study. 3.
Intercultural communication. 4. Identity (Psychology)--Social aspects.
I. Title.
  P53.41155.J33 2008
  418.0071--dc22
                              2007033136

Typeset by Steve Barganski, Sheffield
Printed and bound in Great Britain by Lightning Source UK Ltd, Milton Keynes

Contents

Acknowledgments

This study was generously supported by an RGC earmarked grant from the University Grants Council of Hong Kong (Ref. 2110093) and a Direct grant from the Chinese University of Hong Kong (Ref. 2010244). I wish to express deep gratitude to the students who participated in this study and shared their thoughts and feelings with me as they crossed languages and cultures. This study would not have been possible without their co-operation and candour. They remain anonymous for reasons of confidentiality. Thanks are also due to the research assistants who conducted interviews and transcribed interview or survey data and/or proofread materials: Chan Hoi Wing, Chui Sze Yan (Amy), Pang Soi Mei (Francine), Wu Zunmin, and Pan Ping (Cathy). I am indebted to Chris Candlin and Srikant Sarangi for their wise guidance, encouragement, and critical acumen throughout the writing of this book. Finally, I wish to thank Janet Joyce and her production team at Equinox Publishing, especially Steve Barganski.

1   Introduction

With the push for internationalization on campuses across the globe, a growing number of universities and technical institutions are encouraging their students to take part in study and residence abroad programmes or vocational training schemes (e.g., apprenticeships, work placements) in a foreign language and culture. In 2004 there were 2.7 million students enrolled in higher education outside their home countries (OECD, 2007) and UNESCO estimated that this number would increase to almost 8 million by 2025 (Davis, 2003). Some join 'year abroad' programmes, while many more engage in short-term sojourns, ranging from a week to three or four months (Brockington, Hoffa and Martin, 2005).

Study abroad (SA) has changed in recent years. There is now a wider range of programme options with a greater variety of goals. Some students take part in programmes that are designed to enhance their foreign language and cultural learning; others focus on the acquisition of professional skills in another global market and do coursework in their native language while abroad. Some groups are led by faculty from the home institution; other students travel on their own and take courses with local students in the host institution. While abroad, housing arrangements may also vary (e.g., homestays, dormitories with local and other international students, shared apartments with students from the same ethnic and linguistic groups). This book will primarily focus on SA programmes that aim to enhance the language and cultural learning of participants.

Most language educators assume that informal, firsthand exposure to the native speech community coupled with formal classroom learning creates the optimal environment for learning an additional language and culture; however, what actually happens when students cross cultures in an unfamiliar land? What effect can a sojourn have on their sense of self (identity) and perceptions of the host language and culture? What factors affect their willingness to use their second language (L2) and interact with their hosts in social settings? How might the language and cultural learning of sojourners be supported on stays abroad? What steps can be taken to encourage personal expansion?

1.1   Overview of the book

This book examines the development of bilingual (multilingual) and bicultural (multicultural) identities across time and space. In particular, it explores how adult advanced English as a Foreign Language (EFL) learners view themselves and use language(s) in their home environment before travelling to an English-speaking country. During their sojourn they experience the host culture firsthand and, to varying degrees, move closer towards fluency in their L2. Some also take steps toward intercultural personhood, 'a new, alternative identity that is broader, more inclusive, more intercultural…something that will always contain the old and the new side by side to form "a third kind" – a kind that allows more openness and acceptance of differences in people' (Kim, 2001: 232–33).

Through the analysis of the stories of L2 sojourners, I argue that it is possible for aspiring bilinguals (multilinguals) to strike a balance between two (or more) languages and cultures; they may incorporate new elements into their evolving sense of self and enter the creative world of 'thirdspace'. Their struggles to find themselves and express their ideas and personalities in an L2 extend to sojourners in other parts of the world and, indeed, anyone who crosses cultures and languages, whether in their home environment or in a foreign land (e.g., migrant workers, immigrants, business people in a multicultural environment).

The examples illustrate the experiences of Chinese university students studying in a particular country in a specific SA programme; however, the issues of identity, language choice/use, race, culture, and belonging are of concern to L2 speakers in other contexts. The implications of my findings and their relationship to contemporary sociocultural perspectives are discussed in a wider framework of border crossings.

The book provides a unique, interdisciplinary perspective, addressing issues of importance to professionals in SLA (second language acquisition), second or foreign language teaching, sociolinguistics, SA research and practice, cross-cultural psychology, sociology, postcolonial studies, race relations, antiracist education, speech communication, and intercultural communication. For those who organize, supervise, or teach in SA programmes, a deeper understanding of the cultural and identity factors affecting use of the host language can lead to the planning and implementation of more effective programmes. Host families, as well as SA programme administrators who oversee homestay placements, should also find the book useful.

As the book presents the experiences and voices of L2 students, the writing is appropriate for SA students, graduate students in applied linguistics and/or intercultural communication as well as international educators. Second or foreign language students, international business people, or anyone who crosses cultures may relate to issues that are raised for discussion.

1.2   Research on study abroad (SA)

To place this interdisciplinary book in context, the following section provides a brief chronological review of developments in SA research over the last two decades, drawing on the work of applied linguists, interculturalists, cross-cultural psychologists, speech communication specialists, and international educators.

1.2.1   Insights from SLA (Second Language Acquisition) research

In applied linguistics, Freed's (1995) ground-breaking book, *Second Language Acquisition in a Study Abroad Context*, brought attention to this 'new stream' of SLA research, showcasing studies in the following areas: predicting and measuring language gains in SA settings, comparative investigations of language study at home and abroad, the acquisition of sociolinguistic competence in a SA setting, and diary studies that explore student views of learning abroad. This research ranged from large quantitative analyses to smaller, qualitative case studies; the majority were concerned with individual and group differences in linguistic outcomes (e.g., fluency, lexical and grammatical development, use of communication strategies).

Although the findings were mixed, most lent support to the notion that SA can help learners become 'fluent' speakers of the host language. When compared with foreign language students who remain in their home environment, those who study abroad 'appear to speak with greater ease and confidence, realized by a greater abundance of speech, spoken at a faster rate, and characterized, correspondingly, by fewer dysfluent-sounding silent and/or filler pause' (Freed, 1995: 26). Earlier studies also found that, 'with respect to discourse management and conversational ability, they display a wider range of communicative strategies than students who have not been abroad, demonstrating an ability to initiate, participate in, and maintain an interaction' (Freed, 1995. 26–27).

Freed (1995) also identified gaps and weaknesses in SA research. She observed that testing instruments failed to measure adequately the language growth of the more advanced students. Further, she acknowledged that applied linguists have much to learn about 'how students actually spend their time while abroad, which language they speak with friends and host families, the purposes for which and the amount of time they actually spend using the target language' (Freed, 1995: 28).

In 1995, Parker and Rouxeville's edited collection also appeared, providing insight into the preparation, monitoring, and evaluation of 'year abroad' programmes in Europe. This publication drew further attention to variations in the SA experience. It also pointed to the need for empirical studies on stays abroad as much of the available literature on student mobility was anecdotal and not research-based.

Coleman's (1997) 'state-of-the-art' article, *Residence Abroad within Language*

Study, identified key factors in SLA studies that have relevance for student sojourners, grouping them into five categories: linguistic, biographical, cognitive, affective, and personality. He concluded that there was a need for longitudinal studies of linguistic, cognitive, and affective factors impacting on the learning of L2 sojourners and, on a practical note, emphasized the need to provide adequate preparation and support for stays abroad. The same year, several large-scale projects were initiated to investigate the learning of foreign language students in European year-long SA programmes, namely, the Residence Abroad Project, the Learning and Residence Abroad (LARA) project, and the Interculture Project (Coleman, 2002).

In a review of SA in European settings, Coleman (1998) argued that limiting research to linguistic outcomes 'distorts the experience', as 'language skills are not merely mechanical: sociocultural and intercultural competence are essential elements of the true linguistic proficiency which residence abroad is expected to enhance' (Coleman, 1998: 18). These views were later echoed by Collentine and Freed who warned that 'focusing on traditional metrics of acquisition such as grammatical development might not capture important gains by learners whose learning is not limited to the formal classroom' (Collentine and Freed, 2004: 157).

Nonetheless, much of the research on study and residence abroad for language learners, as in other areas of SLA, has largely been dominated by statistical studies that have focused on proficiency outcomes (Coleman, 1997, 1998, 2006, 2007; Freed, 1998; Huebner, 1998; Isabelli-García, 2003). This product-oriented research largely ignores the social, political, and historical contexts of the learning situation and the increasingly wide range of programme variables that may constitute SA (Coleman, 2006).

More recently, a number of applied linguists have begun to investigate the processes involved in language and cultural learning using introspective techniques (e.g., diaries, first-person narratives, interviews) and such approaches as case studies and ethnographies (e.g., Carson and Longhini, 2002; Jackson, 2005; Mendelson, 2004; Murphy-Lejeune, 2002, 2003; Pellegrino, 2005). These researchers value the voices of individual student sojourners and argue that an examination of their storied experiences can make an important contribution to our understanding of the impact of stays abroad.

In the first in-depth qualitative investigation of student migration within Europe, Murphy-Lejeune (2002) delved into the experiences of 'year abroad' students. In her case studies, she presented a conceptual framework for the analysis of the European student traveller ('the stranger'). The empirical data for her study was derived from interviews with participants from three types of study abroad programmes: Erasmus (a European Commission exchange programme that enables students in 31 European countries to study for part of their degree in another country), bilateral language assistantships, and a French business school programme. Drawing on these oral narratives, Murphy-Lejeune illustrated how the experience of mobility can change students' concepts of 'space' and 'home' as they adapt to their unfamiliar environment and participate in new social scenes. She observed that 'the spatial, temporal, social and symbolical disorientation which strangers experience may provoke a personal 'crisis' during which their identity appears somewhat fragmented or torn' (Murphy-Lejeune, 2002: 27).

Pellegrino (1998, 2005) also drew on the insights of adult L2 sojourners to better understand the challenges they faced and the strategies they employed to overcome difficulties and adapt to the host environment. In her investigation of 76 American learners of Russian who participated in SA programmes in Russia (ranging from four to twelve months), she explored the factors that complicate self-presentation in an L2 (e.g., anxiety, age, gender, risk-taking, self-esteem). Pellegrino discovered that 'learners often reject or reduce their interactions in the second language in order to maintain and protect an ideal self-image. This avoidance of language use ultimately reduces their opportunities for learning and growth and can even inhibit the learner from continuing language study' (Pellegrino, 2005: 2).

She argued that introspective data (e.g., SA narratives) can offer valuable insight into sojourner perceptions of language and help to understand better the quality and impact of their language learning experiences (both inside and outside the classroom). Qualitative data can help gauge their personal, social, linguistic, and academic development during stays abroad and provide vital information for programme administrators and teachers.

Other applied linguists with a particular interest in SA have focused on the cultural dimension in language learning. In Europe, where there is a long tradition of stays abroad, Byram (1997) and Byram and Zarate (1997a, 1997b) examined the nature of intercultural competence and communication, offering a descriptive model of intercultural communicative competence (comprising linguistic, sociolinguistic, discourse, and intercultural components), building on earlier notions of communicative competence put forward by Canale and Swain (1980), Hymes (1972), and van Ek (1986). Byram's (1997) model takes into account linguistic and sociocultural factors in intercultural communication and positions the 'intercultural speaker' as a mediator between the foreign and his/her own language and culture. This has prompted further investigations of the development of intercultural communicative competence in sojourners (i.e., the edited collections of Alred, Byram, and Fleming, 2003 and Byram and Feng, 2006; Medina-López-Portillo, 2004; Pellegrino, 2005).

At the Center for Advanced Research on Language Acquisition at the University of Minnesota in the United States, applied linguists recently joined hands with intercultural educators on a large-scale SA initiative. Cohen, Paige, Shively, Emert, and Hoff (2005) investigated the effectiveness of language and culture strategy materials that were specially designed to enhance the language competence and intercultural communication skills of their students on stays abroad. Their collaborative venture drew further attention to the benefits of integrating language and cultural learning in the preparation and support of L2 sojourners.

1.2.2   Insights from cross-cultural psychology and intercultural/international relations

Applied linguists are not the only professionals interested in SA research and practice. In the last fifty years, a number of cross-cultural psychologists, speech communication specialists in intercultural relations, and international educators have concentrated on the affective, behavioural, and cognitive consequences of sojourns of different types and lengths (Cushner and Karim, 2004; Ward, Bochner, and Furnham, 2001). Their research has examined a range of issues including the variety and impact of pre-sojourn preparation (e.g., Bennett, 1986; Landis, Bennett, and Bennett, 2004). In general, their findings have shown that well-designed training programmes can be beneficial for all phases of the sojourn experience, from pre-departure to re-entry, by providing students with a frame of reference for interpreting and coping with their cognitive, affective, and behavioural reactions to their new environment (Cushner and Karim, 2004).

Other dimensions of the SA experience that have been investigated by inter-culturalists include: the individual, interpersonal, social, organizational, and eco-nomic factors that predict adjustment across cultures (pre-departure variables) (e.g., Kim, 2002; Kim and Goldstein, 2005; Oguri and Gudykunst, 2002; Yang, Noels, and Saumure, 2006).

By way of surveys, Oguri and Gudykunst (2002) investigated the influence of self-construals (e.g., whether individuals consider themselves as separate from others or interconnected with others) and communication styles on the psychological and sociocultural adjustment of 175 Asian international students in the United States. They hypothesized that a close fit between the sojourners' self-construals and the self-construal that predominates in the host culture would predict their psy-chological adjustment. Their study revealed that independent self-construal in this context predicted psychological adjustment whereas interdependent self-construal did not. As expected, sensitivity to others' behaviour and use of direct communi-cation, which is the norm in the host culture, were correlated with successful sociocultural adjustment.

In Canada, Yang et al. (2006) examined how self-construals (an individual's conceptualization of the self) and communicative competence in the language of the host culture contribute to the cross-cultural adaptation of international students. Rely-ing on self-reports, 81 international students with a collectivist cultural orientation were compared with 135 Canadian-born students; hierarchical regression revealed that independent self-construal and English language self-confidence predicted psychological adjustment. Their findings suggested that communicative competence in the host language provides 'a vehicle of self-expression and identity negotiation' which is psychologically beneficial.

As well as the psychological reactions of sojourners to a new cultural environment (e.g., Paige, 1993; Ward et al., 2001), the influence of social interaction and host receptivity on sojourner identity, adjustment, and adaptation has also been on the research agenda (e.g., Bennett, 1998; Kashima and Loh, 2006; Kim, 2002a, 2005; Ting-Toomey, 1999, 2005).

In Australian universities, Kashima and Loh (2006) employed a survey to investigate the acculturation, identity, and social networks of 100 Asian international students who had been in the country for between one month and seven-and-a-half years. The findings suggested that the more local and international ties the students developed in the host culture, the better adjusted they were psychologically. These students also displayed greater knowledge of the host culture than those who were less connected to locals. English fluency facilitated involvement in the host culture and identification with their host institution. Heritage cultural identity was stronger among those who mixed regularly with other international students. Interestingly, the length of their stay in Australia did not play a role. The researchers also observed that the social identities of international students may change dynamically during the course of a sojourn.

Culture learning on sojourns (e.g., M. Bennett, 1993; Bennett and Bennett, 2004), including the development of intercultural competence and intercultural personhood (e.g., Bennett, 1998; Collier, 1989; Gudykunst and Kim, 2003; Kim, 2006; Wiseman, 2002), has been the subject of many studies, although most have focused on outcomes rather than the learning process itself.

At a college in Japan, Ingulsrud, Kai, Kadowaki, Kurobane, and Shiobara (2002) developed a holistic model to assess the cross-cultural experiences of their undergraduates, all of whom were required to participate in a short-term SA programme. Prior to the sojourn, 176 students took a cross cultural communication course and conducted a small-scale ethnographic project in their home environment; during this phase they began developing a cross-cultural portfolio. While abroad, they kept a reflective observation journal and added other material to their portfolio. Post sojourn, multiple raters employed a quantitative instrument to: 1) identify evidence of critical thinking in the student-generated text and 2) measure the degree of cross-cultural awareness. Interrater reliability was high, suggesting that impressionistic evaluation of portfolio contents, coupled with a quantifiable analysis of the text, can provide a useful means of assessing cross-cultural awareness.

SA researchers have also attempted to understand the effect of programme duration on the academic, cultural, and personal development of sojourners (e.g., Dwyer, 2004; Medina-López-Portillo, 2004). As Vande Berg (2004) observed, the conventional wisdom inherited from the 'Junior Year Abroad' paradigm is that if SA is to be meaningful, students must be in the host environment for at least one academic year. But is this the case?

While most research points to the benefits of longer sojourns (e.g., a year abroad), in a survey of 3,700 former SA participants, Dwyer found that, when carefully designed, short intensive programmes can have a substantial impact on student development in personal and cultural domains:

> While it requires very careful educational planning, expert implementation, and significant resources to achieve these outcomes in a shorter-term length, the results of this study should encourage study abroad educators and should reinforce the value of short-term programming of at least six weeks duration. Whether these results would hold for the increasingly popular 1–5 week programs is unknown (Dwyer, 2004: 161).

Chieffo and Griffiths (2004) also explored the merits of short-term SA programmes by way of a self-perception survey that they developed to measure 'global awareness'. This construct included the following elements: intercultural awareness, personal growth and development, awareness of global interdependence, and functional knowledge of world geography and language. They surveyed nearly 1,200 American students in a broad range of academic disciplines and found that those who participated in a five-week sojourn developed more 'global awareness' than those who studied at home during the same time period.

Medina-López-Portillo (2004) measured changes in the intercultural sensitivity and identity of 28 American university students who studied abroad in two language-based programmes in Mexico, one lasting 7 weeks, the other 16 weeks. Making use of pre- and post- measures (both quantitative and qualitative), she found that the two groups differed in the ways they defined culture and discussed cultural differences. Those who spent a longer time in the host environment became more aware of the impact of culture on all aspects of life. They displayed a deeper awareness of cultural differences, a greater depth of knowledge of the host culture, and more cultural sensitivity. Significant differences were also found between the two groups with regard to their perceptions of their cultural identity. Those who had taken part in the shorter programme experienced a greater change, which the researcher attributed to the fact that those in the longer programme had a more strongly defined cultural identity prior to the sojourn. Variations were also found in the groups' perceptions of their home country after their return; those in the shorter programme became more nationalistic than those in the longer programme.

The re-entry culture shock and adjustment of sojourners (e.g., Gaw, 2000; Martin and Harrell, 2004) has not attracted as much attention as other elements of SA, although this is changing. The complex nature of the re-entry process is steadily gaining more recognition. In particular, the challenges it poses to returnees (and their family and friends at home) and the role that it plays in the personal development and identity expansion of sojourners are now being examined from a variety of perspectives.

Citron (1996) investigated the re-entry experiences of 16 American undergraduates who had spent 14 weeks studying Spanish language and culture in Spain. Qualitative data from before, during, and after the SA programme were collected and analysed collectively and individually. The re-entry experience was found to impact on four dimensions of the participants' lives: physical, interpersonal, cultural, and personal. Whether they had lived in Spain according to American cultural norms, the norms of the sub-culture that they had created among themselves or the host culture's norms affected their re-entry. Those who had insulated themselves from meaningful contact with their Spanish hosts experienced fewer symptoms of culture shock on re-entry. By contrast, those who had embraced the host culture (e.g., norms, values, behaviours) were more affected by the re-entry and experienced more changes in the personal domain (e.g., questioning their own lifestyle, developing new career goals).

Sussman (2002) explored the relationship between cultural identity and repatriation experience among 113 Americans whose sojourns in Japan had ranged from 6 to 72 months. Survey results revealed that the repatriation experience was linked to shifts in cultural identity but, unexpectedly, overseas adaptation and repatriation experiences were not found to be directly associated. Home-culture identity strength was found to inversely predict re-entry culture shock; those who suffered the most on re-entry had a weak cultural identity. As predicted by the Cultural Identity Model, ratings of increased estrangement from American culture or feeling 'more' Japanese following a sojourn were correlated with high repatriation distress. Interestingly, those who experienced a more global identity shift displayed higher satisfaction with their lives.

While cross-cultural psychologists and international communication specialists have illuminated our understanding of the impact of sojourns, most have not delved into the actual experiences, perceptions, and transformations of individual L2 sojourners; similar to the SLA field, much of their empirical research has consisted of large-scale surveys and statistical analyses.

1.2.3   Language and cultural learning in situ

Context is now understood to play a significant role in language and cultural learning and identity expansion (e.g., Collentine and Freed, 2004; Dufon and Churchill, 2006; Segalowitz, Freed, Collentine, Lafford, Lazar, and Díaz-Campos, 2004). What are the implications of this? Studies that focus on statistical measures of linguistic and cultural gains will remain important in SLA and intercultural research;

however, we must also look much more closely at the complex, multifarious nature of SA environments and their impact on language and cultural learning. Researchers who investigate the sojourn experience can no longer ignore variations in the design and delivery of SA programmes. It is important to consider the sociocultural, political, and historical factors that may affect a student's intercultural adjustment and willingness to use the host language in social situations.

> [W]hen thinking about what effects study abroad (or any particular learning context, for that matter) might have on second language learning, it is very important to consider more than whether students make greater gains in one environment than in another. Researchers need to look beyond simple quantitative issues such as how much exposure to the target language students have or what level of language ability they bring with them to the learning situation. We need to more fully explore some of the *qualitative* aspects of learning afforded by a particular context. This means looking at the *nature* of the communicative interactions available to the learner and actually entered into, taking into account all communicative opportunities, including what transpires inside, as well as outside, the classroom… We need to ask in what ways the learner is prepared for the special challenges presented by a specific learning context. We also need to consider how those things a student brings to a learning environment change as a function of the experiences afforded by that learning environment (Segalowitz et al., 2004: 15).

To enhance the experiences and development of L2 sojourners, we need to know what actually happens during stays abroad, especially on short-term sojourns, which are growing in popularity but are under-researched. A deeper understanding of the language and cultural learning and identity expansion of student sojourners before, during, and after stays abroad will have implications for others who cross cultures (e.g., immigrants, migrant workers, non-governmental international officers). Finally, SA research and development can benefit from an interdisciplinary approach, bringing to bear different theoretical perspectives and orientations to examine issues of importance to both sojourners and educators.

1.3   Aims of the book

This interdisciplinary book draws on sociocultural notions of language, culture, and identity, integrating recent developments in SLA, social cross-cultural psychology, and intercultural/international relations. It is based on the premise that student sojourners and educators, and, indeed, anyone who interacts across cultures (whether at home or abroad), could benefit from a heightened awareness of the language, identity, and cultural factors that impact on the development of intercultural communicative competence. As such, it provides insight into potential trajectories that may or may not lead to intercultural personhood.

The aim of this book is twofold: first, it makes use of poststructuralist, socio-cultural perspectives to address the nature of language learning, identity (re)construction, and the development of intercultural communicative competence and intercultural personhood in L2 sojourners. For example, Chapter 2 explains the Bakhtinian conceptualization of dialogism (Bakhtin 1981, 1984, 1986), while Chapter 3 outlines the identity negotiation theory (INT) (Ting-Toomey, 1999, 2005), which builds on the earlier work of social identity theorists, symbolic inter-actionists, and relational dialectics theorists. I extend this identity negotiation process to the L2 sojourn, hypothesizing that it may be linked to the willingness of L2 sojourners to use the host language (e.g., in informal, social settings), their degree of participation in the host community (Lantolf, 2000; Lave and Wenger, 1991; Pavlenko and Lantolf, 2000; Wenger, 1998), and the development of their ability to perform appropriate linguistic and nonverbal behaviours when coming into contact with the host culture (Byram, 1997; Byram and Zarate, 1997a, b). Thus, the relationship of identity to intercultural communicative competence is probed along with the notion of 'intercultural personhood' and the creation of 'thirdspace', a dialectical process in which the sojourner sees the relation of Self and Other from a third place and point of view (Bakhtin, 1981, 1986; Kramsch, 1999a; Ting-Toomey, 1999).

The second goal of the book is to test contemporary sociocultural perspectives by investigating the actual experiences of L2 sojourners, following them from their home environment to the host culture and back again. I explore their exhilarating, and sometimes turbulent, journeys of discovery of Self and Other to illustrate the complex, deeply personal processes of language and cultural learning and identity (re)construction. Similar to the work of such applied linguists as Kanno (2003) and Norton (2000), the voices of the often underrepresented and marginalized (L2 speakers) dominate the discussion, recognizing the merits of using first-person narratives to link theory with practice.

Bearing in mind the dramatic increase in student mobility and proliferation of SA programmes, this book aims to inform educators about the complex issues involved when people from different linguistic and cultural backgrounds come into contact. With global markets and enhanced communication networks worldwide, people in professions and workplace situations may also find themselves in intercultural encounters either in their home environment or on assignments outside their own country. As a consequence, language enhancement and intercultural learning are assuming greater value and relevance today and this is certain to increase in the future.

1.4   Outline of content

In Chapters 2 and 3 I provide insight into the theoretical underpinnings of the book. Chapter 2 focuses on Vygotsky's (1978, 1986) SCT (sociocultural theory), Bakhtin's (1981, 1986) conceptualization of dialogism and cultural-linguistic hybridity, and Bourdieu's (1977, 1991) theory of language, power, and social life. Their work has profound implications for our understanding of the language and cultural learning of L2 sojourners.

Building on the constructs presented in Chapter 2, Chapter 3 focuses on post-structural theories of language, identity, and cultural socialization (e.g., Norton, 2000; Ochs, 1991; Weedon, 1987), a contemporary theory of situated learning – communities of practice (CoP) (Lave and Wenger, 1991), and Ting-Toomey's (1999, 2005) integrative identity negotiation theory (INT). Current understandings of 'thirdspace' and the 'intercultural speaker' are also examined in relation to border crossings.

In Chapter 4 I introduce my ethnographic study of Hong Kong university students who took part in a five-week sojourn in England. After describing their SA programme, I introduce the methodological framework for my investigation of their language and cultural learning and identity (re)construction in both their home environment and host culture. I outline my roles and discuss the procedures involved in data collection and analyses. After explaining the rationale for focusing on four of the participants: Ada, Cori, Elsa, and Niki (pseudonyms), I provide an overview of the organization and content of the individual case studies that are featured in Chapters 5 to 8.

In each case-study chapter, I explore the personal journey of discovery of one of the women, travelling with her from Hong Kong to England and back again. Therefore, each chapter is divided into three main parts: pre-sojourn, sojourn, and post-sojourn. In the first part, I offer insight into the young woman's pre-sojourn characteristics, paying close attention to her identities, language, and cultural background. I also reveal her aspirations and concerns about living in an English-speaking country. In the next part, I track her intercultural adjustment during the five-week stay in England. I discuss her growing awareness of the unique aspects of her own culture and identity as she mediated her new world through an L2. To more fully appreciate the nature of her journey, her experiences are presented in chrono-logical order, capturing both highs and lows. For this reason, the sojourn section of each case chapter has multiple sub-sections as each episode is described and analysed in sequence. In the next section, I offer insight into the young woman's post-sojourn perceptions as she reflects on her experiences abroad as well as her re-entry. Throughout I analyse the findings in relation to the theoretical notions pre-sented in Chapters 2 and 3, paying particular attention to language and cultural socialization, and identity formation and change. In the process, I problematize the INT and the construct of CoP, addressing issues of power, access, and agency.

Chapters 5 and 6 present the journeys of Ada and Cori, who seemed to struggle more to come to terms with their identity and use of English in an unfamiliar sociocultural setting. Chapters 7 and 8 focus on Elsa and Niki, women who made further progress down the road to intercultural personhood. While they, too, experienced 'culture bumps' and bouts of homesickness, they were able to push past this and, with a spirit of adventure and a higher degree of openness, more fully embrace their new linguistic and cultural environment.

In Chapter 9 I link the pre-sojourn, sojourn, and post-sojourn findings with the theoretical notions that were discussed in Chapters 2 and 3. In particular, I explore: the links between language, culture, and identity (re)construction and problematize assumptions of the INT and the construct of CoP in relation to stays abroad.

In Chapter 10 I advocate critical praxis as a means of addressing the complex nature of language and cultural learning on stays abroad. Through concrete examples, I illustrate the benefits of engaging in the dialectical process of action-reflection-transformative action to stimulate innovation and change in SA/homestay practices. I also offer suggestions for future research to deepen our understanding of the sojourn experience and, ultimately, to lead to better practices in the design and delivery of SA programmes, including homestay placements.

2 Vygotskian, Bakhtinian, and Bourdieusian perspectives

In Chapters 2 and 3 I outline the theoretical framework for my investigation of the language and (inter)cultural learning of student sojourners, drawing on sociocultural (and social psychological) perspectives that have been put forward by educators from a variety of disciplines in different corners of the globe. In this chapter I synthesize specific aspects of Vygotskian and Bakhtinian theories that link language, culture, context, and identity (selfhood) – core elements in the journeys of L2 sojourners and, in truth, anyone who interacts across cultures. I then discuss the work of Pierre Bourdieu, exploring his concepts of field, habitus, and capital, which heightened my awareness of the complex relationship between power (resistance and inequality), social context, and linguistic practices. This historical groundwork helped to frame my review of poststructuralist notions of identity, language and cultural socialization, and intercultural mediation. The discussion of these contemporary elements is presented in Chapter 3.

For decades, psycholinguistics has dominated applied linguistics research, largely depicting the acquisition of grammatical, lexical, and phonological forms of a language as an isolated individual endeavour (e.g., Mitchell and Myles, 2004). This orientation, however, ignores the situatedness of language learning in particular social, cultural, political, institutional, and historical settings (e.g., Lantolf, 2002; Pennycook, 2001). Recognizing this, interest in sociocultural dimensions of language learning has grown in recent years, raising the profile of SCT (sociocultural theory) in SLA (second language acquisition) research and practice. Social psychological research on language and communication is also gradually developing 'a greater focus and theoretical consideration of the emergent aspects of communication, a more qualitative approach, and greater emphasis on the reciprocal relations among contexts (intergroup and interpersonal, motives, and the interaction process itself)' (Weatherall, Gallois, and Watson, 2007: 2). It is within this context that I surveyed the literature, bearing in mind my investigation of the situated learning of L2 sojourners.

Throughout this chapter and the next, I explain some of the key terms and concepts that resurface when we look at the actual linguistic and (inter)cultural experiences of L2 students, both in their home environment and in the host culture. Chapters 5 to 8, which present their stories, problematize the extent to which these theoretical constructs account for their linguistic and (inter)cultural learning and identity reconstruction.

2.1   Vygotskian and Bakhtinian contributions

To better understand the complex connections between language learning, culture, and identity (the self), I synthesize some elements of the work of two Soviet visionaries: Lev Vygotsky (1896–1934), a developmental psychologist, and Mikhail Bakhtin (1895–1975), a philosopher, literary critic, and cultural theorist. Although from different disciplines, they shared the view that language is always immersed in a social context, and its primary aim is to facilitate communication and understanding between people.

Bakhtin (1981, 1986) theorized about the connections between identity, culture, and language but did not develop an explicit theory of language learning or address pedagogical issues. Nonetheless, his conceptualization of dialogue is very useful for this discussion, especially when linked to Vygotsky's (1978, 1986) psychological theory of cognitive development. In the following sections, I explore connections between Vygotskian and Bakhtinian notions of: language, thought, and dialogicality; the zone of proximal development (ZPD) and 'outsideness'; language, culture, and intercultural dialogue; and identity (re)construction and language development – significant issues in L2 contexts and border crossings.

2.1.1   Language, thought, and dialogicality

Vygotsky is considered the founder of the cultural-historical approach to human development, which is usually referred to as SCT in applied linguistics and SLA research. Despite the label 'sociocultural', Lantolf cautioned that it is 'not a theory of the social or of the cultural aspects of human existence…it is, rather…a theory of mind…that recognizes the central role that social relationships and culturally constructed artefacts play in organizing uniquely human forms of thinking' (Lantolf, 2004: 30–31). For Vygotsky (1978, 1986, 1987), then, cognitive development and higher order psychological functions (e.g., language) are socially and culturally determined. A notion central to SCT is that language, 'the linguistic tool for thought', serves as a significant means of mediation in mental and social activity:

> The central and distinguishing concept of sociocultural theory is that higher
> forms of human mental activity are *mediated*. Vygotsky (1987) argued that

just as humans do not act directly on the physical world but rely, instead, on tools and labour activity, we also use symbolic tools, or signs, to mediate and regulate our relationships with others and with ourselves. Physical and symbolic tools are artefacts created by human culture(s) over time and are made available to succeeding generations, which often modify these artefacts before passing them on to future generations. Included among symbolic tools are numbers and arithmetic systems, music, art, and above all, language. As with physical tools, humans use symbolic artefacts to establish an indirect, or mediated, relationship between ourselves and the world. The task for psychology, in Vygotsky's view, is to understand how human social and mental activity is organized through culturally constructed artefacts and social relationships (Lantolf, 2000: 80).

Through sustained participation in socioculturally and institutionally organized practices, Vygotsky (1978, 1987) argued that we gradually learn the communicative intentions and specific perspectives that are embedded in them. Therefore, in his view, human learning and thinking processes should be located within particular 'activity settings'. That is, the structured social networks and cultural practices available to learners must be acknowledged as well as the mediational processes impacting on learning in those environments (Lantolf, 2000, 2005; Lantolf and Thorne, 2006).

In his work, Vygotsky focused on discourse and interaction between real interlocutors (e.g., pairs, small groups) engaged in educational activities within particular sociocultural and historical contexts. While he concentrated on the language acquisition and cognition of children, his contemporary was preoccupied with dialogue and creative expression in a wider range of verbal texts (both written and oral forms). Even so, there is common ground between them. Both were intrigued by the situatedness of speech (e.g., the use and function of language in specific sociocultural contexts) and were convinced that learning, including language and cultural development, begins in our social worlds.

For Bakhtin, dialogue is the very foundation of culture and human development: 'to be means to communicate dialogically. When the dialogue is finished, all is finished...' (Bakhtin, 1984: 213). In his view, it is a special form of interaction that lies at the heart of the creative nature of our existence. Emerson explained its significance in Bakhtinian terms:

By dialogue, Bakhtin means more than mere talk. What interested him was not so much the social fact of several people exchanging words with one another in a room as it was the idea that each word contains within itself diverse, discriminating, often contradictory 'talking' components. The more often a word is used in speech acts, the more contexts it accumulates and the more its meanings proliferate. Utterances do not forget. And by their nature they *resist unity and homogenization* – two states that Bakhtin…considered akin to death. Understood in this way, dialogue becomes a model of the creative process. It assumes that the healthy growth of any consciousness depends on its continual interaction with other voices, or worldviews (Emerson, 1997: 36).

Throughout his life, Bakhtin argued that the study of language and culture should address dialogic relations between cultures, between people, and between an individual and his/her culture(s) in particular social contexts (Holquist, 2002; Vitanova, 2005). He maintained that these relations, as well as language and cultural development, must be linked to the concepts of identity and difference between Self and Other.

2.1.2   The zone of proximal development (ZPD) and 'outsideness'

One of Vygotsky's most significant contributions to cultural and educational psychology is his construct of the zone of proximal development (ZPD), which he defined as:

> [T]he distance between the actual developmental level as determined by independent problem solving and the level of potential development as determined through problem solving under adult guidance or in collaboration with more capable peers (Vygotsky, 1978: 86).

Participation, collaboration, and social interaction are core elements of the ZPD, and it is in this developmental space that learning is dialogical. In the classic interpretation of the ZPD,[1] participants in this learning process must be different from each other for learning to occur. That is, the interaction should involve an expert who is more knowledgeable and has more experience than the learner or novice (Lantolf and Thorne, 2006).

There are some parallels between Vygotsky's ZPD and Bakhtin's concept of 'outsideness' in dialogue; both involve at least two interlocutors who are different (e.g., in terms of knowledge, expertise, ideas). For Bakhtin, difference is a vital element in the process of communication. Without it, he argued, 'genuine interaction of consciousnesses' is rendered impossible and a monologue rather than a genuine dialogue ensues: '[o]ne voice alone concludes nothing and decides nothing; two voices is the minimum for life, the minimum for existence' (Bakhtin, 1984: 213).

Of particular relevance to this discussion is Bakhtin's (1986) linkage of 'outsideness' to dialogue across cultures. He believed that interlocutors should enter the other culture and attempt to 'see the world through its eyes'. This is akin to the 'ethnorelative perspective' that is advocated by interculturalists today (e.g., Bennett and Bennett, 2004; Ting-Toomey and Chung, 2005) and discussed further in Chapter 3. Bakhtin extended this notion by advising interlocutors to also remain outside the other culture, developing their own unique perspectives. For him, this 'outsideness' is crucial to achieving genuine understanding in intercultural encounters:

> [E]ntry as a living being into a foreign culture, the possibility of seeing the world through its eyes, is a necessary part of the process of understanding it; but if this were the only aspect of this understanding, it would merely be duplication and would not entail anything new or enriching... In order to understand, it is immensely important for the person who understands to be *located outside* the object of his or her creative understanding – in time, in space, in culture...in the realm of culture, outsidedness is a most powerful factor in understanding (Bakhtin, 1986: 6).

It is important to note that Bakhtin and Vygotsky differed somewhat in their perception of the status and roles of interlocutors in a communicative event such as this. For the former, dialogue involves communication between people who are equal but different. Although his notion of 'outsideness' implies a measure of disparity, Bakhtin (1986) did not explicitly acknowledge it; rather, he emphasized the worthwhile contributions made by both interlocutors. In fact, he viewed dialogue as an opportunity for the learning and personal expansion of *both* interlocutors ('equal selves'), irrespective of age, experience, or level of expertise. Vygotsky, on the other hand, spoke candidly about the inequality of interlocutors in the ZPD. In his framework, he referred to the interaction between a learner (novice) and teacher (expert) who do not have equal status or knowledge. As an educational psychologist, he was convinced that children learn best when engaged in activities with people who are more knowledgeable.

Through dialogue with people from other linguistic and/or cultural backgrounds, Bakhtin (1986) argued that one may be exposed to new ideas, utterances, values, and worldviews. If truly open to this process, he was convinced that significant personal growth could occur in both interlocutors: 'The person who understands must not reject the possibility of changing or even abandoning his already prepared viewpoints and positions. In the act of understanding, a struggle occurs that results in mutual change and enrichment' (Bakhtin, 1986: 142). Emerson outlined some implications of Bakhtin's views for those who cross cultures:

> Bakhtin...would recommend that I not seek out people *just like myself* for the sake of security or identity. It narrows my scope and thus is too much of a risk; should I change or the environment change, I might become extinct...

Any instinctive clustering of like threatens to reduce my 'I' and its potential
languages to a miserable dot. Those who surround themselves with 'insiders'
– in heritage, experience, appearance, tastes, attitudes toward the world – are
on a rigidifying and impoverishing road. In contrast, the personality that
welcomes provisional finalization by a huge and diversified array of 'authors'
will command optimal literacy. It feels at home in a variety of zones; it has
many languages at its disposal and can learn new ones without trauma. From
its perspective, the world appears an invitingly open, flexible, unthreatening,
and unfinalized place (Emerson, 1997: 223–24).

While convinced that the learning of another culture or language offers a way to
broaden or enrich oneself, Bakhtin warned against simply replacing one culture or
language with another. He then offered a somewhat idealistic notion of what should
happen in an intercultural event: 'A dialogic encounter of two cultures does not
result in merging and mixing. Each retains his own unity and *open* totality, but they
are mutually enriched' (Bakhtin, 1986: 7). Dialogue, he theorized, 'transcends the
enclosed and one-sided nature of the cultures' respective meanings' (1986: 508).

While he acknowledged differences between speakers, Bakhtin's (1981, 1986)
position minimizes issues of power, status, agency, and access that preoccupy the
contemporary social researchers whose work is reviewed in the next chapter. As
Baynham observed, 'Bakhtinian dialogism…does not capture how speakers position
themselves and are positioned' (Baynham, 2006: 381). For example, Bakhtin did not
speak directly to the power imbalance that may be present when native speakers
interact with non-native speakers. He did not explicitly acknowledge the potential
impact of differing levels of proficiency and linguistic expertise that can exist in
such encounters. Issues of power and inequality are explored further in Section 2.2.2
as well as in Chapter 3.

2.1.3   Language, culture, and intercultural dialogue

One can find congruence between Vygotsky and Bakhtin in terms of their
understandings of culture and its centrality in their beliefs about language development. Vygotsky saw culture as an outcome of social processes that are shaped by
human interaction: 'Culture is in fact the product of human social life and the social
activity of human beings, and therefore the very act of putting the questions about
cultural development of behaviour already leads us directly into the social plane of
activity' (Vygotsky, 1987: 145–46). In his cultural-historical theory of human
development, he portrayed higher psychological functions (e.g., language) as
products of processes that occur within a particular culture and historical context.
From this perspective, the acquisition of culture and the development of 'a cultured
mind' are the ultimate goals of learning.

Bakhtin also considered culture a product of human interaction. As Kostogriz explained, he saw it 'not as a noun but rather as a verb, foregrounding the dynamics of cultural practices and identities between and across constructed and imagined boundaries' (Kostogriz, 2005: 198). In his writings, Bakhtin (1981, 1984, 1986) mused about cultural boundaries and intra- and intercultural interactions. In his view, intercultural communication is vital for human development, including self-awareness. Given the dialogic nature of culture, Bakhtin reasoned that we cannot fully comprehend a culture in the absence of contact with other ways of life:

> It is only in the eyes of another culture that foreign culture reveals itself fully and profoundly... A meaning only reveals its depth once it has encountered...another foreign meaning; they engage in a kind of dialogue which surmounts the closedness and one-sidedness of these particular meanings, these cultures... We raise new questions for a foreign culture, ones that it did not raise itself; we seek answers to our questions in it; the foreign culture responds to us by revealing to us its new aspects and new semantic depths (Bakhtin, 1986: 7).

Bakhtin was convinced that intercultural contact is beneficial for both parties (e.g., resulting in enhanced awareness and appreciation of Self and Other). This rather idealistic notion of mutuality and enrichment is explored further in Chapter 3 when CoP (communities of practice) and the INT (identity negotiation theory) are reviewed.

Another aspect of Bakhtin's work that has implications for intercultural dialogue is his perception of the situated nature of discourse. 'Each sphere in which language is used', he argued, 'develops its own *relatively stable types*...what we may call *speech genres*' (Bakhtin, 1986: 60) and every utterance is 'shaped and developed within a certain generic form' (1986: 78). As Sampson (1993) explained, 'genres are not simply ways of speaking but also ways of seeing, knowing, and understanding. Different genres, then, place us in somewhat different worlds, or at least provide different accentings for experiencing our world, including our selves and others' (Sampson, 1993: 119).

If one lacks an understanding of the speech genre that is culturally appropriate or prevalent in a particular situation (e.g., a relaxed social conversation), miscommunication and misunderstandings are apt to occur. Bakhtin (1986) reasoned that this may, in turn, threaten one's identity, self-image, and willingness to interact further. It would seem reasonable to expect that this might befall L2 sojourners (and other border crossers) who routinely find themselves in settings and situations that are linguistically and culturally foreign to them. Hence, Bakhtin's admonition may have implications for the analysis of critical incidents and pragmatic failures in intercultural encounters.

2.1.4   The role of the Other in identity and language development

For Vygotsky and Bakhtin, dialogue plays a central role in the formation of the self (the development of one's identity). Both theorists rejected structuralist notions of identity as a fixed attribute in the minds of individuals. There are, however, some differences in the ways they conceptualized it. This may be due, in part, to the scope of their research. Primarily concerned with the 'learning self' of children, Vygotsky (1986) saw identity as evolving in a linear way throughout the maturation process. He also maintained that the individual self is formed through the internalization of its sociocultural environment: 'The true direction of the development of thinking', he argued, 'is not from the individual to the social, but from the social to the individual' (Vygotsky, 1986: 36).

While Vygotsky (1987) theorized about 'inner speech' (verbal thought directed at oneself), Bakhtin explored 'the inner other,' which he conceptualized as follows: 'To be means to be for another, and through the other, for oneself. A person has no internal sovereign territory, he is wholly and always on the boundary' (Bakhtin, 1984: 287). Although both philosophers regarded identity as a 'dynamic, evolving entity' there were some differences in their understanding of how selfhood develops and evolves.

Bakhtin's interest in identity was more consuming and broader, extending well beyond educational contexts. In particular, he explored 'how the self emerges in a moral and creative act; how it manifests itself in a dialogical relation with other, equal selves; and how it rebels against the constraints imposed on it by official sociocultural hierarchies' (Marchenkova, 2005: 183). Bakhtin was convinced this process of personal identification and expansion can take place only through contact with an Other: 'I am conscious of myself and become myself only while revealing myself for another, through another, and with the help of another' (Bakhtin, 1984: 287). In his eyes, one's identity is continually subject to change through interaction with Others and is, virtually, 'unfinalizable.'

By engaging in dialogue with Others throughout our lives, Bakhtin (1981, 1986) claimed that we routinely shape and reshape our expressions as well as our sense of self (identity). In this process of personal expansion, we appropriate words and expressions that have been used by others, engaging in the act of 'ventriloquation'. Speakers may then choose to 'bend' these voices to suit their own needs and agendas. Hence, in his eyes, each individual is 'an author who is continuously re-creating her/his lived world' (Vitanova, 2005: 167). From a Bakhtinian perspective, this creative process begins in childhood and continues to evolve throughout our lives. In contrast with Vygotsky, however, he did not believe that it unfolded in a linear fashion.

For Bakhtin (1981), exposure to Others, coupled with 'outsideness', presents an opportunity for self-expansion, bringing about new ways of perceiving the world and the exciting potential of 'highly productive hybridity'.

> The collision between differing points of view on the world…fighting it out
> in the territory of the utterance…unconscious hybrids…are pregnant with
> potential for new world views, with new 'internal forms' for perceiving the
> world in words (Bakhtin, 1981: 360).

For this visionary, hybridity is 'a mode of cultural-semiotic development… a
contestatory energy that exists at and in between cultural boundaries and is, in fact, a
source of productive cultural creativity and new meaning-making possibilities'
(Kostogriz, 2005: 198). In Chapter 3 I link this notion to contemporary understandings of 'thirdspace'.

2.2   Bourdieusian contributions

Pierre Bourdieu (1930–2002), an acclaimed French sociologist, intellectual, and
avid political activist, developed a number of conceptual tools that have relevance
for this discussion. In particular, his notions of field, habitus, capital, and symbolic
violence help to elucidate the complex relationship between language, culture, and
positioning within specific sociocultural contexts. With reference to field research,
his unique perspective on reflexivity, subjectivity, and participant observation also
have implications for ethnographic investigations of L2 learners and sojourners.

Similar to Bakhtin and Vygotsky, Bourdieu recognized that language and social
life are inextricably bound together. In his monograph *Language and Symbolic
Power* (1991), he spoke forcefully against the study of language in isolation from the
social, historical, and political contexts in which it is used:

> Bracketing out the social…allows language or any other symbolic object to
> be treated like an end in itself, [this] contributed considerably to the success
> of structural linguistics, for it endowed the 'pure' exercises that characterize
> a purely internal and formal analysis with the charm of a game devoid of
> consequences (Bourdieu, 1991: 34).

He rebuked formal and structural linguists (e.g., Saussure, Chomsky) for failing
to grasp the socio-political conditions of language development and use. As the
following sections attest, his distinctive *theory of practice*, combined with empirical
data (e.g., fieldwork), represents a major contribution to the study of language,
power, and social relations.

2.2.1   Field, habitus, and agency

In Bourdieusian theory, the concept of field ('market' or 'game') basically refers to a social arena in which individuals ('social agents') manoeuvre and struggle in pursuit of desirable resources (e.g., status, knowledge, wealth). The following definition, which is more complete, is perhaps the best known:

> In analytic terms, a field may be defined as a network, or configuration, of objective relations between positions. These positions are objectively defined, in their existence, and in the determinations they impose upon their occupants, agents or institutions, by their present and potential situation…in the structure of the distributions of species of power (or capital) whose possession commands access to the specific profits that are at stake in the field, as well as by their objective relation to other positions (domination, subordination, homology, etc.) (Bourdieu and Wacquant, 1992: 97).

In Bourdieu's vision, then, a field is a system of social positions and relations structured internally in terms of power differentials. Underpinning this hierarchy are sets of values and worldviews, which determine what 'the social agents' in a particular sociocultural context consider important (e.g., worth striving for). To illustrate this concept, we may consider an L2 classroom a field, bringing to mind Vygotsky's vision of the ZPD. In doing so, it is useful to note that both Bourdieu and Vygotsky acknowledged the power differential and knowledge gap between L2 students and their teachers. Within this 'game', students may struggle to gain access to the knowledge that the teachers possess – if it is prized in their world (e.g., by the students themselves and their parents). Conversely, within this field there may be resistance if, for example, the students believe that the knowledge and skills that are valued in mainstream society (e.g., by the teachers) are beyond their grasp or irrelevant to their lives.

The notion of habitus, which is foundational to Bourdieu's theory of social research, refers primarily to the non-discursive aspects of culture that link individuals to particular social groups. Originally introduced by Marcel Mauss as 'body techniques', Bourdieu (1977, 1991) extended the scope of the term to encompass the totality of learned habits (e.g., daily practices), skills, styles, tastes, values, and beliefs shared by specific groups, societies, or nations. This 'set of dispositions' prompts 'social agents' to act and respond in particular ways in social exchanges or what Bourdieu deemed practices ('actions with a history'). Simply put, habitus, from a Bourdieusian perspective, includes the 'durable motivations, perceptions and forms of knowledge that people carry around in their heads as a result of living in particular social environments and that predispose them to act in certain ways' (Layder, 1997: 236).

Bourdieu (1991) employed the term 'linguistic habitus' to describe the 'sub-set of dispositions' acquired while learning to speak in particular sociocultural contexts (e.g., at home, at school). Like all forms of habitus, an individual's linguistic habitus is a cumulative product of experience and inculcation, providing direction for language use in daily life. It not only affects an individual's linguistic practices, but as Vann (1999) observed, it impacts on one's perceptions of the symbolic value of these practices in various fields. During the language and cultural socialization process, dispositions are also influenced by existing socio-political conditions in 'the field'. Hence, linguistic expressions are the product of the relation between a linguistic market or field and a linguistic habitus.

Within this theory of practice, linguistic exchanges are depicted as 'situated encounters between agents endowed with socially structured resources and competencies' (Thompson, 1991: 2). When individuals use language, Bourdieu (1991) maintained that they draw on their accumulated linguistic resources and adapt their discourse to their audience, which is situated in a particular social field or market. In his eyes, then, every linguistic interaction takes place within a social and historical context and the behaviour of the interlocutors is influenced by the social structure that it both expresses and helps to perpetuate.

When explaining his conception of 'practices', Bourdieu (1991) also drew our attention to the communication and identity misalignments that can arise due to incompatibility between a habitus and a field, as in the following scenario:

> [P]ractices should be seen as the product of an encounter between a habitus and a field which are, to varying degrees, 'compatible' or 'congruent' with one another, in such a way that, on occasions when there is a lack of congruence (e.g., a student from a working-class background who finds himself or herself in an elite educational establishment), an individual may not know how to act and may literally be lost for words (Thompson, 1991: 17).

This 'lack of congruence' can emerge as a consequence of border crossings when individuals lack intercultural awareness and different values collide. For instance, L2 speakers who move into an unfamiliar cultural environment may feel like 'fish out of water', experience symptoms of culture shock (Ward, Bochner, and Furnham, 2001), and be at 'a loss for words' in their new surroundings. As Bourdieu (1977, 1991) explained, when people enter 'new' fields, they naturally bring with them sets of dispositions (habitus); these behaviours and worldviews may not be a comfortable fit within the new field.

Even if border crossers do adjust their behaviour (e.g., acquire the 'right' accent, employ the 'appropriate' communication style) and seek to transform themselves in their new environment, they may not be allowed to fully adopt a new persona and position in the field. As Joseph (2004) has pointed out, existing social networks and hierarchies may still restrict their access and positioning:

> Even the individual who in a wilful, active way undoes the identity they were
> born and socialized into and takes on a new identity (thus undercutting the
> very basis on which the habitus stands) is still going to be perceived, inter-
> preted, and measured by those around them in terms of their relative place
> within a network of social hierarchies based on the distribution of cultural
> capital (Joseph, 2004: 75).

A potential limitation of this conceptualization of habitus and Bourdieu's focus on practices, however, is that they are not objectively determined and, ultimately, are not products of free will. By his own definition, habitus are culturally conditioned structures that inhabit the bodies and minds of individuals ('social agents'). Through practice, fields influence habitus ('dispositions') and habitus, in turn, pervade fields. While practices are presumed to mediate between them, it is not possible to directly observe habitus.

The notion of habitus has also been criticized by Sealey and Carter (2004) and Scollon (2001) for failing to distinguish between culturally based group behaviours and individual differences that may occur in actual social situations:

> The concept (habitus) explains why everyday, routine activities are to some
> degree regular and predictable, since our social backgrounds delineate ways
> of seeing patterns of thought, even physical posture. However, habitus only
> provides a general, loose series of predispositions, and these are not deter-
> mining of what people do in specific social contexts (Sealey and Carter,
> 2001: 54).

While Scollon commended Bourdieu (1991) for 'reminding us that social theory must ultimately ground itself in the concrete realities of the physical and material world' (Scollon, 2001: 70), he had some reservations about habitus. He warned that 'we should not let the concept slip between the material and the ideal or immaterial as Bourdieu allows it to do by sometimes referring to the habitus of a group, class, or most often, a field. Second, we need to remind ourselves of the ultimate fuzziness of the boundary of the biological organism' (Scollon, 2001: 70–71).

For Bourdieu (1991), much of an individual's disposition is predetermined by the social habitus and this, of course, is difficult to change. This has led some critics to argue that he has retained an objectivist bias in his work. Nonetheless, he does seem to allow for agency (the ability to understand and control one's own action) within 'the bounded structures' of society and self. For him, the possibilities of agency must be understood and contextualized in relation to the objective structures of a culture (Webb, Schirato, and Danaher, 2002: ix).

Bourdieu's notions of practice and habitus can also be linked to the construct of communities of practice (CoP), which was more recently developed by Lave and Wenger (1991). As this has profound implications for the language and cultural socialization of L2 learners at home and abroad, this linkage is explored in Chapter 3.

2.2.2   Capital, power, and inequality

In his writings, Bourdieu (1991) discussed various types of capital (e.g., economic, social, cultural, linguistic, symbolic) and their impact on social relations within a system of exchange. Harker, Mahar, and Wilkes (1990) provided insight into the scope of 'capital', a notion that figures prominently in Bourdieu's theory of practice:

> The definition of capital is very wide for Bourdieu and includes material things (which can have symbolic value), as well as 'untouchable' but culturally significant attributes such as prestige, status and authority (referred to as symbolic capital), along with cultural capital (defined as culturally-valued taste and consumption patterns)... For Bourdieu, capital acts as a social relation within a system of exchange, and the term is extended 'to all the goods, material and symbolic, without distinction, that present themselves as rare and worthy of being sought after in a particular social formation (Harker, Mahar, and Wilkes, 1990: 1).

For Bourdieu, economic capital refers to one's financial assets (e.g., material wealth), while social capital covers resources that are based on group membership, relationships, networks of influence and support (e.g., contacts that are important for social and career advancement). The term 'cultural capital' represents resources that are culturally authorized (e.g., tastes, attributes, consumption patterns, academic degrees). Fields, and the actors located within them, determine the value of this capital. Consequently, the specific knowledge, skills, or education associated with higher positions in society vary from one culture to another along with expectations. Drawing on this concept, Sealey and Carter proposed that: 'successful learning of the L2 is an emergent product of cultural capital in combination with a cultured habitus and learners' motivation' (Sealey and Carter, 2004: 207).

In Bourdieu's analysis of social life, he found language to be a significant mechanism of power, observing that the language one uses is linked to one's positioning in a field or social space. In linguistic exchanges, varieties in language use (e.g., code-mixing, accents, vocabulary choices) tend to reinforce the position of each interlocutor, a notion that is explained further in Chapter 3. Linguistic capital, which Bourdieu (1991) defined as the mastery of and worth of a language in a particular sociocultural context, serves as a form of 'embodied cultural capital'. In publications in 1979 and 1982, Bourdieu expressed the belief that 'the production and reproduction of relations of power and inequality are legitimized through ideologies of language and accomplished through local social and discursive practices in specific historical locations and in a number of institutional sites' (Martin-Jones and Heller, 1996: 129). A related notion is that of 'legitimate language', which Bourdieu (1977) formulated to illustrate the ways in which language practices or discourse (e.g., standardized forms of speech used by dominant groups) are legitimized in specific social conditions, reinforcing their authority.

This notion of capital can be employed to analyse inequality in social settings, including linguistic exchanges between native speakers and L2 learners (e.g., hosts and L2 sojourners). Sealey and Carter observed that: 'speakers are not equally placed to realize their linguistic assets as 'capital' (Bourdieu 1986) when the 'correct' accent, for example, or native speaker facility in the dominant language is a pre-requisite for social and occupational mobility' (Sealey and Carter, 2004: 181). This raises important socio-political issues about access to linguistic resources, the positioning of languages in a particular context (e.g., 'legitimate languages', dialects), and inequality in intercultural dialogue. It problematizes Bakhtin's (1981, 1986) idealistic portrayal of 'equal' participants in intercultural exchanges that was discussed in Section 2.1.2.

Bourdieu (1991) was preoccupied with the complex ways in which linguistic practices are shaped by the constraints of society (e.g., power structures that determine one's positioning). Unlike Bakhtin, he made explicit reference to the lack of equality in the status and positioning of actors in a social scene (e.g., interlocutors in an intercultural encounter who have different levels of proficiency in the language used). He described routine linguistic exchanges as 'situated encounters between agents endowed with socially structured resources and competencies' (Thompson, 1991: 2), noting that these differences can have a significant impact on social relations and the communication process.

For Bourdieu (1991), symbolic capital (e.g., prestige, reputation, honour, fame, the right to be listened to) is a crucial source of power. When those with symbolic capital use it to force their will on people in a subordinate position, he deemed this an act of 'symbolic violence'. Over time, he warned that people may come to experience symbolic power and systems of meaning (culture) as legitimate and not challenge them. In his eyes, the act of perceiving symbolic violence as valid makes the agent complicit in his/her own subordination. If an L2 becomes dominant in a particular context and the mother tongue takes a subservient position or even disappears during the process of assimilation, Bourdieu (1991) would characterize this as an act of 'linguistic violence'.

2.2.3   Reflexivity, subjectivity, and the ethnographic gaze

Bourdieu, like Vygotsky, sought to link his philosophy with empirical research.

Grounded in everyday life, his theory of practice combines a structuralist framework with close attention to subjectivity and reflexivity in particular sociocultural contexts. To understand Bourdieu's (1977) argument, it is important to clarify his interpretations of these terms. He saw subjectivism as an intellectual orientation, which aims to access the thoughts, decisions, and actions of individuals positioned within a particular social world. By contrast, he associated objectivism with the notion that objective social structures (e.g., those related to class, ethnicity, gender, language) determine people's actions and attitudes. Viewing reflexivity primarily in terms of social research, Bourdieu maintained that 'the researcher is seen as being inserted into a social field, with specific relationships of competition and power conditions generating a particular "habitus", that is, a pattern of action dispositions, among the participants' (Alvesson and Sköldberg, 2004: 5).

Advocating a method of 'reflexive sociology', Bourdieu employed 'double participant observation' in investigations of social practices with the explicit aim of balancing subjectivity and objectivity. While he identified limitations in each, he was more accepting of the latter: 'The chief merit of objectivism is that it breaks with the immediate experience of the social world and is able thereby to produce a knowledge of the social world which is not reducible to the practical knowledge possessed by lay actors' (Thompson, 1991: 11). In Bourdieu's theory of practice, a key factor in achieving a balance between subjectivity and objectivity was the link that he envisaged between habitus and field (sets of relations in the world) via practices.

Stressing the importance of reflexivity in social research, Bourdieu, Chamboredon, and Passeron (1991) advised researchers to reflect on how forces (e.g., social, linguistic, and cultural background, their position within particular fields) may influence the way they view the cultural scene under study. In a kind of double participant observation, they argued that researchers should take on the perspectives of both research subject and observer. This balancing act combines the objective study of the world with reflexive knowledge of the subject(s) of the study. Hence, in social research, Bourdieu and his co-researchers advocated a mix of 'emic' perspectives ('the rules, concepts, beliefs, and meanings of the people themselves, functioning within their own group' (van Lier 1990: 43)) and 'etic' interpretations (outsider's/ researcher's analyses):

> It is not sufficient for the sociologist to listen to the subjects, faithfully recording their statements and their reasons, in order to account for their conduct and even for the reasons they offer; in doing so, he is liable to replace his own preconceptions with the preconceptions of those whom he studies, or with a spuriously scientific objective blend of the spontaneous sociology of the 'scientist' and the spontaneous sociology of his object (Bourdieu et al., 1991: 37).

Bourdieu and Wacquant (1992) warned researchers to avoid the trap of falling into 'a naivety imbued by unconscious, ideological, and thus prescientific frames of reference'. This view was echoed by Sealey and Carter (2004) when they criticized researchers (e.g., Norton, 2000) who claim to have relied solely on the actual words of the 'social actors' under study and not questioned their informants' perspectives. In line with Bourdieu et al. (1991), Sealey and Carter (2004) argued that embracing 'the "emic" categories used by those who participate in the processes we are researching' and neglecting an etic perspective can result in 'a different set of epistemological problems' (p. 105). 'Thick description and holistic accounts', in their view, are simply inadequate. They called on social researchers to apply their knowledge and expertise to develop theoretical accounts of the cultural scene, making use of *both* 'emic' and 'etic' viewpoints.

In his own fieldwork, Bourdieu preferred to be situated as the professional or familiar stranger. In this position of marginality, 'the ethnographic gaze is predicated on some mixture of distance and familiarity with one's object' (Reed-Danahay, 2005: 3). To understand the subjective-objective nature of social and cultural practices, Bourdieu et al. (1991) argued that the ethnographer must consider the viewpoints of both participant (research subject) and observer (researcher). This stance combines the objective study of the world with reflexive knowledge of the participant(s) under investigation. As Jenkins (1992) explained, what Bourdieu advocated was 'double objectification' as a method in field research: 'First, there is the work done in the act of observation and the objectification of distortion of social reality which it is likely to produce. Second, there is an awareness of that distortion and of the observer as a competent social actor in his/her own right' (Jenkins, 1992: 50).

2.3   Implications for ethnographic investigations of L2 sojourners

Vygotskian and Bakhtinian theories link language, culture, context, and identity (selfhood) – core elements in the journeys of L2 sojourners and, in truth, anyone who interacts across cultures. Bourdieu's notions of field, habitus, and capital also heightened my awareness of the complex relationship between power (resistance and inequality), social context, and linguistic practices. Not surprisingly, the work of these visionaries has had a significant impact on the direction of social research today. Bourdieu's notion of 'double objectification', for example, has profound implications for ethnographic studies of the language and cultural development of L2 sojourners. For this reason, his advice resurfaces in Chapter 4 when I describe the methodological approach that I employed in my study.

In Chapter 3 I now turn to contemporary views of identity, language and cultural socialization. I also explore current understandings of intercultural mediation that helped to further inform my analysis of the ethnographic data that I gathered both in Hong Kong and England.

Notes

1   The notion that participants in the ZPD must differ from each other (e.g., in terms of knowledge, expertise, ideas) for learning to occur remains a contentious issue as noted by Chaiklin (2003) and Lantolf and Thorne (2006). Some contemporary sociocultural theorists have reinterpreted the ZPD and extended it to peer interactions.

3 Contemporary poststructuralist notions of language, culture, and identity

Building on the earlier work of Vygotsky, Bakhtin, and Bourdieu that was discussed in the previous chapter, I now move to more recent poststructuralist conceptions of language, identity, and culture. In particular, I investigate socio-cultural understandings of the relationships between these constructs, highlighting the importance of power, agency, and investment in language and cultural learning, and identity expansion. Border crossings and the potential for identity reconstruction are also discussed in relation to current notions of 'thirdspace' and the 'intercultural speaker'.

I begin by explaining terms that are essential to frame a discussion of current understandings of these constructs. This sets the stage for my critique of communities of practice (CoP), a concept developed by Jean Lave and Etienne Wenger (1991) that has gained prominence in education, management, and social science, especially in the last decade. I conclude my review by focusing on the identity negotiation theory (INT), which Stella Ting-Toomey (1999, 2005) proposed to explain the potential impact of culture and identity on intercultural communication.

3.1 Language, identity, and culture

3.1.1 Multifaceted identities: cultural, ethnic, social, and global

As this book centres on the experiences of L2 sojourners who move from their home culture (where they are members of the ethnic majority) to another culture (where they become visibly different members of an ethnic minority), it is important to examine current understandings of the constructs of cultural identity, ethnicity, and social identity. As the students are learning English, an international language, this section also explores the development of a global identity.

Most interculturalists maintain that we develop our cultural group membership through the guidance of our family and peers as children and adolescents. In addition, 'physical appearance, racial traits, skin colour, language usage, self-appraisal, and other-perception factors all enter into the cultural identity construction equation' (Ting-Toomey and Chung, 2005: 93). Strong associations of membership affiliation with one's culture reflect high cultural salience; conversely, weak associations of membership affiliation reflect low cultural identity salience: 'The more strongly our self-image is influenced by our larger cultural value patterns, the more we are likely to practice the norms and communication scripts of the dominant, mainstream culture' (Ting-Toomey and Chung, 2005: 94). This is not as straightforward as it seems, however; as Bhabha explains, cultural identity involves a struggle between alternative positionings and is not constant. For this reason, he argued that notions of 'inherent originality or purity of cultures' are indefensible (Bhabha, 1994: 20).

Ethnicity, which can be based on national origin, race, religion, or language, is linked to feelings of belonging to a particular ethnic group due to historical and emotional ties. Ting-Toomey and Chung defined it as 'an inheritance wherein members perceive each other as emotionally bounded by a common set of traditions, worldviews, history, heritage, and descent on a psychological and historical level' (Ting-Toomey and Chung, 2005: 97). Referring to ethnicity as 'a problematic concept', Smith, Bond, and Kağitçibaşi (2006) cautioned that 'a person's self-identified ethnic identity does not always coincide with his or her ethnicity as identified by others' (Smith, Bond, and Kağitçibaşi, 2006: 276). Clément, Noels, and MacIntyre agreed, noting that ethnic identity is 'highly variable and responds to contingencies of the situation in which it is played' (Clément, Noels, and MacIntyre, 2007: 65).

Norton, an applied linguist and poststructuralist, also argued that ethnicity is best understood as 'being produced in specific circumstances of social, economic, and historical relations of power that are reinforced and reproduced in everyday social encounters' (Norton, 2000: 13). Noting that 'ethnicity, gender, and class are not experienced as a series of discrete background variables', she argued that they are 'in complex and interconnected ways, implicated in the construction of identity and the possibilities of speech' (Norton, 2000: 13).

In their ethnography of urban American youth, Heath and McLaughlin (1993) discovered that their participants' embedded identities or 'multilayered self-conceptions' represented much more than simple labels of ethnic or racial membership. Similar to Clément et al. (2007) and Norton (2000), these linguists advised educators to refrain from making assumptions about ethnic and cultural identification, noting that the youth in their study regarded ethnicity as 'a label assigned to them by outsiders,' rather than 'an indication of their real sense of self' (Heath and McLaughlin, 1993: 6). In keeping with a poststructuralist perspective, Heath and McLaughlin emphasized that ethnic identity is flexible and may vary across individuals and situations.

The conceptualization of social identity also merits our attention. According to social identity theory (SIT), it consists, in part, of cultural, ethnic, or social group membership affiliations (Tajfel, 1981, 1982) as well as the 'emotional significance' of that membership. SIT suggests that individuals prefer to be attached to groups that afford them a positive social identity and tend to perceive 'ingroup members' in a more favourable light (Tajfel and Turner, 1986). Ting-Toomey and Chung observed that social identity accounts for 'how different groups perceive their own and others' group membership identity issues. It is also about marking ingroup/ outgroup boundaries as well as majority/minority group relations issues' (Ting-Toomey and Chung, 2005: 102). Further, according to Ochs, social identity comprises 'participant roles, positions, relationships, reputations, and other dimensions of social personae, which are conventionally linked to epistemic and affective stances' (Ochs, 1996: 424).

McNamara, an applied linguist and social theorist, stressed that social identity is partially dependent on 'the particular intergroup setting in which one finds oneself' (McNamara, 1997: 564). Our sense of self (identity) may develop when we are children within a particular sociocultural context (e.g., family, ethnic group) but may change due to contact with others and the desire or willingness to open up to new environments and ideas. This notion of identity as dynamic and evolving over time and space is in line with Bakhtin's (1981, 1986) conceptualization that was discussed in the previous chapter.

At this juncture, it is important to acknowledge the role that the process of globalization is now playing in the reconstruction of identities. Arnett, for example, has argued that young people today may develop both local and global identities that afford them 'a sense of belonging to a worldwide culture' (Arnett, 2002: 32). In some contexts, according to Ryan, the global identity may 'override other social identities, such as nationality and ethnicity' (Ryan, 2006: 33).

> If we accept the construction of a social identity as a site of struggle and conflict, it would be possible to argue that globalization does not necessarily present individuals with an 'either/or' choice; it creates contextually dependent hybrids of local and global values... The task for individuals is to construct their own identity with reference to this 'local manifestation of global values' (Ryan, 2006: 33).

The notions of hybridity, thirdspace, and identity reconstruction are explored further in Sections 3.1.4, 3.2.3, and 3.3.2.

3.1.2   Language, identity, and the sociocultural dimension

Our understandings of the relationship between identity, language, and culture learning have evolved over time. In traditional psycholinguistic approaches to SLA (second language acquisition), language learning is deemed an internal, biological process of linguistic system-building; by contrast, socioculturalists view it as 'the jointly constructed process of transforming socially formed knowledge and skills into individual abilities' (Hall, 2002: 66). While recognizing the importance of innate, biological capability to learn language, SCT (sociocultural theory) posits that what and how we learn is shaped by 'our history of lived experiences in our communicative environments' (p. 66). For this reason, when we learn a language, we are also learning a culture and forming our sense of self (identity).

According to Ting-Toomey, 'language infiltrates so intensely the social experience within a culture that neither language nor culture can be understood without knowledge of both' (Ting-Toomey, 1999: 93). Ochs explained this inextricable link between language and culture learning in this way:

> The acquisition of language and the acquisition of social and cultural competence are not developmentally independent processes, nor is one process a developmental prerequisite of the other. Rather the two processes are intertwined from the moment a human being enters society (at birth, in the womb, or whatever point local philosophy defines as 'entering society'). Each process facilitates the others, as children and other novices come to a perspective on social life in part through signs and come to understand signs in part through social experience (Ochs, 1996: 407).

To fully comprehend these 'intertwined' processes we must understand and take into account the sociocultural context where the learning is taking place.

Researchers working within critical and poststructural traditions consider identity to be socially situated, arguing that a language learner should be conceptualized as 'a social agent, located in a network of social relations, in specific places in a social structure' (Kress, 1989: 50). As Norton and Toohey observed, this reflects a rather dramatic shift in our view of the learner and the role the environment plays in human development:

> While humanist conceptions of the individual – and many definitions of the individual in SLA research – presuppose that every person has an essential, unique, fixed and coherent 'core' (introvert/extrovert; motivated/ unmotivated), poststructuralism depicts the individual – the subject – as

diverse, contradictory, dynamic and changing over historical time and space (Norton and Toohey, 2002: 121).

Within contemporary sociocultural approaches, then, identity is construed as 'a contingent process involving dialectic relations between learners and the various worlds and experiences they inhabit and which act on them' (Ricento, 2005: 895). In other words, it is recognized that individuals (e.g., language learners) are influenced, to varying degrees, by the social, historical, economic, cultural, and political contexts of their environment. As a consequence, one's sense of self is not fixed and static; in poststructuralist terms, it is 'multiple, changing, and a site of struggle' (Norton and Toohey, 2002; Pavlenko and Blackledge, 2004). Therefore, self-identity is best understood as 'a "production" which is never complete, always in process, and always constituted within, not outside representation' (Hall, 1994: 392).

To more fully grasp this complex relationship between identity, culture, and language learning, it is essential to delve into the processes involved in identity formation and language and cultural socialization. Norton and Toohey provided insight into this phenomenon:

> Language learning engages the identities of learners because language itself is not only a linguistic system of signs and symbols; it is also a complex social practice in which the value and meaning ascribed to an utterance are determined in part by the value and meaning ascribed to the person who speaks it… Thus, language learners are not only learning a linguistic system; they are learning a diverse set of sociocultural practices, often best understood in the context of wider relations of power (Norton and Toohey, 2002: 115).

Within this sociocultural orientation, then, identities and beliefs are thought to be 'co-constructed, negotiated, and transformed' on an ongoing basis by means of language (e.g., Norton Pierce, 1995; Ricento, 2005). Drawing on Bourdieu's (1991) notions of linguistic capital and 'legitimate languages', Norton argued that, 'SLA theory needs to develop a conception of identity that is understood with reference to larger, and frequently inequitable, social structures which are reproduced in day-to-day social interaction' (Norton, 2000: 5). What does this mean in practice?

It is vital that we acknowledge the 'complex and powerful regulations of what can and cannot be said and by whom, and ways in which speaking positions are made available in particular discourses and genres' (Baynham, 2006: 382). Educators need to be sensitive to the conditions under which language learners use their L2, whether in their home environment or abroad. As Norton and

Toohey have cautioned, these situations are often 'highly challenging', impacting on the identities of the speakers in 'complex and often contradictory ways' (Norton and Toohey, 2001: 312). This again raises our awareness of the potential impact of access, power, and agency on language learners in a particular context. Pavlenko and Piller stressed that these factors may, ultimately, result in different learning outcomes:

> While many SLA theories view L2 learners as passive vessels for input and output, poststructuralist approaches portray them as agents in charge of their own learning. This view implies that in some cases L2 users may decide to learn the second, or any additional, language only to a certain extent, which allows them to be proficient, but without the consequences of losing the old and adopting the new ways of being in the world. In other contexts, their L2 learning may be accompanied by a full transition to the new linguistic community and L1 loss. And yet in others they may resist the language that positions them unfavourably. Moreover, an individual's choice is only part of the story in the poststructuralist framework which sees agencies as co-constructed and learning options as predicated on language ideologies and power structures within a particular society (Pavlenko and Piller, 2001: 29).

From a poststructuralist perspective, agency is defined as the 'socioculturally mediated capacity to act' (Ahearn, 2001: 112). As noted by Kress (1989), L2 learners are viewed as 'agents' who play a key role in shaping their own learning. How might this relate to the sojourn experience? In the host culture some L2 sojourners ('social actors') may decide to learn and use their L2 only to a certain extent (e.g., to express their basic needs and wants), avoiding new 'ways of being' in the world. Some may resist the language of the host community, believing that it positions them unfavourably or disrespects their first language. By contrast, others may embrace the new linguistic community, interact more frequently across cultures, and experience identity expansion. Those who opt to permanently reside in the host community may even fully assimilate and gradually lose their first language, an outcome that troubled Bakhtin (1986). (See Sections 3.1.3 and 3.2.4 for a related discussion of the communication accommodation theory (CAT) and the ecological notion of affordance.)

3.1.3   Identity, language choice, and investment

By speaking a common language, interculturalists Ting-Toomey and Chung observed that, 'members signal equal ingroup linkage and outgroup differentiation. The core symbols and linguistic categories of a group often express ethnic and nationalistic sentiment' (Ting-Toomey and Chung, 2005: 158). Consequently, language can be a powerful and visible symbol of a group's identity or an individual's affiliation with a group. In essence, it may function as 'an emblem of group solidarity'.

SLA researchers have long recognized the importance of studying how individuals use language to display their identities and group memberships in particular sociocultural settings. Zuengler (1988, 1989; Dowd, Zuengler, and Berkowitz, 1990), for example, investigated the relationship between identity, L2 pronunciation, interlanguage development, and context. She discovered that the strength of a learner's cultural identity and ethnicity may have an effect on the variety of language used as well as the individual's attitudes towards it. In particular, the use of a social marker (e.g., phonetic variant) may signal 'the influence, in the person's speech, of a particular social or social psychological state, such as feelings of identity, beliefs, motives, etc.' (Zuengler, 1988: 33).

In a review of research on the identity and language choice of L2 speakers, Zuengler (1989) observed that learners sometimes opt to use a language according to 'status or solidarity' criteria. In other words, they are mindful about who they wish to identify with. Pressure for group solidarity among peers and whether or not their interlocutor shares the same ethnic identity may influence their language choices.

In intercultural encounters, an interlocutor's perceived empathy (or lack of it) towards the non-native speaker's ethnicity and culture has also been linked to an individual's interlanguage performance and willingness to communicate (WTC) in the target language (Clément et al. 2007; Zuengler, 1989). WTC is defined as: 'a situationally-determined volitional choice to speak at a particular time with a specific person or group' (MacIntyre, Clément, Dörnyei and Noels, 1998). Within the context of L2 use, this construct incorporates such variables as anxiety, confidence in language ability, and self-efficacy (the ability to perform successfully) (Dörnyei, 2005; Pellegrino, 2005).

The impact of sociocultural factors on code-switching (i.e., switching languages or dialects at sentence boundaries) and code-mixing (i.e., switching languages or dialects within a sentence) has also been investigated by sociolinguists. Auer (2005), McKay (2005), and Meyers-Scotton (1993, 2006), for example, found that both of these modes of communication may be used by L2 speakers to increase or decrease intergroup distance or affiliation (e.g., social identity) in certain contexts.

In addition, social psychologists have developed frameworks to explain language attitudes and behaviours (e.g., code-switching) in multilingual and multiethnic societies. Bourhis, el-Geledi, and Sachdev (2007) drew on the communication accommodation theory (CAT), the interactive acculturation model (IAM), and elements of the ethnolinguistic vitality theory and inter-cultural adaptation theory

(Berry, 1997) to explore language choice and use. Bourhis et al. (2007) argued that the following factors play a role: intergroup dynamics (e.g., the status of a linguistic minority relative to the majority language), interpersonal relations (e.g., degree of harmony between groups), and structural influences (e.g., level of institutional support for language variety). Bourhis et al. further suggested that 'the acculturation orientations of minority and majority group speakers can have an impact on the intergroup communication strategies they adopt during their intercultural encounters, resulting in harmonious, problematic or conflictual relational outcomes' (Bourhis et al., 2007: 15). The findings of sociolinguists and social psychologists raise our awareness of the need to pay attention to the language attitudes, motives, emotions, and self-construals of L2 speakers on stays abroad.

In Norton's longitudinal case studies of the language learning of immigrant women in Canada, she proposed the notion of investment, to represent 'the socially and historically constructed relationship of learners to the target language' (Norton, 2000: 10). Building on the earlier work of Bourdieu (1991) and Weedon (1987), a feminist poststructuralist, Norton challenged static conceptualizations of motivation for failing to capture 'the complex relationship between power, identity and language learning' (Norton, 2000: 10). She pointed out that language learners have a complex social history and multiple desires that shift over time as circumstances change. Through the act of expressing their thoughts and ideas, learners constantly organize and reorganize their sense of self and how they see their position in the social world they inhabit. For Norton, 'an investment in the target language is also an investment in a learner's own identity, an identity which is constantly changing across time and space' (Norton, 2000: 11). In a later publication she expanded on her interpretation of this process:

> If learners 'invest' in a second language, they do so with the understanding that they will acquire a wider range of symbolic and material resources, which will in turn increase the value of their cultural capital. As the value of their cultural capital increases, so learners' sense of themselves and their desires for the future are reassessed. Hence, the integral relationship between investment and identity (Norton and Toohey, 2002: 122).

Although Norton (2000) addressed issues of power, investment, and the emergence of new social identities, Byram observed that she overlooked 'the psychological impact of being obliged to learn another language and the effect on the individual's existing social identities' (Byram, 2003: 53). For those who live in (post)colonial settings or cross cultures to live (immigrate), work, or study, these issues merit serious attention.

The unique status of English, a global language, further impacts on how foreign language speakers of the language may view themselves in non-English-speaking contexts. Arnett (2002), Kanno and Norton (2003), and Kramsch (1999b), for example, have argued that the language can provide young 'EFL' learners with a sense of affiliation with a 'constantly evolving imagined community' of world citizens. As noted in Section 3.1.1, their 'global self' may even become an integral part of their local identity (Ryan, 2006). This may then deepen their investment in mastering English, the language which functions as an emblem of their international persona.

3.1.4   The 'intercultural speaker': linguistic and identity expansion

This review would be incomplete without an examination of current theoretical perspectives that specifically link identity and the experiences of foreign-language learners who cross cultures and borders. For this I turn first to Byram's (1997, 2003; Alred and Byram, 2002) notions of the 'intercultural speaker' or 'intercultural mediator', which were created when formulating the following vision of intercultural communicative competence (ICC) (Byram and Zarate, 1997a, 1997b).

> [S]omeone with Intercultural *Communicative* Competence is able to interact with people from another country and culture in a foreign language. They are able to negotiate a mode of communication and interaction which is satisfactory to themselves and the other and they are able to act as mediator between people of different cultural origins. Their knowledge of another culture is linked to their language competence through their ability to use language appropriately – sociolinguistic and discourse competence – and their awareness of the specific meanings, values and connotations of the language (Byram, 1997: 71).

Within this orientation, according to Byram, the L2 sojourner becomes mindful of 'the multiple, ambivalent, resourceful, and elastic nature of cultural identities in an intercultural encounter' (Byram, 1997: 56). In essence, through an L2 the individual mediates between two, or more, cultural identities and, over time, may undergo a 'restructuring' of her/his identity. This vision of personal expansion is congruent with contemporary poststructuralist notions of identity, which depict it as socially constructed, hybrid, fluid, plural, and relational (e.g., Bhabha, 1994; Byram and Feng, 2004, 2005; Guilherme, 2002). In their study of 'border crossers' in Germany and Poland, Meinhof and Galasiński offered the following definition of identity, integrating many of these elements:

Identity is a discourse of (not) belonging, which is continually negotiated and renegotiated within a localized social context. It is therefore an ongoing process of becoming: always provisional, always subject to change… Finally, identities are necessarily relational – as much as identity is about who 'I am', it is also about who 'I am not'. Identities need the 'constitutive outside' (Hall, 1996). It is only through the Other that 'we' can establish our own identity, through what we are not (Meinhof and Galasiński, 2005: 8).

Through intercultural mediation, Meinhof and Galasiński (2005) and other social theorists (e.g., Giroux, 2002; Guilherme, 2002) have argued that L2 sojourners may fuse feelings of belonging with a sense of detachment. These 'border crossers' may then enter a 'state of in-betweeness' as they negotiate their 'own cultural, social, and political identifications and representations with the other's' (Kramsch, 1998: 26). Ricento explained the process of cultural and linguistic expansion in this way: 'One's linguistic competence in a new culture reflects a process of transformation rather than one of replacement, in which the ultimate outcome represents an identity that is not exclusively anchored in one culture/language or another' (Ricento, 2005: 904). For Kramsch (1999b), a 'bicultural identity' that integrates elements of the local and global is essential for learners of English in today's globalizing world.

This creative intercultural space, which is sometimes referred to as 'thirdspace' or 'thirdness', has captured the attention of such critical social theorists as Bhabha (1994), Guilherme (2002), Kramsch (1993, 1999a, 2000) and Soja (1996) among others. As Kostogriz explained: 'The dialogical principle of intra- and intercultural interaction emphasizes those processes that occur on the boundaries between the self and the Other or between cultural-semiotic spaces, resulting in the production of Thirdness – new texts, meanings, and identities (Kostogriz, 2005: 198). (This concept is expanded on in Sections 3.2.3 and 3.3.2.)

To understand this process of identity expansion and the complex relationship between 'border crossers' and their hosts, we must delve into the context of the intercultural experience and the access that newcomers have to community resources. For this, I now move to the notion of 'communities of practice' (CoP), which also has profound implications for L2 sojourners.

3.2   Communities of practice and situated L2 learning

Jean Lave, a social anthropologist, collaborated with Etienne Wenger, a social learning theorist, to develop a model of situated learning that has become prominent in social, educational, and management sciences in recent years. For these theorists, learning involves a process of engagement in what they termed a 'community of practice' (CoP). In their path-breaking publications, *Situated Learning: Legitimate Peripheral Participation* (Lave and Wenger, 1991) and *Communities of Practice: Learning, Meaning, and Identity* (Wenger, 1998), they drew our attention to the need to understand knowledge, informal learning, and identity reconstruction in social context.

This review also draws on a book edited by David Barton and Karin Tusting (2005) entitled *Beyond Communities of Practice: Language Power, and Social Context.* Based on empirical research, the contributors (linguists and educational researchers) underscored the importance of incorporating thinking about language-in-use, power and conflict, and social context into CoP. They articulated concepts that have implications for our understandings of informal L2 learning and cultural development.

The following sections problematize key elements of CoP and the relationship between identity, L2 discourse, and practice in social context. Throughout, I return to issues that were foregrounded in my review of Bakhtin's, Vygotsky's, and Bourdieu's work in the previous chapter. Central to this discussion is the relationship between language and power in bilingual/multilingual contexts, and selfhood (identity) – issues that are particularly relevant to L2 learners and the sojourn experience.

3.2.1   The construct of community of practice (CoP)

Drawing on Vygotsky's SCT (sociocultural theory) as well as aspects of social theory and anthropology, Lave and Wenger (1991) and Wenger (1998) argued that people everywhere come together in groups to perform activities throughout the course of their daily lives – at home, in the community, and in the workplace. Over time, members build up relationships as they participate in informal activities, which are organized around a particular skill or knowledge base. Wenger explained the formation of a CoP in this way:

> Being alive as human beings means that we are constantly engaged in the pursuit of enterprises of all kinds, from ensuring our physical survival to seeking the most lofty pleasures. As we define these enterprises and engage in their pursuit together, we interact with each other and with the world and we tune our relations with each other and with the world accordingly, In other words we learn.

> Over time, this collective learning results in practices that reflect both the pursuit of our enterprises and the attendant social relations. These practices are thus the property of a kind of community created over time by the

sustained pursuit of a shared enterprise. It makes sense, therefore to call these kinds of communities *communities of practice* (Wenger, 1998: 45).

To better grasp this notion from a sociolinguistic perspective, Eckert and McConnell-Ginet provided a description of a CoP that is especially apt for this discussion:

> A community of practice is an aggregate of people who come together around mutual engagement in some common endeavour. Ways of doing things, ways of talking, beliefs, values, power relations – in short, practices – emerge in the course of their joint activity around that endeavour. A community of practice is different as a social construct from the traditional notion of community, primarily because it is defined simultaneously by its membership and by the practice in which that membership engages. Indeed, it is the practices of the community and members' differentiated participation in them that structures the community socially (Eckert and McConnell-Ginet, 1992: 464).

Within the framework of CoP, a 'practice' has the following dimensions: first, the 'social actors' engage in a 'joint enterprise' or common endeavour, which they continually renegotiate to accomplish their goals. Secondly, through the act of 'mutual engagement' members interact with each other in a variety of ways; this process binds them together into a social unit. Lastly, they gradually build up 'understandings' (learning) and 'a shared repertoire of communal resources' (e.g., vocabulary, ways of talking, stories, routines, beliefs, values). These features are an integral part of the formation of their identities as members of that community (Lave and Wenger, 1991; Wenger, 1998, 2005). Accordingly, through a succession of mediated actions (Scollon, 2001), social practices are presumed to develop in the 'habitus' (Bourdieu, 1991; Wilson, 2001) (see Section 2.2.1). These practices ('shared doings') and related identities of the participants evolve and change over time; they are essentially 'unfinalizable' (Bakhtin, 1984; Scollon, 2001).

This conception of CoP, which is fundamental in situated approaches to learning, is not without its critics. Scollon, for example, cautioned that the term 'proves rather difficult to use with much assurance that one has not been pulled at least metaphorically back into presupposed and unexamined bounded social entities' (Scollon, 2001: 146). His concern is shared by other linguists and social theorists (e.g., Candlin and Candlin, 2007), who have noted that the emphasis on commonalities in the community largely ignores diversity, 'multiple memberships', and conflict. Engeström, for example, observed that, 'the instability and inner contradictions of practice are all but missing from Lave and Wenger's accounts' (Engeström, 1999: 12).

Several authors in Barton and Tusting's (2005) book also drew attention to the lack of a theory of language-in-use in Lave and Wenger's model of CoP (e.g., Creese, Rock, Tusting). They argued that the role of language should be made much more explicit, especially in relation to the negotiation of meaning within the community, which is, by nature, discursive, semiotic, and language-based. Following Bourdieu (2001), they stressed that power relationships are conveyed and sustained through language use in CoP. While Lave and Wenger (1991) acknowledged that problems of access may curtail the personal expansion of newcomers, they did not sufficiently emphasize the 'discursive processes of conflict, instability and power negotiations' (Barton and Tusting, 2005: 9). A focus on language can challenge assumptions about homogeneity, which are implicit in much of the literature on this model of situated learning.

3.2.2   A social apprenticeship: legitimate peripheral participation (LPP)

In the CoP framework, learning is viewed as a socially situated endeavour in which newcomers interact with more experienced 'core' members in a range of tasks or activities that contribute to the overall aims of the community. Initially, the 'apprentices' observe and participate in simple but productive tasks. As they gain in experience and confidence, they become acquainted with the vocabulary, routines, and organizing principles of the social group and eventually become full members of the community – a process called 'legitimate peripheral participation'. Lave and Wenger explained this social learning process and the nature of situated learning (engagement in CoP) in this way:

> Learners inevitably participate in communities of practitioners and… the mastery of knowledge and skill requires newcomers to move toward full participation in the socio-cultural practices of a community. 'Legitimate peripheral participation' provides a way to speak about the relations between newcomers and old-timers, and about activities, identities, artefacts, and communities of knowledge and practice. A person's intentions to learn are engaged and the meaning of learning is configured through the process of becoming a full participant in a socio-cultural practice. This social process, includes, indeed it subsumes, the learning of knowledgeable skills (Lave and Wenger, 1991: 29).

Simply put, a CoP conceptualizes the learning and socialization of newcomers as a process of gradually gaining competence and membership in a given community. When new arrivals (e.g., sojourners) meet a group of people with shared practices (e.g., their host family), in Lave and Wenger's (1991) view, they need to learn to participate in the group's activities to gradually become 'full-fledged' members of that community. If learners (e.g., L2 sojourners) are to become more fully engaged in the host community, they must be favourably positioned as 'legitimate peripheral participants'. Without access and support, they may be sidelined and 'disempowered'.

> Legitimate peripherality is a complex notion, implicated in social structures involving relations of power. As a place in which one moves toward more-intensive participation, peripherality is an empowering position. As a place in which one is kept from participating more fully – often legitimately, from the broader perspective of society at large – it is a disempowering position (Lave and Wenger, 1991: 36).

Critical to this theory then is the opportunity that newcomers have to gain entry and exposure to situated social practices as a resource for learning, as Lave and Wenger explained: 'To become a full member of a community of practice requires access to a wide range of ongoing activity, old-timers, and other members of the community; and to information, resources, and opportunities for participation' (Lave and Wenger, 1991: 100–101).

Although these social theorists acknowledged the importance of access in CoP, they have been criticized for failing to sufficiently address the implications of inequality and the subsequent distribution of roles and responsibilities (Barton and Tusting, 2005; Candlin and Candlin, 2007; Scollon, 2001). The reality is that power relations within a CoP may seriously curtail entry and participation. We simply cannot ignore issues of power, access, and transparency. The differential opportunities that novices actually have to actively engage in in the social practices of the community must be taken into account. Moving towards full membership in a CoP not only involves a significant amount of time, effort, and motivation on the part of the newcomers, but the willingness of the hosts (the 'core' members) to share their expertise and resources with them (Bourdieu, 1991; Pavlenko and Lantolf, 2000; Wenger, 1998, 2005).

3.2.3   New trajectories and identities

This critical theory of situated learning posits that 'apprentices' who have adequate access to the CoP and remain committed to the process of becoming full-fledged members ('master practitioners') are apt to experience a change in their identities and social relations. Extending this notion to intercultural communication, Corder and Meyerhoff (2007) observed that participants who actively engage in 'cultural performances' within the CoP may find themselves transformed in some ways. How does this happen? Over time, the newcomers may learn to speak, act, and improvise in ways that make sense or are deemed culturally and socially acceptable in the community. To borrow from Bakhtin (1981, 1986), they may appropriate the voices of core members, engaging in the act of 'ventriloquation' (see Section 2.1.4).

This process may also be connected to the communication accommodation theory (CAT), a social psychological perspective. Through the act of 'convergence', it is hypothesized that 'individuals adapt their communicative behaviours in terms of a wide range of linguistic (e.g., languages, accents, speech rates), paralinguistic (e.g., pauses, utterance length), and nonverbal features (e.g., smiling, gazing) in such a way as to become familiar to their interlocutor's behaviour' (Bourhis et al., 2007: 37). Within the CAT, these language convergence strategies are thought to lead to 'harmonious relational outcomes' and a shift in one's identity.

This resonates with Lave and Wenger's assertion that 'when central participation is the subjective intention motivating learning, changes in cultural identity and social relations are inevitably part of the process...' (Lave and Wenger, 1991: 112). Similar to Bakhtin's (1981, 1986) notion of 'the relational nature of self-understanding', this theory links exposure to the Other (e.g., the new CoP) with enhanced awareness of the self, a key element in the pathway to identity expansion:

[M]embership in a community of practice translates into an identity as a form of competence. An identity in this sense is relating to the world as a particular mix of the familiar and the foreign, the obvious and the mysterious, the transparent and the opaque. We experience and manifest ourselves by what we recognize and what we don't, what we grasp immediately and what we can't interpret, what we can appropriate and what alienates us, what we can press into service and what we can't use, what we can negotiate and what remains out of reach. In practice, we know who we are by what is familiar, understandable, usable, negotiable; we know who we are not by what is foreign, opaque, unwieldy, unproductive (Wenger, 1998: 153).

For Lave and Wenger and other poststructuralists, identity is 'something we constantly renegotiate during the course of our lives' (Wenger, 1998: 154) as we encounter new CoPs. Newcomers may initially have a peripheral status but their identities, to varying degrees, are invested in their future participation and membership in the host community (Bourdieu, 1991; Norton and Toohey, 2002). It is through this process of engagement with 'experts' in the community that newcomers may broaden themselves.

While Lave and Wenger did not use the terms 'thirdspace' or 'cultural hybridity', their understandings of identity reconstruction parallel those of other sociocultural theorists (e.g., Bakhtin, 1981, 1986; Bhabha, 1994; Kramsch, 1993,

1999a). In his 1998 publication, for example, Wenger mused about the novel, creative ways that newcomers may express themselves when interacting with others in their new environment:

> [N]ew trajectories do not necessarily align themselves with paradigmatic ones. Newcomers must find their own unique identities. And the relation goes both ways; newcomers also provide new models for different ways of participating. Whether adopted, modified, or rejected in specific instances, paradigmatic trajectories provide live material for negotiating and renegotiating identities (Wenger, 1998: 156).

As they engage in new CoP, newcomers come face to face with unfamiliar expressions, practices (e.g., 'speech genres'), and 'ways of being' (Bakhtin, 1986), which reflect views and values that may conflict with their own. Familiar ways of interacting may no longer be effective in the new context and, if used, may lead to misunderstandings and disappointments, or what interculturalists refer to as critical incidents or 'culture bumps':

> 1) different ways of engaging in practice may reflect different forms of individuality; 2) different forms of accountability may call for different responses to the same circumstances; 3) elements of one repertoire may be quite inappropriate, incomprehensible, or even offensive in another community... Reconciling these aspects of competence demands more than just learning the rules of what to do when. It requires the construction of an identity that can include these different meanings and forms of participation into one nexus... The work of reconciliation may be the most significant challenge faced by learners who move from one community of practice to another. For instance...when an immigrant moves from one culture to another... (Wenger, 1998: 160).

Similar to Bakhtin (1986), Wenger (1998) argued that this firsthand experience with difference and the struggle to find oneself can lead to a restructuring of one's identity. If newcomers are to broaden their sense of self, however, they need to be flexible and resilient enough to cope with difference and learn from it.

3.2.4   Affordance: mutuality and engagement

Wenger also drew our attention to the importance of 'mutuality' and 'engagement', in determining the outcomes of CoP:

> At the core of processes of identification through engagement is the direct

experience of mutuality characteristic of communities of practice. By recognizing each other as participants, we give life to our respective social selves. Within the bounds of engagement, our identities constitute each other through direct interactions so that identification is a two-way process. The mutuality of this process of giving and receiving can be very fulfilling. It can make a community of practice the source of great social energy. For that very reason, however, we can become hostage to this experience and fail to move on. And for that reason also, a lack of mutuality in the course of engagement creates relations of marginality that can reach deeply into our identities (Wenger, 1998: 193)

When extended to the sojourn experience, this raises some rather intriguing questions. It suggests that those who perceive their hosts to be receptive and supportive may find their stays fulfilling and, subsequently, be more open to personal/linguistic expansion and identity reconstruction. This resonates with the self-determination theory, a social psychological premise, which posits that 'intrinsic and self-determined motivation [to use the L2] are sustained to the extent that significant others foster a sense of autonomy, competence and related-ness, by providing choice, informative feedback, and a warm caring environment' (Clément et al., 2007: 55).

However, 'mutuality of experience and sharedness of goals among members [in CoP] cannot be equally counted upon', (Candlin and Candlin, 2007: 209). L2 sojourners may experience 'a lack of mutuality' in the host environment (e.g., be confounded by new routines and modes of communicating) and never fully engage in the community. They may even feel alienated to the extent that their identities are threatened. One might expect that this would reduce their willingness to communicate (WTC) in the host language.

Within the CoP framework, the language and cultural learning of L2 sojourners would be characterized as a social 'apprenticeship' to the practices (including discourse, activities, worldviews, values, and belief systems) of a specific situated community in the host culture (e.g., homestay family). Lave and Wenger (1991) have argued that this engagement affords the opportunity for *both* parties (e.g., hosts and sojourners) to 'negotiate and renegotiate' their identities. This is similar to Bakhtin's idealistic notion of what should unfold in intercultural encounters. While this seems straightforward, it is problematic. One cannot assume that newcomers will find their hosts welcoming or that L2 speakers will develop 'a sense of belonging' in the new linguistic environment (Corder and Meyerhoff, 2007). In fact, they may perceive their hosts to be unfriendly and distant or even racist. Also, for a variety of reasons (e.g., historical, political, social, economic, personal) learners may resist their positioning as 'apprentices'. They may fight to stay true to their current sense of self (identity) and hold steadfast to familiar habits and modes of behaviour. This could then limit their exposure to the discourse and practices in the new CoP and, subsequently, curtail personal expansion.

This notion of 'resistance' may be linked to the communication accommodation theory (CAT), which was discussed in the previous section. Within this theory, language 'maintenance' is defined as 'a speech act involving non-convergence with the other but, instead, sustaining one's own personal or own group language usage' (Bourhis et al., 2007: 37). An act of 'divergence' is 'a dissociative strategy where individuals change their communicative behaviours to become less similar to their interlocutor's behaviour' (Bourhis et al., 2007: 37). Both communicative strategies may be used to express group affirmation and differentiation. In contrast with 'convergence', both are linked to 'problematic relational outcomes' and critical incidents (Bourhis et al., 2007). Applying the CAT to the CoP framework, 'apprentices' who adopt maintenance or dissociative linguistic behaviour would be seen as less willing to change and become 'full-fledged members' in the new community.

Just as newcomers may be resistant, one cannot assume that hosts (the 'experts' in the CoP) will regard the hosting experience as an opportunity to broaden themselves. While some may take a genuine interest in the language(s), cultural background, and personal experiences of the sojourners, others may not. It is naive to make assumptions that a homestay will automatically provide a site for the expansion of both parties. They may have different agendas or perceive certain barriers that limit their participation and learning in particular social contexts. In social psychological terms, some may 'converge', while others opt to 'diverge' or 'maintain' their communicative behaviours and identities for a variety of internal or external factors (Bourhis et al., 2007; Gallois, Ogay, and Giles, 2005).

In SA programmes where much of the learning takes place out of class, we cannot ignore the potential impact of the host environment on the language and cultural learning of L2 sojourners. Researchers and educators must be sensitive to the opportunities (or lack of them) that newcomers have for language-mediated engagement with the host culture and related social practices. As well as host receptivity, the learner's degree of participation in linguistic activities (e.g., effort and willingness to engage in social functions/conversations in the host cultures) should not be overlooked.

Of relevance to this discussion is the ecological notion of affordance, which refers to the reciprocal relationship between properties of the environment and the learner (Gibson, 1979; van Lier, 2000, 2004). What are the implications for L2 learners and sojourners? Positioned in a similar linguistic and cultural environment, replete with both invitations and constraints, individual L2 learners may perceive their world quite differently. Those who are open and receptive to the world around them are apt to take advantage of linguistic affordances and play a more active role in their language and cultural learning. By contrast, those who see only obstacles and rejections may withdraw and opt for a more passive role, thereby reducing opportunities for linguistic and cultural enhancement. As well as environmental factors, this perspective cautions researchers to be mindful of a language learner's response to them.

3.3 The identity negotiation theory (INT): an integrative perspective

Stella Ting-Toomey (1999, 2005), an interculturalist and speech communication researcher, developed a theoretical basis to explore the struggles and transformations of those who cross cultural boundaries. Her identity-based framework has the potential to deepen our understanding of the impact that such crossings can have on the language and cultural learning, intercultural adjustment, and identity reconstruction of sojourners.

The identity negotiation theory (INT) (1993, 1999, 2005) weaves together strands of social identity theory (e.g., Tajfel, 1981, 1982), symbolic interactionism (e.g., Stryker, 1994), the identity negotiation perspective (e.g., Ting-Toomey, 1993), and relational dialectics (e.g., Baxter, 2004). Table 3.1 presents the ten core assumptions that Ting-Toomey formulated to explain her theory, which stemmed from extensive informal ethnographic observations of intercultural encounters. The concepts that are particularly relevant to the journeys of L2 sojourners are the focus of the following sections. When appropriate, reference is also made to the notion of CoP and other issues that were presented earlier.

Table 3.1 Core assumptions of the identity negotiation theory (INT)

1. The core dynamics of people's group membership identities (e.g., cultural and ethnic memberships) and personal identities (e.g., unique attributes) are formed via symbolic communication with others.
2. Individuals in all cultures or ethnic groups have the basic motivation needs for identity security, inclusion, predictability, connection, and consistency on both group-based and person-based identity levels. However, too much emotional security will lead to tight ethnocentrism, and, conversely, too much emotional insecurity (or vulnerability) will lead to fear of outgroups or unfamiliar strangers. The same underlying principle applies to identity inclusion, predictability, connection, and consistency. Thus, an optimal range exists on the various identity negotiation spectrums.
3. Individuals tend to experience identity emotional security in a culturally familiar environment and experience identity emotional vulnerability in a

culturally unfamiliar environment.

4. Individuals tend to feel included when their desired group membership identities are positively endorsed (e.g., in positive ingroup contact situations) and experience identity differentiation when their desired group membership identities are stigmatized (e.g., in hostile outgroup contact situations.)

5. Individuals tend to experience interaction predictability when communicating with culturally familiar others and interaction unpredictability (or novelty) when communicating with culturally unfamiliar others – thus, identity predictability leads to trust, and identity unpredictability leads to distrust, second-guessing or biased intergroup attributions.

6. Individuals tend to desire interpersonal connection via meaningful close relationships (e.g., in close friendship support situations) and experience identity autonomy when they experience relationship separations – meaningful intercultural-interpersonal relationships can create additional emotional security and trust in the cultural strangers.

7. Individuals tend to experience identity consistency in repeated cultural routines in a familiar cultural environment, and they tend to experience identity change (or at the extreme, identity chaos) and transformation in a new or unfamiliar cultural environment.

8. Cultural, personal, and situational variability dimensions influence the meanings, interpretations, and evaluations of these identity-related themes.

9. A competent identity negotiation process emphasizes the importance of integrating the necessary intercultural identity-based knowledge, mindfulness, and interaction skills to communicate appropriately and effectively with culturally dissimilar others.

10. Satisfactory identity negotiation outcomes include the feelings of being understood, respected, and affirmatively valued.

Ting-Toomey, 2005: 218 (reprinted with permission)

3.3.1   Identity, language, and negotiation across cultures

Within Ting-Toomey's theoretical framework, identity is defined as 'reflective self-images constructed, experienced, and communicated by the individuals within a culture and in a particular interaction situation' (Ting-Toomey's, 2005: 217). In stark contrast with structuralists who portray identity as fixed and static, she argued that identities, like cultures, can and do change over time: 'We are the recipients and also the preservers of our culture via the daily messages that we trade. However, culture is not a static web. It is a dynamic, evolutionary process. Human beings are also not static individuals – they are changeable' (Ting-Toomey, 1999: 23). Her views are in line with Bakhtin (1981, 1984, 1986) and contemporary sociocultural theorists.

In the INT the role of language is implicit. A review of the core theoretical assumptions in Table 3.1 does not reveal any direct reference to the impact of language on intercultural encounters. Nonetheless, when laying the groundwork for her theory, Ting-Toomey drew a link between language (e.g., pragmatic rules), culture, and identity within the context of intercultural relations. She maintained that an individual's cultural and ethnic identities are typically expressed through language, and can pose challenges when crossing cultures:

> Intercultural frictions can easily occur because of the ways we name or 'catalog' the different groups of individuals or behaviours around us. For example, how we catalog 'outsiders' and 'insiders,' 'strangers' and 'hosts' and the proper behaviours associated with each category can profoundly influence our communication with them (Ting-Toomey, 1999: 85).

As language permeates our social experience, in her view, it shapes our 'cultured and gendered expectations and perceptions' (1999: 95). Similar to Lave and Wenger's (1991) model of CoP, the INT could be strengthened if the role of language was made more explicit in the core theoretical assumptions.

Besides identity, another aspect that is central to Ting-Toomey's theory is the concept of negotiation, which she defined as 'a transactional interaction process whereby individuals in an intercultural situation attempt to assert, define, modify, challenge, and/or support their own and others' desired self-images' (Ting-Toomey's, 2005: 217). This negotiation takes place through both verbal and non-verbal means; it is discursive and semiotic.

Some individuals may be oblivious to the identity negotiation process, while others are 'mindful' about the dynamics involved. Within this framework, mindfulness is 'a learned process of attuning to self-identity reactive issues plus engaging in intentional attunement to others' salient identity issues' (Ting-Toomey, 2005: 217). By contrast, 'mindlessness' refers to 'the heavy reliance on familiar frames of reference, old routinized designs or categories, and customary ways of doing things' (Ting-Toomey, 1999: 46).

To be mindful communicators, individuals need to be empathetic, respectful listeners and pay attention to pragmatic rules across cultures (LoCastro, 2003; Spencer-Oatey, 2000). 'Sensitive language usage', Ting-Toomey explained, is 'a pivotal vehicle in reflecting our mindful attitudes in communicating with dissimilar others' (Ting-Toomey, 1999: 85). She argued that we must be open to different ways of viewing and experiencing the world and the possibility of identity change. This is congruent with Bakhtin's (1981) stance, although she was less idealistic, acknowledging more explicitly that a lack of desire for openness and change and/or weak intercultural skills could curtail personal growth and identity expansion.

From Ting-Toomey's (1999, 2005) standpoint, successful intercultural communication is achieved through a joint function of *both* communicators successfully attending to their 'mutual identity needs, expectations, attunements, and cravings'. Acknowledging the 'dialogic nature of Self' (Bakhtin, 1981, 1986), she defined competent intercultural communicators as 'resourceful individuals who are attuned to both self-identity and other identity negotiation issues. They are also mindful of 'structural, historical, and situational scripts' as they shape and reshape 'a multifaceted identity' (Ting-Toomey, 2005: 229).

To communicate successfully across cultural boundaries, Ting-Toomey (1999, 2005) argued that individuals must be sensitive to the cultural beliefs and values that underpin different verbal expressions and communication styles, practise mindful listening skills, master culturally appropriate forms of nonverbal communication and pragmatic rules of verbal communication, and make use of culture-sensitive paraphrasing skills. Although the significance of the linguistic element is not apparent in her list of theoretical assumptions, her (1999) book, *Communicating across Cultures*, revealed that it was very present in her mind when formulating the INT.

The construct of CoP is also not mentioned in Ting-Toomey's writings; however, her explanations of the processes involved in intercultural adjustment and identity change are very much in accord with Lave and Wenger's (1991; Wenger, 1998) views about the situated learning and socialization of novices. She, too, theorized that newcomers who find their host environment welcoming and supportive are likely to develop more positive attitudes towards the host culture (and language) and, as a consequence, make more of a concerted effort to become 'full-fledged' members. By contrast, those who find the journey too daunting may retreat, reducing opportunities for personal and linguistic expansion.

> [T]o be a resourceful communicator in a new culture, one has to constantly walk a narrow path while balancing different identity acts. One has to forgo stability in order to regain stability. One has to experience differentiation in order to regain inclusion. One has to risk losing trust in order to regain trust. Finally, a newcomer has to be willing to 'become' an anonymity in the unknown territory in order to 'be' a full-fledged, recognized member of the new culture. While some travellers view the journey as difficult and hazardous, others take advantage of traversing the hills and valleys along the way as part of a long-term learning process (Ting-Toomey, 1999: 259).

Similar to Bourdieu (1991), Ting-Toomey recognized the significance of power, access, and agency in determining the outcomes of border crossings. She hypothesized that those who believe that their access to the host environment is blocked or feel that their identities are continuously misunderstood or not respected may remain disconnected from the host culture (and language), suffer more symptoms of culture shock (Ward et al., 2001), and adhere to old, familiar 'identity habits' and behaviours.

Ting-Toomey maintained that 'core' members of the host culture ('master practitioners') should be gracious, respectful hosts, while newcomers (the 'apprentices' or 'peripheral members') must initially be 'willing-to-learn guests' who are 'open to constructive identity change'. Without this collaborative effort, she warned that the new arrivals and their hosts may end up with 'great frustrations, miscommunications, and identity misalignments' (Ting-Toomey, 2005: 221), reinforcing ethnocentric tendencies and stereotypes. Notions of mutuality, engagement, and agency are complex. A range of internal and external factors may impact on intercultural relations and the adjustment of sojourners.

3.3.2   Liminality: dynamic in-betweeness and identity transformation

Through ethnographic investigations of cultural rituals, folklorists and ethnologists have explored liminality, a notion that may be extended to Ting-Toomey's (1999, 2005) depiction of border crossings and Lave and Wenger's (1991) construct of CoP. It helps to conceptualize the process of engagement and change that can occur when novices enter a new environment and gradually through practice become full-fledged members in the host culture and new CoP – provided that they are open to change and conditions are favourable.

From the Latin word *limen* for 'boundary or threshold', liminality refers to a rite of passage in which the participants cross boundaries and are transformed (e.g., in terms of their social status or identity). Typically, individuals are separated from their social group and undergo a period in which they are 'betwixt and between' or in a state of 'in-betweeness' (Ting-Toomey, 1999; Turner, 1969). During this uncertain time (liminal stage), they neither have one status nor the other:

> The attributes of liminality or liminal personae ('threshold people') are necessarily ambiguous, since this condition and these persons elude or slip through the network of classifications that normally locate states and positions in cultural space. Liminal entities are neither here nor there, they are betwixt and between the positions assigned and arrayed by law, custom, convention, and ceremonial (Turner, 1969: 95).

In Rampton's (1995) ethnography of British adolescent friendship groups, he linked this notion of liminality with 'language crossings', a phenomenon wherein people who belong to one ethnic group adopt the 'identity signals' of another group of lower social status (e.g., the use of Punjabi by those of Anglo descent). Liminal activity, he explained, 'departs from the patterns of conduct and systems of classification that are dominant in a society' (Rampton, 1995: 197). When the adolescents deviated from the norm and 'crossed languages', in effect, they entered 'an unofficial zone of alternative communicative possibilities' (1995: 196). During these 'occasions of relative uncertainty', Rampton found that 'the ordered flow of social life was loosened and normal social relations could not be taken for granted' (1995: 193).

This may be extended to the experiences of other 'border crossers' (e.g., long- and short-term sojourners) who enter the unknown. Ting-Toomey explained that newcomers must 'learn to experiment and reinvent new ways of coping, thinking, feeling, and behaving on a daily basis. The costs of such internal and external struggle and constant reinvention can include everything from identity rejection to identity loss' (Ting-Toomey, 1999: 258). Adjusting to a new culture and language involves an 'oscillating, dialectical process' which can be destabilizing for some. Gradually, over time, as 'border crossers' undergo socialization in the new environment (e.g., gain exposure to new CoP), they may assume a new social status in the final or postliminal stage (e.g., become full-fledged members of the host community) (Trubshaw, 2001). This 'rite of passage' is therefore a way of moving from the known to the unknown.

L2 sojourners, for example, may be separated from their parents and closest friends to travel to a foreign land, where they live with people ('strangers') from the host culture (e.g., in a homestay). During their stay abroad, the students may gain exposure to new linguistic and cultural practices (to varying degrees) and enter a 'liminal state' (transitional phase). Short-term sojourners may experience 'temporary liminality' as they participate in activities which allow them to transform from one social state to another without permanent change. During this phase, they may initially be treated as 'guests' or 'peripheral members' of the host culture and not be expected to perform the full range of tasks that are required of 'core' members in the homestay.

Entering uncharted waters may pose threats to the identity of the sojourners and challenge their equilibrium as they are exposed to ambiguous, unfamiliar situations. Conversely, border crossings offer the opportunity for sojourners to try new things and step outside of themselves and their social positions. Those who are open to their new environment, find their hosts receptive, and actively engage in their activities may incorporate novel expressions (e.g., colloquialisms) into their linguistic repertoire and take on board aspects of the host culture (e.g., communication styles, cultural practices).

From her observations of people who cross cultural boundaries (e.g., immigrants, student sojourners, international business people), Ting-Toomey concluded that such experience has the potential to be life altering: 'As a result of sustained first-hand contact with persons from the host culture, individuals often undergo external and internal changes in their adventurous adaptive journey' (Ting-Toomey, 1999: 233).

While sojourners may not become 'full-fledged' members of the host culture during their stay, they may gradually feel less like 'fish out of water', become comfortable in new CoP, and even begin to feel 'at home' (e.g., like family members in their homestays). In the process of adjustment, some may broaden their identity and develop new, unique perspectives.

In the same vein as Bakhtin (1981, 1986) and Lave and Wenger (1991; Wenger, 1998), Ting-Toomey (1999) theorized that some border crossers develop a 'third culture perspective'. This brings to mind notions of 'thirdspace', 'new trajectories', and 'cultural hybridity' which were discussed in Sections 2.1.4, 3.1.4 and 3.2.3. From this potentially empowering position, border crossers may 'integrate the best practices and approaches of the two cultures and work out the task and relational issues synergistically and creatively' (Ting-Toomey, 1999: 259).

This notion may also be linked to Janet Bennett's (1993) concept of 'constructive cultural marginality' and Yoshikawa's (1987) description of 'dynamic in-between-ness'. In this state individuals are able to recognize, interpret, and act from different cultural frames of reference and feel 'authentic' in each. The new identity that these border crossers acquire may be 'more inclusive, more intercultural'; in essence, what Kim (2001, 2006) defined as 'intercultural personhood'.

For many border crossers, these developments (e.g., identity expansion) may not be apparent until they return to their home country and discover that they see the world differently. They may long for the practices (e.g., linguistic and cultural) and values that they had come to accept while abroad and find it difficult to accept former 'ways of being' (Bakhtin, 1986). Their altered or expanded identity may confound and disturb their relatives and friends. 'By transcending the boundaries of respectability and orthodoxy', Trubshaw explained that those who cross boundaries and enter a state of liminality may 'bring back from the Otherworlds tales of a wisdom which the respectable remainder cannot grasp for themselves. Like all the rituals and metaphors of liminality, all this is part and parcel with the process of proceeding from the known to the unknown' (Trubshaw, 2001: 9). Conversely, some sojourners may discover that they feel out of place in both contexts and enter an unsettling state of what J. Bennett (1993) coined 'encapsulated marginality'. A complex intertwining of both internal and external factors may account for variations in the situated learning, intercultural adjustment, and identity reconstruction of those who cross cultures.

3.4   Implications for ethnographic investigations of L2 sojourners

Systematic, longitudinal studies of 'border crossers' are essential (e.g., ethnographic accounts of L2 sojourners) to check and validate the theoretical notions that have been put forward by contemporary social theorists. In particular, the construct of CoP and the INT need to be explored in relation to the actual experiences of short-term sojourners. Will these theories resonate with the trajectories of L2 students at home and abroad? Can these notions account for variations in sojourn outcomes (e.g., differences in language and cultural learning/ identity expansion)?

In Chapters 5 to 9, these concepts are problematized when I examine the language learning and (inter)cultural experiences of emerging bilinguals (multi-linguals) as they travel from their home country to an unfamiliar linguistic and sociocultural environment and back again. I now turn to an account of how I carried out my study.

4 Research site and methodological framework

In this chapter I introduce the Special English Stream (SES), a short-term study and residence abroad programme for English majors at the Chinese University of Hong Kong. After briefly describing the elements of this programme, I discuss the methodological framework for my investigation of the language and cultural learning and identity reconstruction of SES students at home and abroad. Focusing on the third cohort, I outline the central research questions that guided my ethnographic study and discuss the roles that I played. The remainder of the chapter provides a detailed description of the procedures and modes of analysis that I employed, as well as the rationale for focusing on four of the participants. I conclude the chapter by providing an overview of the structure and content of the illustrative case studies that are presented in Chapters 5 to 8.

4.1 The Special English Stream (SES)

To enhance the education of our second-year English majors, the English department established the SES, an enrichment programme which centres on a five-week residency in an English-speaking country. As the trip to England would be fully funded by a language enhancement grant, the department set an 'English only' policy for the sojourn to encourage the students to become fully immersed in the host culture and maximize the opportunity provided by the grant.

The following framework, adapted from Byram (1997) and Byram and Zarate (1997a, b), helped target specific competencies for the SES sojourners:

Attitude shift – Abandon ethnocentric attitudes towards other cultures and heighten awareness and understanding of the differences and relationships between their own and a foreign culture.

Skills of observation and discovery – Observe and analyse how people of another language and culture perceive and experience their world; become aware of the beliefs, values, and meanings they share.

Literary and cultural knowledge – Become aware of aspects of English literature and culture (e.g., beliefs, values, and meanings), which help natives of that culture to communicate without making these assumptions explicit.

Skills of interaction – Draw upon the previous three areas in real time to interact successfully with English people in England.

Critical cultural awareness – Make use of specific criteria to critically evaluate perspectives, practices, and products in both their culture and English culture.

As well as enhancing their linguistic and intercultural communication skills, the sojourn was intended to spur intellectual growth (e.g., the ability to synthesize and solve problems) and the refinement of interpersonal and social skills. It was also hoped that the participants would become more independent, self-confident, and willing to take the initiative to interact in English in a wide range of settings, including informal social situations (e.g., homestay activities).

To fully maximize their stay abroad, we aimed to provide adequate pre-sojourn preparation, ongoing support, and encouragement during the sojourn, as well as post-sojourn debriefing. A unique feature of the SES is that all of the elements are credit-bearing and fully integrated into the three-year Bachelor of Arts (BA) curriculum.

4.2   The project

4.2.1   Methodological framework

Similar to my pilot study of the first intake of SES students (Jackson, 2005, 2006a, b), the methods of data collection and analysis that I adopted for this investigation were aligned with ethnography, which has its roots in anthropology (Agar, 1996; Hammersley and Atkinson, 1995). Brewer offered a basic definition of this mode of research that is relevant for this study:

> Ethnography is the study of people in naturally occurring settings or 'fields' by means of methods which capture their social meanings and ordinary activities, involving the researcher participating directly in the setting, if not also the activities, in order to collect data in a systematic manner but without meaning being imposed on them externally (Brewer, 2000: 10).

Ethnography emphasizes systematic observation and inquiry of a culture or particular social context for a sustained period in order to obtain an 'emic' (insider's) perspective and a holistic view of what is being studied. As noted by Hornberger, ethnographers focus on 'what people say and do in a given context and across contexts in order to arrive at a fuller representation of what is going on' (Hornberger, 1994: 688). To accomplish these goals, ethnographers typically observe participants in situ and then interview or converse with them to gain insight into their perspectives. A long period of engagement allows the researcher to delve more deeply into the cultural scene. This also provides more opportunity to check for misinterpretations. Triangulation, making use of multiple data sources and methods, can help to verify the researcher's ('etic') interpretations of what is under investigation.

It is important for ethnographers to bear in mind Bakhtin's (1986) notion of 'outsideness' in dialogue across cultures. As discussed in Section 2.1.2, he advised interlocutors to try to see the world through the eyes of those from the other culture and, at the same time, 'remain outside it', developing their own interpretation. In essence, he advocated the inclusion of both 'emic' and 'etic' perspectives to achieve a deeper level of understanding. This 'balancing act' also resonates with Bourdieu et al.'s (1991) recommendation that social researchers engage in what he termed 'double objectification' (see Section 2.2.3).

Relevant to this study, ethnography can play a valuable role in demystifying the learning processes and development of students over time. Schensul, LeCompte, Hess, Nastasi, Berg, Williamson, Brecher and Glasser (1999) explained this application in this way:

> Ethnography is critical to describing and monitoring the process of change. It is also an approach that is useful in studying natural phenomena. Thus, it can provide the methodology for describing the evolution of the intervention process and its effects on individual and environmental factors. Using ethnography involves an iterative or recursive process of continuous data collection, analysis, and reflection that results in changes in intervention (Schensul et al., 1999: 44–45).

Similar to such SA researchers as Murphy-Lejeune (2002) and Pellegrino (2005), I have found qualitative research a useful way to investigate the language and cultural development of my students. As much of their learning was ethnographic in nature and they were undertaking their own small-scale ethnographic research projects, the choice of this mode of research was particularly appropriate. It was also ideally suited to a small-scale programme like the SES as I had the opportunity to develop a close relationship with the participants and continuously collect ethnographic data for almost two years. In this way, I was able to build up a 'thick, rich description' of the learning situation, which helped me to identify the factors (e.g., individual, sociocultural) that influenced the students' language and cultural learning and identity (re)construction in both their home and host culture environments.

This mode of research is not without limitations. One of the major challenges of ethnographic research is how to strike a balance between insider and outsider perspectives. This concern is addressed in Section 4.2.4.

4.2.2   Guiding questions

The broad questions guiding this research were: a) how are the participants' socio-cultural identities and views about language and cultural learning negotiated and transformed in different contexts (at home and in England) and b) what factors are associated with those changes? Ultimately, I hoped to better understand the relationship between language, culture, and identity over time and space. In particular, I aimed to identify the factors that impact on the development of linguistic and intercultural communicative competence and intercultural personhood in a study abroad setting.

4.2.3   Background and roles of ethnographer

As ethnography is an interpretive endeavour, it is important to acknowledge the background, biography, and identities of the researcher (ethnographer) as noted by Bourdieu et al. (1991). For the present study it is relevant to note that I am a female Canadian (Caucasian) professor who is a native speaker of English. I have taught Hong Kong Chinese university students for more than thirteen years and researched their language choices, linguistic attitudes, and identities both pre- and post-Handover (the return of Hong Kong from Britain to Mainland China in 1997) (Jackson, 2002a, 2002b). As an undergraduate major in French, I took part in a 'Junior year abroad' programme at a French Canadian university around the same age as the Hong Kong students who participated in the present study.

My relationship with the participants developed over the course of the study and was very complex as I balanced many roles (e.g., teacher, research advisor, participant observer, interviewer, evaluator, confidante, fellow researcher/explorer, motivator, photographer) (Denscombe, 2003; Jackson, 2006b; Knapp, 1999). I taught two of the pre-sojourn SES courses: ethnography and intercultural communication and, during the five-week sojourn in England, I supervised their ethnographic research, helped facilitate weekly debriefing sessions, and joined the students on excursions. Following the sojourn, I led debriefing sessions and, in the ethnographic research report-writing course, helped them make sense of the data they had gathered in England. I also had the opportunity to observe the sharing session they facilitated for the next group of SES students.

4.2.4   Issues of consent, confidentiality, and bias

At the beginning of the study, in keeping with the ethics guidelines for my university, the students were asked in writing if they would be willing for me to analyse their SES work and follow their progress throughout the programme. They were assured that their participation in the study or lack of it would not affect their grades and they would be given pseudonyms in any reports. All agreed to participate and, as in the pilot study with the first cohort, they were offered the option of withdrawing from the study at any time. None did.

The success of a study of this nature depends on the willingness of the participants to freely disclose their thoughts and feelings. Similar to the pilot study, a review of the narratives (both oral and written) revealed that the students had been introspective and frank. While the grading of some sources of data (e.g., diaries) might have affected their comments, this did not appear to be the case, as a range of both positive and negative views were offered by the participants. Most were very open about critical incidents they had experienced and their reactions to them.

A major challenge of ethnographic research involves the balancing of insider and outsider perspectives as noted by Bourdieu et al. (1991). If ethnographers are too familiar with a particular context or group of participants, they may have biases, which may distort their interpretations. On the other hand, if they are not familiar enough with the cultural scene and are not close to the participants, they may not be able to gain access to an insider's views. For educators who become ethnographers, achieving a balance between these two extremes is challenging, as Hornberger warns: 'Classroom teachers researching their own culture must simultaneously maintain membership for the sake of their identity and detach themselves from the culture sufficiently to describe it' (Hornberger, 1994: 689–90). Throughout the course of my study, I was mindful of these issues as I sought to develop a relationship with the participants and simultaneously analyse their behaviour and identity reconstruction.

4.2.5   Participants

In the third cohort of the SES there were 15 full-time English majors in the second year of a three-year BA programme. All had a grade point average of 3.3 or higher. They had an advanced level of proficiency in English (an average of B on the 'Use of English' A-level exam at the end of their secondary schooling). All were female Chinese students who were born in Hong Kong. They ranged in age from 19 to 22 on entry into the programme, with an average of 19.7 years. Fourteen spoke Cantonese as a first language; one student, who spent most of her childhood in the Mainland, spoke another Chinese dialect as her mother tongue. Before the SES sojourn, five had visited an English-speaking country on trips, ranging from a few days to three weeks. For most, personal contact with non-Chinese had been very limited.

4.2.6   The data collection process

The sections that follow describe the data collection process in detail, revealing how

I sought to better understand the complex relationship between identity, culture, and language as the students moved from their home environment (Hong Kong) to an English-speaking country (England) and back again. Table 4.1 provides an overview of the data that were gathered during the various stages of the study: pre-sojourn, during the five-week sojourn, and post-sojourn. Unlike most investigations of SA, this study has a longitudinal dimension that permits a deeper understanding of the processes involved in language and cultural learning and identity expansion both at home and abroad.

4.2.6.1   September to December 2003: pre-sojourn preparation

In early September, four months after they were interviewed and accepted into the SES, the students began taking courses that were specially designed to prepare them for the sojourn. In the literary studies seminar, they discussed the works of British authors to set the stage for their literary site visits. In my intercultural communications course, I introduced the fundamental concepts of this field of study (e.g., the values, behaviours and beliefs that can differ across cultures and impact on the communication process) and provided culture-specific preparation for England. This element included a focus on discourse and pragmatics related to the homestay as all of the students would live with an English family. This was added to the pre-sojourn phase as the first cohort had found informal conversations and relationship-building across cultures very challenging (Jackson, 2005, 2006b).

In the intercultural communications course the students wrote a narrative in which they reflected on their cultural identity and how their cultural background and experiences might impact on their communication with people from other cultures. For this assignment, I provided a list of guiding questions to stimulate their reflection about events and people that had impacted on their sense of self and their attitudes towards the various languages they spoke. In October all of the students submitted their written narratives, which ranged from 10 to 18 double-spaced pages (2,473 to 5,628 words); the average length was 12.4 double-spaced pages (3,169 words).

Throughout the course the students kept a journal in which they reflected on their intercultural encounters, their perceptions of their intercultural communication skills, their interview with a previous SES student, and their aspirations, concerns, and beliefs about the impending sojourn. The length of their journals ranged from 12 to 23 double-spaced pages (3,023 to 7,077 words); the average length was 17.5 pages (3,941 words).

The students completed surveys that provided information about their family background, their A-level scores in English, their perceived proficiency in the various languages they spoke, their formal English language learning experiences, intercultural experiences, and previous travel outside Hong Kong (if any). I also facilitated both small- and full-group discussions to encourage the students to reflect

Table 4.1   Data collection process

Timeframe	Location	Dates	Activities	Data collected
Pre-sojourn	Hong Kong	June 2003	SES selection process at CUHK	Application essay Notes taken during interviews
Pre-sojourn	Hong Kong	Sept. to Dec. 2003	SES coursework at CUHK: Literary studies Intercultural communication	Biographical survey Homestay form Interview (1) Cultural identity narrative Intercultural reflections journal Ethnographic conversations Group discussions Field notes
Pre-sojourn	Hong Kong	Jan. to April 2004	SES coursework at CUHK: Ethnography Theatre appreciation Sojourn orientation	Interview (2) Pre-sojourn surveys 'Home' ethnography projects Homestay placement form Group discussions Field notes
5-wk sojourn	England	May to July 2004	Homestay with English family Coursework at the host institution in England: Literary studies Cultural studies Weekly debriefing Excursions to cultural and literary sites Ethnographic research Individual or small group explorations during free time	Diary Language use log Weekly survey Weekly debriefing sessions Ethnographic conversations Group discussions Ethnography projects Field notes A visual record of sojourn (digital images)
Post-sojourn	Hong Kong	July to August 2004	Submission of sojourn diary	Interview (3) Field notes
Post-sojourn	Hong Kong	Sept. to Dec. 2004	Post-sojourn debriefing Coursework at CUHK: SES research report-writing (ethnography or literature-based)	Post-sojourn survey Ethnographic research survey Ethnographic conversations Ethnographic project reports Group discussions Field notes
Post-sojourn	Hong Kong	Jan. to May 2005	SES students' orientation session for next cohort	Ethnographic conversations Field notes

on the challenges and benefits of the 'English only' policy. Their comments were then recorded in my field notes.

In October 2003, a female bilingual (Chinese-English) research assistant (RA) interviewed each student individually in a quiet research office. All of the students opted to use Cantonese. The RA followed a semi-structured format to gather essential data from each participant and, at the same time, to encourage freedom of expression and input in areas that I might have overlooked when preparing the interview protocol. Nearly all of the questions and probes were open-ended and delved into such areas as their academic and family background, their perceived strengths and weaknesses, their perceived adaptability to change, their language learning experiences, and their personal, academic and career goals. Some of the questions were designed to clarify comments and responses in their questionnaires. These initial interviews lasted between 29 and 90 minutes, with an average of 55 minutes. The interviews were tape-recorded using a Mini-Disk recorder, translated, and transcribed.

4.2.6.2   January to April 2004: additional pre-sojourn preparation

In the theatre appreciation course, the students were provided with background information about some of the plays that they would see in England. They also saw a Shakespearean play together in Hong Kong; for most, this was their first visit to the theatre.

In the applied English linguistics seminar, I helped the students hone the skills necessary to carry out an ethnographic project (e.g., participant observation, note-taking, diary-keeping, reflexive interviewing, the recording of field notes, the audio-recording and analysis of discourse). Through weekly tasks outside of class, I encouraged them 'to make the familiar strange' and become more aware of aspects of their culture that they took for granted. After they had developed basic ethnographic research skills and begun to move from description to analysis and interpretation, they undertook a small-scale project to explore their own cultural world. This was intended to foster a systematic approach to cultural and intercultural learning in preparation for the sojourn (Jackson, 2006a; Roberts, 1997, 2003; Roberts, Byram, Barro, Jordan and Street, 2001). Their projects focused on such diverse topics as the discourse and culture of mahjong players, code-mixing in a local Chinese family, and 'Yum cha' (dim sum) – a daily habit of the elderly.

From late-January until mid-February, the participants were interviewed a second time, addressing such topics as language use by family members, language choice, attitudes towards languages and code-mixing, intercultural/travel experiences, pre-sojourn concerns and aspirations, and the 'English-only' policy. The RA followed a semi-structured format and encouraged the students to expand on comments made in their narratives and surveys. The interviewees again opted to express their views in Cantonese. The sessions ranged from 34 to 63 minutes, with an average of 49 minutes.

In late February, the students completed a pre-sojourn self-assessment scale; using a five-point Likert-scale, they expressed their views about 25 statements related to language, culture, personal traits, and intercultural adjustment. In particular, they responded to statements that provided insight into their tolerance for ambiguity, willingness to use English in social situations, adaptability/flexibility, and interest in England and English culture. The survey included ten open-ended questions that encouraged them to reflect on their goals, expectations, and concerns about the sojourn, and the 'English only' policy.

4.2.6.3   29 May to 3 July 2004: the five-week sojourn in England

For their five-week stay, the students and I were based in Kenilworth, a town in central England with a population of 20,000. It was close to the university where the students would take their courses. This institution was selected as it was able to offer a specially designed, thematically linked programme that would fully integrate the literary and cultural visits (e.g., plays, tour of Blenheim Palace) and academic course-work (e.g., lectures, workshops, discussions). Like the first group, each student was placed in a homestay situation to more fully experience English life (with one SES student per family). On most afternoons and Sundays they were free to explore or conduct their small-scale ethnography projects.

On weekdays, at the University they took literary and cultural studies courses as an intact group due to the specialized nature of their studies. In one joint class and during breaks they were able to interact with other international students. Through-out their stay, they attended many events (e.g., Shakespearean plays) and visited literary and cultural sites. As I accompanied the students on the excursions, I was able to observe them in a variety of settings and intercultural situations; I also had the opportunity to meet their host families during our stay and, on occasion, observe the students' interactions with them. Some students approached me about difficulties they were having (e.g., in their homestays), providing further insight into their inter-cultural communication skills and adjustment. Their comments and observed behaviour and my reactions were then recorded in my field notes.

Under my guidance, the students conducted ethnographic research on a cultural scene of their choice (e.g., gardening, keeping pets, a charity shop) to build a relationship with their cultural informant(s) and have more opportunity to converse in English informally (Jackson, 2006a, b).

To encourage the use of English, each student filled in a 'language use log' which consisted of a chart with a box for each day of the sojourn. They indicated how much English they used each day (e.g., 100%, 75%), jotting down a few notes explaining their rating (e.g., spent day in English with hosts on excursion). They also completed a 'daily rating log' in which they assessed each day using a scale of 1 to 10, with 10 being a fantastic day, 5 an average day, and 1 a terrible day. Similar to the previous chart, they wrote a brief note in each box to explain their daily rating, providing insight into their intercultural adjustment and investment in language and cultural learning. After the sojourn, the charts could be triangulated with other data that was dated (e.g., language use, diary entry).

As part of their credit-bearing fieldwork course, the students kept a detailed diary to record their observations and reactions to each day's activities, including their homestay, intercultural encounters, excursions, research, and lessons (Berwick and Whalley, 2000; Jackson, 2005, 2006b). They were encouraged to describe confusing or disturbing intercultural experiences as well as those that were particularly rewarding or memorable. They were also asked to describe and reflect on their language choices and any steps they were taking to enhance their communication across cultures.

Each Monday morning, a cultural studies specialist from the host institution facilitated an hour-long debriefing session in which the students raised questions and expressed their views about what they had observed or experienced that had caught their attention, annoyed them, or left them confused. I recorded their comments and these became part of the fieldwork journal that I kept throughout the sojourn. These sessions gave me further insight into the students' linguistic and cultural awareness, intercultural adjustment, and coping strategies at a particular point in time.

During the sojourn, the students completed surveys at the beginning of the second, third, fourth and fifth weeks to prompt further reflection on their sojourn experiences and provide insight into their language- and cultural-learning processes. I designed each survey to facilitate a comparison of their attitudes, perceptions, and concerns over time. The open-ended questions covered such topics as their goals for the sojourn, their reactions to their new environment, their contact with locals, perceived host receptivity, their stress level (degree of culture shock), their coping strategies, their awareness of cultural differences, their evolving sense of self, their relationship with their hosts, new behaviours they had adopted or rejected, their language choices, the 'English only' policy, perceived language gains, their attitude towards the English language, England and English people, and their perceptions of their intercultural communication skills. The survey administered in the last week solicited comments about their overall impression of the sojourn and its impact on their identity. It asked them to reflect on their pre-sojourn goals, the highlights of their stay, their linguistic and cultural gains, personal change/growth, their emotional state, and their thoughts about returning home.

4.2.6.4   July to August 2004: post-sojourn reflection

Back in Hong Kong, the students sent their diary entries to me by email as part of the requirement for their fieldwork course. They had been asked to make a minimum of three entries per week but there was considerable variation in the length and depth of their entries. Their diaries ranged in length from 27 to 95 double-spaced pages (7,275 to 25,405 words); the average was 47 double-spaced pages (13,529 words).

The third interview took place in July–August 2004, shortly after the students had returned from the sojourn (and their extended travels in Europe, in some cases). The topics included: feelings on re-entry, reaction to Hong Kong/L1, positive and negative elements of the sojourn, perceptions of hosts/host culture and language, intercultural adjustment in England, personal change/gains due to sojourn, the 'English only' policy, and advice for the next SES cohort.

As in the first two interviews, each participant was invited to use either Cantonese or English; this time, nearly half (seven) of the fifteen students used only English, two used mostly English with some code-mixing and the remaining six opted for Cantonese as in their earlier interviews. The interviews ranged from 30 to 83 minutes, with an average of 55 minutes per interview.

4.2.6.5   September to December 2004: post-sojourn reflection and report-writing

Two months after the sojourn, the students completed a post-sojourn self-assessment survey that mirrored the one that they had filled in prior to their stay in England. Using a five-point Likert-scale, they expressed their views about 25 statements related to language, culture, and intercultural adjustment. They rated such aspects as their English language skills, intercultural adjustment, and understanding of their own culture/English culture and also completed several open-ended questions about their sojourn experiences. This allowed me to draw a comparison with their pre-sojourn views and supplement the information they had provided in their post-sojourn interview.

In September the students began the research report-writing course; half opted to work with the ethnographic data that they had gathered during the sojourn, two went on a full-year exchange programme and were absent from CUHK for that semester, and the rest wrote a literary report related to the sojourn.

I met with the ethnography students on a regular basis from September until early December, providing guidance for the analysis and writing-up of their projects. This afforded me the opportunity to do further debriefing and gain more insight into the impact of crossing cultures. At the end of the semester, the students gave a presentation about their ethnographic research and invited the other SES classmates to attend. This session provided additional information about their current use of English and attitudes toward the sojourn as several of the topics and discussion centred on language use and intercultural adjustment.

4.2.6.6   January 2005 to May 2005: clarification of data

Throughout this semester, I reviewed the data and contacted participants when necessary to clarify any ambiguous comments in their oral and written narratives. In March, four of the participants participated in an orientation for the new cohort of SES students. They selected digital images of the sojourn and prepared a 20-minute PowerPoint presentation. This was followed by a question-and-answer session in which they talked about their sojourn experiences and offered advice about the homestays. This helped me to gauge the impact of their stay in an English-speaking country, nine months after their return.

4.2.7   Organization and ongoing analysis of data

Once the SES students had agreed to participate, as with the pilot study I set up a project database on QSR NVivo (Gibbs, 2002; Richards, 2002), a software program that facilitates the organization, coding and analysis of qualitative data. Each piece of data (e.g., interview transcript, survey, sojourn diary, digital image) was entered into the database soon after it was gathered. Consistent with ethnographic methodology, I coded and analysed the data in an ongoing fashion throughout the study; as I reflected on the material and gained new insights, I modified the data collection instruments and codes (Agar, 1996; Denzin and Lincoln, 2003; LeCompte and Schensul, 1999).

To better understand their personal journeys of discovery of Self and Other, I adopted a reiterative, interpretive mode of analysis throughout the study, triangulating data types and sources (Cortazzi, 2001; Reissman, 2002a, 2002b). I hoped to discover how the students made sense of experiences (e.g., how they reacted to intercultural encounters, how they felt when interacting with native speakers of English in Hong Kong and England, how their self-perceptions were influenced by encounters with Others). In my investigation of their 'versions of reality' (Ochs and Capps, 1996), I examined how their intercultural stories were constructed, mindful of the elements of narrative context (e.g., the purpose of their diary entries or ethnographic conversations, the cultural context and time frame in which they occurred). Since all of the data was dated and linked to individual participants, it was possible to compare and contrast their language and cultural learning processes throughout the programme and detect changes in their identity over time.

In my analysis, I examined the expressions they used to convey their ideas and emotions. I also noted repetitions and patterns in their narratives, the ordering and sequencing of their accounts, and the issues and themes that caught their attention at various stages of the programme (Bailey and Ochsner, 1983; Reissman, 2002a, b). Triangulation figured prominently in the collection and analysis of the data.

Heeding the advice of Bourdieu et al. (1991) and Sealey and Carter (2004), my analysis went beyond the students' perspectives. Drawing on my knowledge and expertise in the field and review of the literature, I made use of both 'emic' and 'etic' viewpoints to analyse the language and cultural learning and identity (re)construction of the participants both at home and abroad.

After actively recording data for almost two years, my NVivo database contained thousands of pages of narrative (oral and written) data and visual clips (e.g., digital photos of the sojourn). Throughout the study, this data was coded (indexed into categories and themes) and analysed to create a rich, hypermedia account. As well as providing a comprehensive picture of the group as a whole, NVivo allowed me to isolate the data (e.g., surveys, interviews, narratives) and coding related to each individual participant to construct case profiles for each student.

4.3   The illustrative case studies

4.3.1   Selection of case participants

To better illustrate the connections between language, culture, identity, and context, and not lose sight of the personal dimension, I decided to focus on the journeys of several participants instead of limiting my analysis to the group as a whole. As I was particularly interested in the impact of the sojourn, I began the selection process by eliminating those with previous SA experience. Next, I reviewed the cultural identity narratives, sojourn diaries, surveys, and interview transcripts of the remaining participants to identify those who had supplied very detailed, candid information about their language use, culture, and identities before, during, and after the trip to England. From this database, I selected six individuals and developed their cases; however, I found them so rich in detail that I needed to reduce the number further due to the confines of this book. I then chose four of these cases to represent a range of sojourn experiences and outcomes.

While all of the selected participants had received the same pre-sojourn preparation, the ways in which they viewed and responded to their sociocultural environment differed. Elsa and Niki (pseudonyms) took more advantage of linguistic affordances in England and made greater strides in their language and cultural development than Ada and Cori (pseudonyms). Perceiving their hosts to be welcoming and supportive, they experienced identity expansion and developed a deeper understanding and appreciation of both Chinese and English cultures. By contrast, Ada and Cori sensed 'a lack of mutuality' in the host environment; they were more resistant to cultural differences, language learning, and identity reconstruction.

4.3.2   The structure and content of the illustrative case studies

Chapters 5 to 8 present the ethnographic case studies of the selected participants, Ada, Cori, Elsa, and Niki (pseudonyms), following them from their childhood in Hong Kong through the sojourn in England and back again. Each chapter is divided into three main sections, pre-sojourn, sojourn, and post-sojourn so that the reader can better understand the nature and impact of each woman's experiences as they occurred.

These situated and personalized accounts illuminate the kinds of issues that L2 learners grapple with when crossing languages and cultures (e.g., identity misalignments, sociopragmatic failures, culture shock). Incorporating both descriptive and interpretive elements, the cases allow access to the 'real world' of the L2 learner/ sojourner. As such, they offer insight into how each participant interpreted experiences and constructed her own understandings of her language and cultural learning both at home and abroad. Blending proximity with distancing (as recommended by Bourdieu et al., 1991), I draw the reader's attention to details in the young women's stories, noting the specificity, complexity, and interconnectedness of their situations. By way of analytic commentary, I explore possible factors influencing their behaviour (e.g., linguistic choices), linking their reflexive knowledge and experiences to the theoretical constructs discussed in Chapters 2 and 3. This format involves a dialectic of the particular with the general, encouraging reflective, multiple, and critical interpretations of their storied lives to emerge.

Throughout the case chapters, the voices of the individual learners dominate, bringing their journeys and emotions to life. All of the quotes from written narratives (e.g., cultural identity narrative, surveys), which were written in English, are presented in their original form. For interviews, the students had the option of Cantonese or English. Interestingly, all chose to reveal their thoughts and feelings in their mother tongue prior to the sojourn, while on re-entry some opted to switch to English to discuss their sojourn experiences. For interviews that took place in Cantonese, efforts were made to retain the nuances and emotions of their discourse in the translations. By presenting a detailed account of their background and experiences, readers may draw their own conclusions about the relevance of their stories to their own situations.

Each case chapter begins with a profile of the Chinese university student whose story is in the spotlight. To better understand the impact of residency in an English-speaking country, the first section explores the young woman's personality, cultural/ family background, pre-sojourn identities, and language use/attitudes within a Hong Kong context. This provides insight into her character and childhood, offering a context for understanding her experiences and reactions to them. I also discuss her pre-departure aspirations, expectations, and anxieties about the impending five-week stay in England.

Her sojourn experiences are then recounted in chronological sequence to better understand her intercultural adjustment, linguistic and cultural development, and identity reconstruction over time and space. As her story unfolds, we gain insight into her evolving perceptions of the homestay experience and attempts to build a relationship with her hosts. We also see how she grapples with symptoms of culture shock and critical incidents across cultures. On the eve of departure, we discover her perceptions of her accomplishments and disappointments during the sojourn. Therefore, the sojourn section has numerous sub-sections, reflecting the sometimes turbulent nature of intercultural adjustment and personal expansion of L2 sojourners.

In the final part of each chapter, we return with the young woman to Hong Kong, where she grapples with re-entry and reflects on her sojourn experiences. Her candid thoughts and emotions offer an indication of the impact of the stay abroad on such aspects as her attitudes towards English, the host culture, and Hong Kong, her willingness to communicate (WTC) in English (Clément et al., 2007), her sense of self (identity), and her future goals. At the end of each case chapter I then provide a summary of the young woman's journey.

This approach captures the complexities of individual experience, the dynamic, relational nature of identity, and the situated nature of language learning and use. In each case chapter, I draw comparisons and contrasts across the data as I examine each woman's lived experiences. I also link their 'emic' perspectives with my interpretations and the theoretical constructs presented in Chapters 2 and 3.

What follows, in the next four chapters, are their unique, individual stories.

5   Ada's journey

My divided identity appears in the different names I have in
Chinese and English. I feel more myself when being called by my
Chinese name, Sze Ying, than my English (Christian) name, Ada.
(pre-sojourn cultural identity narrative, Ada)

5.1   Pre-sojourn

5.1.1   Profile and family background

When I first met Ada she was a rather quiet, reserved twenty-year old. The first member of her family to attend university, she was highly motivated to excel academically. A self-professed introvert, she described herself as a 'quiet, hardworking person' who liked to read and was 'willing to learn'. In an interview she added:

> I don't have any special interests besides reading books and
> studying. I like to read short stories, mostly in English. For
> Chinese, the variety is broad. I would read books about cooking
> skills, weaving, planting flowers… Sometimes I would listen to
> the radio but since I find it difficult to find a programme I am
> interested in, I will then turn it off.

While she had several close friends, she preferred to spend time alone. In secondary school, she served as a prefect and was a member of a civil education team as well as her class society. When she joined the SES, she was the secretary for a college English society. She did not take part in any other social or physical activities, preferring to focus on her academic work.

When asked about personal goals for her life, she disclosed her pragmatic nature and again emphasized the importance of her studies. She aimed to achieve good academic results so that she could eventually become a secondary school teacher of English. Interestingly, she did not cite areas of personal or social development.

A native speaker of Cantonese, Ada had spent her whole life in Hong Kong and had led a sheltered life with very limited intercultural contact outside academic settings. Prior to the sojourn, the only trip she had made outside the city was a three-day visit to her family's ancestral hometown in Mainland China.

When this study began, Ada lived at home with her widowed mother and younger sister, a secondary school student. Mrs Chan (a pseudonym) spoke Cantonese and Putonghua (Mandarin) but did not understand English and had little contact with people from other cultures. Raised in the Mainland, she worked in a factory after finishing secondary school. After her husband died, she became the sole provider for her family when Ada was just a toddler. It was difficult for her to make ends meet and Ada was acutely aware of the struggles her mother had faced to take care of her and her sister. What follows is Ada's journey of discovery of Self and Other.

5.1.2   Identity

5.1.2.1   Relational self-construal

In the cultural identity narrative that she wrote seven months prior to the sojourn, Ada candidly discussed the factors affecting her identity and positioning in the world around her. Until the age of thirteen, she saw herself as a 'Hong Konger' or 'Westernized Chinese' and was proud of this status as it differentiated her from Mainlanders. Growing up, she was aware of Hong Kong's colonial status and was affected by messages from her environment: 'Hong Kong was governed by the United Kingdom as a colony during my childhood. At that time, I saw Hong Kong as a modern, Westernized Chinese region, as advocated by textbooks and the mass media… I took in every word that was said, and was proud of being a Westernized Chinese.'

When Hong Kong was returned to Mainland China in 1997, she was an impressionable fourteen-year old. Not surprisingly, this event had a significant impact on her sense of self and attitudes towards the British and Westerners, in general. In her narrative she recounted her initial resistance to the pressures she felt to embrace a broader Chinese identity and move away from English to Putonghua (Mandarin), the official language of Mainland China.

```
When the handover of Hong Kong to China came closer, things
began to change. There was a sudden shift of emphasis from
English to Putonghua and the advocacy of identifying with the
Chinese Mainlanders. At first, I was quite opposed to this new
emerging identity, which was so sudden and quite unmatched with
my perception towards Hong Kong and my identity: Hong Kong is
modern and westernized, while the mainland China is backward and
traditional. Later, I started to accept such a change. After
all, I am a Chinese: yellow-skinned like the Mainlanders.
```

> However, I could only say that I am a Hong Konger, nothing more,
> nothing less. (cultural identity narrative)

Due, in part, to the influence of her mother and political events, she harboured reservations about being linked to the Motherland and still preferred the label 'Hong Konger' after the Handover. Before the sojourn, she accepted her Chinese ethnicity but 'denied her identity as a Chinese from the country China'. By comparing herself with Mainlanders, Ada engaged in the process of 'otherness' (Bakhtin, 1981). She articulated a sense of who she was by referencing that which she was not.

> Today, Hong Kong is a Special Administrative Region of China. My
> identity as a Hong Konger is still very strong, with a varying
> degree of identification towards the Mainland Chinese. Not that
> I deny my Chinese ethnic origin but the cultural differences
> between Hong Kong and Mainland China make me feel strong for
> Hong Kong and remote from Mainland China. Traditional, lack of
> civil education and non-democratic are my impression towards the
> Mainlanders, which is so different from that of the Hong Kong
> people. After the big demonstration against the China-appointed
> Hong Kong Chief Executive and the quest for universal suffrage,
> an even stronger sense of belonging towards Hong Kong and
> alienation to the Mainland built in my mind. Such a divergent
> view on democracy between us and the Chinese central government
> illustrates the big cultural difference and prevented me from
> saying whole-heartedly, without doubt, that I am a Chinese… From
> the stories told by mother in bedtime when I was small, I know
> the hardship she and her family came across in the Mainland.
> Maybe this gives me a bad image towards the Mainland and poses a
> hidden reason for me to refuse to identify wholly with the
> Mainland Chinese. As a result, together with the political
> background of Hong Kong mentioned above, I identify myself more
> as a Hong Konger. All these leave me to behave as a Chinese yet
> denying my identity as a Chinese from the country China.

While holding many negative stereotypes of Mainlanders, she recognized the impact of Chinese values on the wider Hong Kong community and her own identity. Western cultures and languages (e.g., English) had also influenced the formation of her sense of self, but to a much lesser degree. All of her friends and family were ethnic Chinese and, throughout her formative years, they had shaped her value system, worldview, and identity. Ada rejected some values and behaviours that she perceived as Western and realized that her core values were Chinese. At this stage, she saw herself as fundamentally Chinese.

> Hong Kong is perceived as a 'modern and westernized' society
> since I was very small. Yet, from the expectations towards the

social roles mentioned above, it seems that Hong Kong is indeed
not thoroughly westernized. The traditional Chinese philosophy
is still deeply rooted in everyone's heart. As a comparison, in
the western country, the taking care of old parents is done
through providing them insurance and other institutions, not by
the children themselves and a student may call their teachers by
their first names. Equality, instead of seniority, is emphasized
in western culture. From this perspective, I am a Chinese,
because I hold most of the Chinese expectations towards my
identity.

Although Ada felt more closely linked to her Chinese identity, many of her comments reflected a weak attachment to the Motherland and larger ethnic group. Her revelations also lent support to Vygotsky's (1986) notion that the individual self is formed through the internationalization of its sociocultural environment.

5.1.2.2   A divided, dual identity

A common practice among bilingual Hong Kongers is to have both Chinese and English names (Chan, 2000; Li, 1997; Scollon and Wong-Scollon, 2001). Most young people have a Chinese name given by their parents (in Chinese script), the anglicized version of this, and an English or Western-style name. In some cases, parents who are proficient in both languages may give their children 'official' English names that appear on legal documents (e.g., birth certificates, ID cards); however, the vast majority of students choose an 'unofficial' English name or are given one by an English teacher (a local Chinese). Sometimes students come up with a name that sounds similar to their Chinese name or is close in meaning; others simply pick a word from a dictionary, adopt the name of someone they admire, choose a name to indicate a religious affiliation, or create a 'fanciful', unique name of their own.

Li's study found that, while 'the majority seem to have little or no concern about the loss of Chinese identity' (Li, 1997: 508), by following this dual-naming practice, some resist this trend as it would make them feel 'un-Chinese' to have a Western name. Hence, this 'Englishisation' of names (Li, 1997; Tan, 2001, 2004) can lead to inner conflicts and psychological resistance in some. In Ada's case, for example, she sometimes felt that she possessed a 'divided' identity by having both English and Chinese names. Sze Ying (a pseudonym), the Chinese name her parents gave her, conveyed her true self and had a special meaning for her. She was emotionally connected to it as it linked her to her family and culture. By contrast, her English name, Ada, was more detached from her; in fact, she declared that it conveyed a 'superficial' side of her and primarily served a functional purpose. In her cultural identity narrative, she explained:

My divided identity appears in the different names I have in

> Chinese and English. I feel more myself when being called by my
> Chinese name, Sze Ying, than my English (Christian) name, Ada.
> The latter seems to perform a functional role only for the
> easiness of others to remember me, while the former one not only
> has its literal meanings as being a decent and elegant person
> but also incorporated the expectations and blessings of my
> parents. Most of my closer friends know and call me by my
> Chinese name. I treat it as the expression that they know the
> real me, not the superficial me. However, this kind of feeling
> towards my name, as well as my divided identity, is diminishing
> when my English name is used more and more frequently among my
> friends.

Interestingly, when asked what name she preferred to be called in class, she wrote down 'Ada' on the form. While she felt much closer to her Chinese name, within the context of English-medium lectures she opted for her 'superficial' label, similar to the majority of her peers (English majors).

5.1.3   Languages

5.1.3.1   Language ability and usage

Ada spoke two languages: Cantonese (her mother tongue) and English. She considered herself 'fluent' in the former but was much less confident in her English language skills, convinced that she was 'not up to standard'. While she had received a 'B' on the A-level 'Use of English' examination at the end of her secondary schooling, she only rated her proficiency in the language as 'fair' (in the middle of a six-point scale). Although she considered her writing and understanding of the language to be 'very fluent', in an interview she commented that she sometimes could not 'catch the meaning when native speakers speak very fast'. She was less certain about her reading and speaking skills, rating them 'fairly fluent'.

Within the confines of her home, Ada 'lived in' Cantonese. She preferred not to use English due to her sensitivity to the feelings and 'education standard' of her family members, especially her mother: 'I do not feel good when I deliberately speak a language that my mother would never understand because I feel I'm not showing respect to her. She would feel offended.' The only time she spoke English at home was when she helped her sister prepare for her A-level exam. Once it was over, she stopped practising the language with her. Ada seldom watched TV programmes or movies in English because she found it 'exhausting' to try and understand the dialogue.

Ada attended a Chinese-medium primary school and took English language lessons with local Chinese teachers. Her Christian secondary school officially used English as the medium of instruction; however, she pointed out that, in reality, there was a lot of code-mixing (Cantonese and English). At university, all of her classes in the English Department were taught in English, but some of her General Education electives were in Chinese, in keeping with the University's bilingual policy. In English-medium lectures, Ada used English to communicate with her professors; she usually code-mixed or spoke in Cantonese with her classmates unless a professor approached (interview).

Ada stated that she had few opportunities to speak English in Hong Kong due to the Cantonese environment. Her cultural identity narrative revealed that her use of English was limited to formal, classroom situations and never social contexts; the language served a 'functional purpose' for her:

```
Though Hong Kong claims itself to be a bilingual region, our use
of English does not have an equal status with that of Chinese.
We will not normally talk to each other in English unless we are
doing oral drills; and we do not expect a person randomly picked
on the street will understand and be able to use English... I
seldom speak English to a Hong Kong person unless it is
required, such as when I am giving a presentation or doing some
oral activity, i.e., in a classroom context. English serves, in
this light, a functional purpose only.
```

In Ada's writing, it was interesting to note that she often alternated between 'we' and 'I', blending her collectivist perspective (inclusive social self) with the more Western-oriented (individualized) sense of self.

5.1.3.2 Attitude towards languages

Ada was much more comfortable using her mother tongue than English, as she found it difficult to express her emotions and ideas in a foreign tongue:

```
I feel more at home when I hear or speak Cantonese than English
although I am an English major. In my daily life I can express
my thoughts and feelings more spontaneously and accurately by
using Cantonese; whereas for English I sometimes need to think
for a second before the words actually come out of my mouth.
(cultural identity narrative)
```

Later, in the same interview, Ada stated that she felt 'inferior' when speaking English with a native speaker, a view shared by many of her peers before the sojourn.

```
If the speaking content is the same, my feeling would be
different when I speak English with a Chinese speaker or a
native speaker of English. I would feel inferior when I speak
```

> English with a native speaker. For example, when I see a group
> of native speakers discussing and when they speak very fast, I
> feel they have an advantage. This is because as a Chinese
> speaker, my reaction is too slow. I can't compare with them. On
> the other hand, I feel better when speaking English with a
> Chinese speaker as we know each other's situation well. When we
> speak English, we would not fight for the chance to speak.

This lack of confidence in her oral English contributed to her ambivalent and sometimes negative feelings about the language. Her situation is not unique. Learners in other foreign language settings may also be detached from the language they are learning in classrooms. Feelings of inadequacy, especially when interacting with speakers who are more proficient, may lessen their willingness to practise it.

For Ada, English was a 'tool' for communication, something external to her sense of self, reflecting a strong instrumental orientation (primarily learning the language for pragmatic purposes) (Gardner and Lambert, 1972; Ricento, 2005). 'For me, English is a language to use. It is something like a tool for me to communicate with rather than part of myself.' Her strategic, grades-oriented perspective became apparent in the following excerpt from an interview that took place in Cantonese:

> RA: Does your use of English vary depending on the
>   context?
> Ada: Yes. If it is something like a tutorial, where you can
>   gain marks only if you speak, I would speak for sure
>   but if it's just casual talk, where we are aiming at
>   building up a relationship or getting to know each
>   other better, I would tend to be passive and speak
>   less. If I am chatting with a person that I am
>   familiar with, I feel better if I speak Cantonese, and
>   of course I would be more talkative. But if it is a
>   person I am not too familiar with, even if both of us
>   are Chinese speakers, I would remain quiet. If that
>   person is a native speaker, I would be even quieter.

Ada's view that communicating in English involved a constant struggle resurfaced when she offered an explanation for the reluctance of Hong Kong English majors to use English with each other. She associated the language with hard work, emphasizing the need to occasionally escape from it.

> RA: Many Hong Kong Chinese students who are English majors
>   use Cantonese when talking with each other outside of
>   class. Why do you think there is a reluctance to use
>   English outside situations in which it is required?
> Ada: I think it is to get a release from English. When you
>   speak in English, you would feel like you are studying

Ada felt detached from English and experienced psychological pressure when forced to use it. How would she react to the English-language policy that would be in place during the sojourn? Would exposure to an English-speaking environment change her perceptions of the language and deepen her level of investment or would she retreat to the warm embrace of her L1?

Similar to many of her peers, Ada considered it unnatural for Chinese speakers to use English with each other when not absolutely required. In an interview, she said: 'if both of us are Chinese and can speak Cantonese, it's strange to speak in English but when I speak English with a native speaker, I think it's okay to do so because it's quite difficult for Westerners to learn Cantonese'. Her comments may strike a chord with foreign language teachers around the globe who struggle to motivate their students to practise the language with each other (in and outside of class).

5.1.3.3 Code-mixing

Ada frequently code-mixed when communicating with her peers; that is, she added English words to her largely Cantonese discourse. In an interview she revealed that she was conflicted about this practice: 'I use code-mixing as it's more efficient. I can finish a sentence faster when I express myself in this way. Sometimes I speak too slowly in English. When code-mixing I feel good but later I feel I'm not good in either language.' Influenced by the constraints of society, Ada held very definite views about how much English should be added to Cantonese discourse. Her tendency to be rather judgmental became evident when she disclosed the criteria she used to brand a speaker a 'show-off':

5.1.3.4 Language, culture, and identity

As a schoolgirl in colonial Hong Kong, Ada recognized the power of English and felt compelled to master the language to 'survive' in her environment: 'Before the Handover, the education system put a lot of emphasis on English, such as the use of English as the medium of instruction in almost all secondary schools, and teachers' emphasis that "if you know no English, you cannot survive in Hong Kong".' In Bourdieu's (1977, 1991) terms, Ada's narrative disclosed her awareness of the linguistic capital, legitimacy, and authority of English. As a consequence, she felt societal pressure to gain prestige ('cultural capital') for herself and her family by becoming proficient in the language she associated with colonialism.

As a university student, Ada was becoming more cognizant of the complex relationship between language, culture, and identity. In her narrative, she reflected on the hybridity of Hong Kong – the intertwining of Chinese and Western values and languages. Distinguishing herself from Mainlanders, she contemplated the impact of her identity and culture on her indirect style of communication. Her mixed views about English, 'an interference' with her mother tongue, exposed a complex love–hate relationship with the language. Her comments highlight the need for applied linguists and EFL teachers to be mindful of Byram's (2003) warning about the potential psychological impact of being forced to learn another language on one's existing social identities.

```
Who am I?


Hong Kong, with its claim as a modern, westernized, and
international city, allows the wide usage of both Chinese and
English in the society. At the same time it attracts people from
different cultural background to come to Hong Kong. These
factors affect the formation of my identity and attitude towards
the two languages. On one hand, I am educated in English and
exposed to a wide range of English media; on the other hand, I
live mostly in Cantonese and Chinese culture, with the
occasional interference from other languages. The political
background of Hong Kong and the language background of my family
all give birth to my dual identity both as an acculturated
Chinese and an English language user – a unique 'self',
different from both the (Mainland) Chinese and western culture.
While indirect communication style is mostly used, conforming to
the Chinese tradition, code-switching is a prominent feature of
communication among Hong Kong people. Too much code-switching,
or the overuse of English overriding the use of Cantonese
(Chinese), however, is regarded as showing off. A complicated
sense of both admiration and despise exists towards the varying
extent of the use of English. All the above show that I am a
'Hong Kong Man', who has taken advantage of the British colonial
```

```
rule to be able to get in touch with both Chinese and western
cultures, possessing a unique cultural identity. (cultural
identity narrative)
```

Ada's views provide further evidence of the socially constructed, evolving nature of the self and illustrate how language can be used to display identities and memberships in groups (Zuengler, 1988, 1989). As Pavlenko and Lantolf (2000), Wenger (1998), and other sociocultural theorists have pointed out, identity is an ongoing process of negotiating the self, and issues of power and belonging play a central role. This socially situated view of identity and language use helps to better understand the complexity of the lived experiences of foreign-language learners, like Ada, and highlights the limitations of SLA research that overlooks sociocultural and sociopsychological factors.

5.1.4   Pre-departure aspirations, expectations, and anxieties

Prior to the sojourn each student was asked to set goals for their five-week stay in England. Ada's aspirations were far ranging. As this would be her first trip away from home, she anticipated becoming more mature, independent, and broadened in some ways:

```
My personal goals of this trip include to become more
independent, to be able to put myself into a wider worldview and
to know how people of a different place from mine live. I expect
this sojourn will change me to a certain degree. After all, I
will have gone to a place that is different from my living place
and met people that I otherwise will not meet. I hope I would
become more mature in dealing with people and things happening
around me. After living so many years in a protective
environment, this is time and chance for an adventure to the
unknown. (intercultural reflections journal)
```

By crossing boundaries, Ada expected to become more aware of her culture, identity, and personality: 'I hope to understand the differences between the Asian world and the Western world, and thus establish my individuality, my self-concept as a human being' (pre-sojourn survey). She also had rather high hopes for the enhancement of her oral English skills: 'I expect that I will be able to speak English fluently after the trip to Britain' (interview).

Before departing for England, the students were asked their views about the 'English only' policy that would be in place for the sojourn. Ada felt 'it would be a good idea to get a total immersion', noting that she would not have the opportunity to 'speak English for 24 hours a day in Hong Kong!' Nonetheless, like many SES sojourners who had preceded her, she conceded that it would initially seem 'unnatural' or 'weird' to communicate with her SES friends in English. Ada also doubted that she had sufficient command of the language to use it on a daily basis and was not sure that she would be able to stick to the policy unless someone constantly reminded her to do so.

In the weeks leading up to the departure, in a survey, Ada also divulged additional fears about a wide range of issues:

```
Living in a completely strange environment – new places, new
setting, a language not often used, all of this is going to be a
great challenge for me. I'm always nervous with changes… I'm
worried about being robbed… I'm also worried that I'll get lost…
I'm worried about how to start talking with my homestay family.
As this is the first time for me to go abroad, I'm worried over
security, safety and health and the fieldwork we will do and the
financial situation.
```

Her low tolerance for ambiguity and lack of self-confidence contributed to her malaise. While many of her peers shared some of her concerns (especially about living with strangers from another culture), Ada displayed a more elevated level of stress than usual and was very worried about her ability to 'survive' on her own. In a step towards independence, she moved into a hostel on campus a few months before the sojourn. She explained that she hoped that this time away from home (on weekdays) would help her mature and become better prepared for life with strangers.

Previous research on student sojourners has found that pre-departure stress and undermet expectations are strong predictors of adjustment difficulties while abroad (Ward et al., 2001). Would any of Ada's unrealistic goals and anxieties lead to disappointment and frustration during her stay in England?

5.2   The sojourn

Near the end of May, after two semesters of preparation (September to April), the fifteen sojourners boarded a plane with me in Hong Kong and 13 hours later landed at Heathrow airport in London where we were met by an International Student Support Officer from the host institution. The weary travellers then boarded a bus for the two-hour trip to the University. Soon after our arrival, the students were introduced to their hosts one by one and whisked away to Kenilworth and a different way of life.

5.2.1   From euphoria to disillusionment

Ada was initially filled with excitement and anticipation, a common experience for newcomers. In this honeymoon stage of intercultural adjustment, 'sojourners

perceive people and events through pleasantly tinted (or "rose-colored") lenses…
Overall, they are cognitively curious about the new culture and emotionally charged
up at meeting new people' (Ting-Toomey and Chung, 2005: 128). The first entry in
Ada's diary reflected this euphoric state: 'All the scenery from the bus trip to the
homestay was like magic; everything was so beautiful, like pictures and fairy tales.'
Later, on the same day, she added: 'I rode in my host father's car and looked around.
Riding in a private car is a rare experience for me in Hong Kong. And now is the
second time already in just the first day of my stay here. I feel quite satisfied.'

Her buoyant mood was short-lived, however, which is not unusual. While everything may seem 'fresh and exhilarating' at first, sojourners may also experience
'mild bewilderment and perplexity about the new culture' and 'bursts of loneliness
and homesickness' (Ting-Toomey and Chung, 2005: 128). By the middle of the first
week, Ada began to show the strains of trying to function in English in an unfamiliar
land and sometimes lapsed into her mother tongue and a darker mood: 'It is really
hard to use English all the time because it means you have to do translation work 24-
hrs a day. Sometimes, by instinct, Cantonese slips in' (sojourn survey, beginning of
the second week).

While she yearned to become fluent in the language, after only a few days in an
English-speaking country she had become very self-critical and felt incapable of
achieving her goals. In social psychological terms, she was experiencing low self-
efficacy; her mind was full of self-doubts and negativity as fatigue and stress
engulfed her.

```
I really think that my English is not okay. I need time to
translate what I want to say: grammar and articles and tenses
are all wrong… And it's so tiring to use English all day. I find
that my English vocabulary is not enough. And the translation is
really killing me!… It is getting harder and harder for me to
translate and I feel tired. I just speak Cantonese by instinct.
I saw some of the classmates do this too. It is hard, really
hard, to speak English all the time — those tenses and 's', etc.
I think my mind will burst… I have started to have problems in
translation; maybe I am too tired for that because I need to do
it all day long for 5 days already. Really killing me. My
English proficiency is dropping and my mood is on the drop.
Really bad… Maybe there is a maximum capacity of learning a
foreign language/second language that prevented my further
improvement? (diary, first week)
```

Did her negative expectations about her adjustment become a self-fulfilling
prophecy?

5.2.2   Identity misalignments and perceptions of discrimination

To complicate matters, early on, Ada experienced a threat to her identity. Her hosts mislabelled her as Japanese, a very common occurrence for my students. While we had discussed this possibility before our departure for England, experiencing it firsthand was very upsetting to her: 'My host family always mistake me as a Japanese: "How are things like in Japan…I mean, Hong Kong?" Whenever they look at me: dark hair and yellow skin, I think, it reminds them of the Japanese student they had before' (diary, first week).

Her comments support Assumption 4 in Ting-Toomey's Identity Negotiation Theory (INT) (See Table 3.1), which emphasizes the need for 'desired group membership identities' to be 'positively endorsed' if intercultural encounters are to be successful. In Ada's situation, her hosts failed to understand the identity domains that she considered salient; as a consequence, she experienced 'identity differentiation' and did not feel recognized or accepted.

In the first week the students and I went to Coventry as a group to collect our bus passes; other customers in the queue watched as we filed up to the wicket one-by-one. Ada interpreted their stares as 'discrimination of yellow people' rather than mere interest or annoyance at having been made to wait longer. In her diary, she wrote: 'I think here, there is really some discrimination when it comes to business with yellow people. On the street, they won't stare at you. But in offices, they will, maybe because we'd made a scene there, I mean at the place where we made our bus pass.'

This was Ada's first trip outside Hong Kong and her first taste of being a visible minority. She found the situation unnerving and was plagued by insecurities: 'Feeling at ease in a foreign place is difficult… The locals see us as foreigners… When there are lots of blonde hair, blue eyes around you, it is easy to forget that you are black hair, black eyes but you know you are not one of them.' Sensitive to these differences, Ada was on edge and fearful: 'There are miscommunications everywhere. Once you're out of home, you are different from others. You need to take care of yourself' (sojourn survey, beginning of second week).

In the INT, identity security is defined as 'the degree of emotional safety concerning one's sense of both group-based membership and person-based identities in a particular cultural setting' (Ting-Toomey, 2005: 219). By contrast, identity vulnerability refers to 'the degree of anxiousness or ambivalence in regard to group-based and person-based identity issues' (2005: 219–20). According to Assumptions 2 and 3 of this theory, 'we often experience emotional insecurity or vulnerability because of a perceived threat or fear in a culturally estranged environment' (2005: 219). Ada's revelations support the notion that 'emotional issues' (e.g. anxiety, fear, displacement, insecurity) are closely linked to 'self-conception or identity issues' (2005: 219) and intercultural adjustment.

From the onset, Ada's fears held her back from exploring her new surroundings: 'It is stressful here in terms of finding my way, avoiding getting lost, and staying safe… Sometimes to have enough security I stick into a group, but I know it is no good' (sojourn survey, beginning of second week). She longed for the security and familiarity of home, believing that she needed to be on guard against 'those white people' who discriminate against her ethnic group. She eyed the host culture with suspicion and fear.

```
I miss the connections I have in Hong Kong, the feeling of
belonging to Hong Kong, and having all the people and things
that I know there. I feel more secure in Hong Kong because,
although UK is quite international, people of all colours are
here, I think there is still some discrimination. Sometimes I
think the discrimination is valid, that is, some doings of the
Chinese people is worthwhile to be discriminated by the people
here, because sometimes the Chinese shout or talk loudly to each
other and make a scene, which is very horrible. Those white
people won't do this often. No wonder they discriminate us.
(diary, first week)
```

Ada's comments lent support to Assumptions 4 and 5 of the INT, which centre on the themes of ingroup/outgroup-based boundary maintenance issues. 'Identity differentiation is defined as the degree of remoteness (i.e., emotional, psychological, and spatial distance) we perceive in regulating our group-based boundary with either ingroup or outgroup members' (Ting-Toomey, 2005: 220). 'Too much group-based differentiation', she explained, 'may cause us to feel unwelcome or excluded' (2005: 220). This appeared to be the situation for Ada.

5.2.3   An ethnocentric mindset

Ada's diary and sojourn surveys offered insight into the difficulty she faced in accepting aspects of life that differed from what she was used to. While she had hoped to become more open, she found herself judging everything from her culture's standpoint. Her high level of ethnocentrism held her back from fully enjoying her stay and created a negative mood that permeated her discourse:

```
Water in UK is directly drinkable from the tap, which is new to
me. But I can sense that this is the same water source to flush
the toilet so it's a bit disgusting to think in this way… Weird
rice here, too. The chicken is TASTELESS, maybe they are just
those frozen chicken, not the fresh one. We Chinese, especially
the Cantonese people, are really picky at eating! (diary, first
week)
```

For the first time in her life, Ada found herself exposed to concepts of health and wellness that differed from her own. This, too, was very unsettling for her and difficult to accept. To borrow from Bourdieu (1977, 1991), she entered a new 'field' with a set of dispositions (habitus) that had been formed in another cultural setting; her beliefs, behaviours, and worldview were an uncomfortable fit in the new environment, leaving her confused and out of sorts. She began to notice cultural differences and responded to most with annoyance or hostility. While she indicated that she 'tried' to accept differences, her mindset, at this stage, predisposed her to reject anything that was different from what she was used to.

```
There are a lot of differences between me and my host family.
Like they eat the skin of potatoes (which is said to be
poisonous by my mum), and they eat the burnt toast (black part)
(which is said to be leading to cancer). They like pets,
gardens, keep clean and beautiful everywhere. More decorative
than functional home; more to the look than for use. And they
have vinegar for chips not tomato ketchup. I tried to accept the
difference, but if it is concerning health, I won't do that.
(diary, first week)
```

In her diary, Ada also wrote about a 'critical incident' that had taken place in the first week. Icy, an SES student, had invited Ada and four other friends, to her homestay to show off her room. Unfortunately, Icy had not talked to her host beforehand and the woman's reaction was one of surprise and annoyance. After much reflection, Icy wrote a lengthy entry in her diary in which she considered the situation from the perspective of her host, acknowledging that it was not considerate to arrive unexpectedly with a large group of strangers. In stark contrast, Ada was very critical and unforgiving, unable to consider another viewpoint or recognize that some social norms in this context might have been broken: 'After lunch today, I went to visit four houses of my SES friends. Icy's host gave a stern "no" to our visit. She said that it was a time for her and her husband, not for us so we had to leave immediately. I think the host was very impolite, and Icy was embarrassed' (diary, second week). In Ting-Toomey's (2005) terms, Icy displayed 'mindfulness', whereas, Ada was not able to shift her frame of reference and remained entrenched in a state of 'mindlessness'. Her lack of openness and rigidity stymied her inter-cultural adjustment.

5.2.4   The psychological impact of L2 use

Prior to the sojourn, Ada had had high aspirations for the enhancement of her English-language skills. By the end of the second week in England, however, she was thoroughly discouraged and down on herself. She discovered that her mother tongue had a tight grip on her. At this stage, English was still just a 'foreign language' to her. Ada was clearly suffering from the strain of trying to function in an L2 in daily life. Her admission provides concrete evidence of the potential psychological impact of being pressed to use another language:

```
My language skills are worse. Every time after seeing a play, I
am going to say something in Cantonese. Every time! So last
night after Macbeth, I deliberately shut my mouth for a moment
to let my Cantonese instinct go. Then I could talk in English
again. Maybe my first language really has a strong hold over me;
English is probably a foreign language, rather than a second
language, to me.
```

Ada criticized her accent in English and lamented her use of code-mixing. What is noteworthy is her use of 'we' and 'our' when discussing her habit: 'Yesterday I would rate my language use at 80%. It seems that we were all tired of English; the code-mixing phenomenon is more frequent now' (diary, second week). In reality, most of her classmates were using English not Cantonese or code-mixing; she was experiencing much more difficulty functioning in English.

```
What we usually do when we find words that we don't know in
English, we just use Cantonese, that is, code-mixing! This trip
will certainly enhance our skills in code-mixing rather than
English speaking. Sadly, it maybe true. I was foreseeing that
when I go back to Hong Kong, I would not be able to speak either
Cantonese or English purely and properly, but all mixed up. Too
bad! I certainly realize my weakness in spoken English through
these 2 weeks. I would forget tenses, 's', wrongly used verb
form, using 'is it?' for all kinds of question tags, etc. and I
feel that my accent is becoming more Hong Kong like than British
or American-like. Very ugly! I should pick up the RP here,
instead of Hong Kong accent, right? Just speaking makes me feel
tired of all the translations! Horrible. Please let me have the
enlightenment moment, the light bulb moment, which I suddenly
grasp the secret of using spoken English. Things don't usually
happen this easily, do they? (diary, second week)
```

An entry that she made in her diary in the second week also caught my attention. It revealed that she had not come to terms with the notion of Chinese communicating naturally with each other in English, which was, to her, a foreign tongue: 'Despite my Cantonese instinct, I am now used to speaking and hearing English. Really strange! For the ABC (American-born Chinese), it must be strange to have the combination of yellow skin but speak and be acculturated in another culture.'

5.2.5   Feeling misplaced, homesick, and insecure in an alien environment

Ada's homesickness and negativity continued. In her diary, at the end of the second week, she wrote: 'We are all fed up with sandwiches. I think today, I have a bit of homesick as I'd like to have normal Chinese meal, the soup, etc, and sense of security. Really boring here, too, I mean the life here.' While most of her classmates seemed to be enjoying themselves, Ada made use of the collective 'we' when describing her negative feelings and longing for 'normal' food. A few days later, in her survey, she admitted that she had not adjusted well in this alien environment: 'I expected to feel misplaced, and it is true for the time being. I expected to feel tired, and it is still true.'

'In the hostility stage', according to Ting-Toomey and Chung, 'sojourners experience major emotional upheavals. This is the serious culture shock stage in which nothing is working out smoothly. This stage can occur rapidly right after the glow of the honeymoon phase is over and reality sets in sooner than expected' (Ting-Toomey and Chung, 2005: 129). Not surprisingly, in this liminal, transitional state, sojourners often experience a significant reduction in self-confidence and disorientation (Trubshaw, 2001). Like Ada, they may feel emotionally drained, inept, and misplaced.

This novice sojourner continued to worry a great deal about her personal wellbeing, which slowed her adjustment: 'As there is no lock on my door, I don't feel safe in my room… Last night, after coming back home, I couldn't sleep well. I heard noises (proved to be the cat this morning) and barely sleep. I even woke up at 4 am to check the time. Really horrible' (diary, second week). Like most of the women, Ada lived in a crowded public housing estate in Hong Kong and was not used to open, empty spaces and the silence of the night:

```
I would like to be more independent. It is not so good to be
alone in a foreign country, actually because it is not safe.
More people is safer. I would like to feel more comfortable at
home (stop reading too much in my room, try to find something to
interact with my host, e.g., football watching). I feel unsafe
at night, which is really a pity. (sojourn survey, second week)
```

In her anxious state, Ada's imagination ran wild and this hampered her willingness to interact and use English. Her revelations lent support to Assumption 3 of the INT (identity negotiation theory); a high level of insecurity in an alien environment appeared to have a significant negative impact on her intercultural adjustment and sense of self.

5.2.6   Lack of mutuality and engagement

Near the end of the second week, Ada plucked up the courage to talk about her fears with her hosts (white, middle-aged, middle-class Anglo-Saxons who had grown up in the area and were native speakers of English). While the couple had travelled extensively in Europe and beyond, they failed to grasp why she was so anxious about her personal safety, as Kenilworth is a small, quiet town with a very low crime rate. In their eyes, it was much safer than most places they had visited. Ada saw herself as a 'helpless female' and did not feel that her hosts understood or cared about her. She was disappointed and resentful, which made her even more anxious and unsettled. Not surprisingly, she became less willing to develop a relationship with them. This also impacted negatively on her attitudes towards the host language and culture and her willingness to communicate (WTC) (Clément et al., 2007).

```
It is good to have my host family's assurance [about personal
safety] but I am still not secured. They just keep on saying,
'If that is elsewhere, I can't be sure but here, in Kenilworth?
No, nothing will happen. You are safe here...' Why is it safe for
me to walk alone at night (or with one more young helpless
female)?... My host is hoping that the best, instead of the worst,
would happen. I mean, why [does] no one think 'precaution is
better than regret'? I am really unhappy about this. (Ada,
diary, second week)
```

Ada's entry brings to mind Wenger's (1998) conception of 'mutuality and engagement' in communities of practice (CoP), which suggests that newcomers who perceive their hosts to be supportive and understanding may find their sojourn fulfilling and take a more active role in their new environment. By contrast, those who experience 'a lack of mutuality', like Ada, may feel alienated and fail to fully engage in new social practices and make less of an effort to become 'full-fledged' members of the host culture (Ting-Toomey, 1999).

Shortly after her disappointing discussion with her hosts, Ada admitted that she was still homesick and having difficulty coping. She felt 'trapped' by her fears, which continued to limit her exploration of the world around her:

```
Maybe at home in Hong Kong I will feel safer and freer; here, I
feel a bit trapped so as to be safe. Symptoms: stomach ache,
wind inside it, making me feel uncomfortable and preventing me
to eat whatever I want. I took some medicine and skipped a meal
once but it's still not okay. May be cured only when I go back
to Hong Kong. (sojourn survey, beginning of the third week)
```

As a consequence of culture shock, she became moody and withdrawn, a typical response in the 'hostility stage' (Ting-Toomey and Chung, 2005; Ward et al., 2001).

5.2.7   Feeling out of place and detached from English

Midway through the sojourn, Ada still found informal, social discourse in English confounding and had difficulty building a relationship with her host family. To cope, she often hid in her room, limiting her contact with them: 'When my host family talks with me, it's like an interview or they are trying to entertain me in my opinion. My hosts may feel that I am easily contented because I usually want less food and usually stay in my room. But how far do I fit in their eyes? I don't know' (sojourn survey, beginning of the third week). As she did not always understand what they said, this further hindered her communication with them: 'I feel a bit out of place because sometimes I have no idea what my hosts are talking about.'

Bakhtin (1986) put forward the notion that, if one lacks an understanding of the 'speech genre' in a particular situation, miscommunication and misunderstandings can occur, which may threaten one's self-image and willingness to engage. In Ada's case, she was not familiar with the 'habitus' (learned habits) of her host family (e.g., the particular ways in which they acted and responded in informal social exchanges) (Bourdieu, 1977, 1991). In these events she was exposed to unfamiliar 'ways of seeing, knowing and understanding' (Bakhtin, 1986:78) that placed her in a 'different world'. Feeling uncomfortable and out of place, she responded with hostility and withdrew.

At this stage of the sojourn many of Ada's peers were buoyed by enhanced self-confidence in their oral English and a few even claimed to be thinking or dreaming in the language. By contrast, she still felt detached from it and did not feel that it 'belonged' to her. Using English in unfamiliar situations was 'highly challenging' for Ada. As Norton and Toohey warned may occur in L2 speakers, this impacted on her sense of self in 'complex and often contradictory ways' (Norton and Toohey, 2001: 312). While she wished to speak more fluently in English, she was very negative about herself and her language skills:

```
I can feel that my English standard is falling, and I have
increased code-mixing. I have never dreamed in English.
Yesterday, I feel that I have difficulty in expressing myself in
English accurately and quickly. Maybe because I am tired of
translating things in my mind? English doesn't seem to belong to
me. There are so many lively and accurate and precise
expressions in Cantonese that cannot be expressed in English,
which is quite sad. I feel my accent become strange too. Not
good. (sojourn survey, beginning of fourth week)
```

Ada had hoped to speak English 'fluently' by the end of the trip, and when her progress was less than expected, she became disillusioned. While some of her peers also experienced disappointments, they were able to reset their goals and motivate themselves to make the most of their short stay. Ada appeared to find it more difficult to remain positive and was more self-critical throughout much of the sojourn.

5.2.8   Identity misalignments: feeling misunderstood and misplaced

According to the INT, if intercultural encounters are to have satisfactory outcomes, the participants must feel that they have been understood, respected, and 'affirmatively valued' (Ting-Toomey, 2005). What happens when newcomers, like Ada, do not believe that their desired identities have been 'authentically understood'?

As well as being discouraged about her perceived lack of progress in English, Ada continued to feel misunderstood by her hosts, who failed to recognize her preferred self-construal (Hong Kong Chinese). In her diary, at the beginning of the fourth week she was still referring to locals as 'those British people' and clearly did not feel at ease or happy in this context. Her reaction supports Ting-Toomey's (2005) assertion that communicators who feel that their desired identities have been 'mindlessly bypassed, misunderstood, and/or insulted' are apt to experience 'a low sense of identity satisfaction' and have prolonged adjustment difficulties.

```
My host family sometimes forgets that I am from Hong Kong, like
yesterday, my host dad said, 'Does Professor Jackson teach you
in Japan?' which really makes me feel confused: does he mean
whether my professor teach me in Japanese or teach me Japanese,
the language? But then he realised that he was wrong, 'Oh, no,
how can I forget…' I think, to them, or to those British people,
Asian equals Japan; they look alike, speak alike. Japan is a
strong country here. They also seem to have the impression that
Asia is bad, always transmits diseases to us (the British).
Maybe to them, China is bad; Japan is good. To them, I am just a
Chinese, not specifically from Hong Kong. And they don't know
much about Hong Kong or China. It's just too far away from them.
They know more of the Indians, who, according to my host dad,
settled and mixed well with the British people since 1960s. But
we, the Chinese, have just come here (which, to me, is not very
true). (diary, third week)
```

Being mislabelled Japanese, coupled with a growing awareness of ways in which she differed from locals (e.g., appearance, communication style, medical beliefs, habits, values), put Ada on the defensive and heightened her awareness and acceptance of her racial/ethnic identity. In essence, her unsatisfactory encounters with Others (e.g., hosts) served as identity triggers, making her 'ethnically conscious', stimulating further reflection on her place in the world. 'Usually people ask us whether we came from Japan. Asian = Japan? Quite worrying. Maybe Japan is too powerful. And I realize that I am Chinese. I need Chinese medicine to help me cope with the food here. By nature, from body to mind, we are Chinese' (sojourn survey, beginning of fourth week).

```
Although we think that Hong Kong is modern, etc., indeed we are
Chinese. Some things we've acculturated can't be changed, like
the belief of 'heaty' versus 'cold' food. It seems that after
coming here, I become more aware of my Chinese side: I drink
'cold' tea to put out the heat from the western food, and take
Chinese medicine to prevent sore throat. The westerners and I
are just very different. (diary, third week)
```

Similar to many of her fellow sojourners, she was dismayed to discover that, although she considered herself very different from Mainland Chinese, most English people did not make this distinction or understand why it mattered to her. This was very deflating. She felt a significant cultural distance between herself and 'Westerners' and frequently believed that she was being discriminated against. This prompted her to continue the 'them vs. us' theme in her discourse. Her reaction to feeling different led her to withdraw to the safe confines of her own racial/ethnic group.

```
Identity: Hong Kong, westernized Chinese. But to them, the
British, we are Chinese. They don't accept us to be in their
country. Discrimination is still there, though there may be laws
to protect you… Now I feel more about my Chinese identity, it
will never equal to western people. We are too different. We
don't understand, or refuse to understand, each other fully.
They are too ahead of us. (I notice the use of 'we', 'I' versus
'they' here; there is really a distinction) (diary, third week)
```

Ward et al. have observed that it is not unusual for international students to perceive prejudice and discrimination in intercultural encounters; they explained that, 'these perceptions are often stronger in students who are more culturally dissimilar from members of the host population' (Ward et al., 2001: 153). In other words, students who are visibly different, speak the host language with a different accent, and have significantly different values and behaviours may experience more adjustment difficulties.

By the middle of our stay, most of the students were exploring the nearby towns and cities in their free time, but Ada was still feeling too insecure and homesick to share in their fun: 'What I feel is still misplaced… Just saw an aeroplane pass by, feel a bit like flying back to Hong Kong' (diary, third week). Her fears and difficult adjustment compelled her to seek out people 'just like herself' (e.g., her SES peers/ female members of the same ethnic/linguistic group) for the sake of security or identity. From Bakhtin's perspective, this set her on a 'rigidifying and impoverishing' path (Emerson, 1997: 223–24).

As the weeks passed, Ada continued to be exposed to cultural practices ('actions with a history') (Bourdieu, 1991) that differed from what she was familiar with in Hong Kong; her written narratives (diary and surveys) laid bare a discourse of resistance. She was uncomfortable being positioned as a 'social apprentice' in CoP that were new to her, and she reacted negatively to the pressure that she felt to conform: 'Now I know more of how to behave and why they behave that way but it doesn't equal to I accept it' (survey, beginning of fourth week). As Bourdieu (1991) warned, identity misalignments and hostility can arise due to incompatibility between a habitus and a field, especially when different values collide. Ada's unbending personality and tendency to be judgmental made it more difficult for her to fully participate in the homestay.

```
Disgusting thing: Today's breakfast is really shocking, because
I found the bread has turned bad. It's all in blue colour.
Really horrible. This is the first time that I have seen
something turn bad so completely and so ugly. I think my host
mum was embarrassed because I am still a guest to them but I saw
something so nasty in her house. So this morning, I could only
have cereal for breakfast. (diary, fourth week)
```

Later that week, she wrote about an incident on a bus and again made use of the collectivist 'we' in a disparaging comment about England: 'We really don't like this culture.' When reading the following excerpt, it is relevant to note that her university in Hong Kong has a very large campus and a bus system is used to transport students from one area to another; the bus drivers frequently have to call out for passengers to make room for others. What she witnessed on the bus in England was not new to her. Her hostile reaction to the girl (and the host culture) reflected the irritable, grumpy state of culture shock that had a tight grip on her.

```
On the bus, we saw a girl occupying two seats with her bag in
front of us. Zoe started to scold her in Cantonese, which is
really a good tool in my opinion as she won't know what we were
talking about and she won't get angry with us; at the same time,
we can release our anger towards her. We really don't like this
culture. Why they need two seats actually? Because they need
more personal space? I really don't understand. (diary, fourth
week)
```

5.2.9   Enhanced awareness and appreciation of cultural differences

Much of Ada's discourse revealed a rigid character and rejection of the host culture.

However, I did discover examples of her attempts to open herself up to new modes of behaviour and even appropriate some local practices (e.g., expressions of appreciation): 'The politeness of English people is really amazing: they say "thank you" every time to the bus driver when they get off the bus. When I first noticed it, I felt odd but now I imitate them. We should appreciate the efforts of others who serve us' (survey, beginning of fifth week). Ada was tentatively repositioning herself as a 'willing-to-learn guest' in the host speech community as she experimented with what Bakhtin (1986) referred to as 'ventriloquation'.

In spite of the difficulties she'd experienced, in the same survey, Ada described the homestay experience as 'valuable', since it had provided her with the opportunity to 'really see what is happening in an English family'. One of her pre-sojourn goals had focused on developing a better understanding of cultural differences, and she felt that she had accomplished this: 'The differences of culture (in terms of how to greet each other, how to keep the house clean and beautiful, how they view TV or history) between the host family and my own family broaden my horizons.' Ada was beginning to notice visible cultural differences; however, she was not yet able to recognize or adjust to more complex variations (e.g., values, worldviews).

Feeling more positive, Ada had begun to make more of an effort to interact with her hosts instead of hiding in her room: 'Usually, at the beginning of the sojourn, when I had lunch or dinner, that would be the only time I went downstairs to the kitchen. After their invitation, and much emphasis, I now stay for a while after dinner, just to chat' (sojourn survey, beginning of fifth week). Through 'shared doings' (e.g., cooking with her host mother) she began to develop a deeper understanding of social practices in this CoP. Although she still struggled to fully express her ideas and emotions in English, she had started to communicate more easily with her host mother and felt closer to her due to their collaboration:

```
Last night, I made pizza with my host mother. This makes me
think of mother-daughter relation. Really nice experience… I'm
getting along with my host family. I'd say that we both enjoy to
talk to each other. I can converse with them naturally. I spent
most of my evening with them. We had dinner together, watch TV
and talk. I watch my host embroidering and walk the dog with
them. It's getting easier to communicate with them and I'm less
tense so I can joke with them. (diary, beginning of fourth week)
```

5.2.10   Racial/ethnic realization

In an ethnographic conversation with me on the fourth week of the sojourn, Ada indicated that she had adjusted to life in England. In her diary, however, she wrote that she still felt like a foreigner, noting that her physical appearance differed from that of the locals: 'Today is quite a depressing day. I do not feel I belong here. I miss the belongingness I felt in Hong Kong. Here, I am just a foreigner. In their hearts, I am still a foreigner, never a part of them' (diary, fourth week). A few days later, she wrote: 'I can't say that people here make me upset but, anyhow, I am different from them. Sometimes, I know that people are staring just because I am a Chinese – black hair and yellow skin. The level of comfort is definitely different from when I was in Hong Kong' (sojourn survey, beginning of fifth week).

'New racial/ethnic realization', according to Ting-Toomey (2005), may be awakened in minority group members because of a 'racially shattering' event (e.g., encountering racism), which makes them realize that they are different and not fully accepted by the majority group. This appears to be a straightforward explanation of Ada's experience, yet it is not that simple. Students of colour, unfortunately, may indeed encounter racism in their travels; however, feeling vulnerable in unfamiliar settings and CoP can also lead to *perceptions* of discrimination, which may only exist in the mind of the minority member (Ward et al., 2001). In this heightened state of alert, sojourners may feel different and expect to be mistreated. This reaction to their environment must not be overlooked. It can serve as a powerful and even traumatic jolt to their sense of self and feelings of security. It can also negatively impact on their willingness to participate in new CoP.

Regular debriefing sessions can provide a venue for these feelings and insecurities to surface. A skilful, sensitive facilitator can listen empathetically and provide reassurance, motivating L2 sojourners (e.g., minority group members) to become more engaged in new CoP and adopt a more balanced view of the host culture (and home culture). By emphasizing the natural ebbs and flows of the adjustment process, those who are particularly anxious and fearful, like Ada, may look more positively on their journey.

The experience of living in a foreign country raised Ada's awareness of her personality and place in the world, further illustrating the relational nature of identity (re)construction: 'I'm more aware of my Chinese identity and my weaknesses. I am proud of who I am and hope to change my weaknesses and be a better person in terms of personality. Be stronger' (sojourn survey, beginning of fifth week).

```
I know more about myself: what I want, what sort of life I
prefer to have, what my weaknesses are… I feel more of my
Chinese identity. Before coming here, I didn't know that Hong
Kong is really so Chinese. But after the comparison, I know that
although Hong Kong is a modern city, it's not so westernized.
And I am just a Chinese both to myself and how the foreigners
see me. My identity as a Chinese is built through this trip. I
can still feel that Hong Kong is different from the Mainland. My
identity is, therefore, Hong Kong Chinese to me. (dairy, fifth
week)
```

Ethnicity, as defined by Ting-Toomey, involves 'a subjective sense of belonging to or identification with an ethnic group across time' (Ting-Toomey, 2005: 215), while ethnic identity salience refers to 'the subjective allegiance and loyalty to a group large or small, socially dominant or subordinate with which one has ancestral links'. In Ada's case, she struggled between the perception of her own ethnic identity and Others' questioning of it. Throughout much of her stay, she resisted the labels assigned to her by Others; on many occasions her self-construal had neither been validated or respected. In response, her allegiance to her ethnic group grew stronger.

5.2.11   Plagued by emotional vulnerability

While most of her peers were sad to be leaving England after such a short stay, Ada was still suffering from culture shock, often feeling out of sorts and dissatisfied. In her diary, she vented: 'I am not satisfied here… I think my homesickness is getting worse now. And I feel that I want to go home. I feel tired here, and there is nothing hot here: I have never drunk hot water here. Everything is expensive here.' Ada never fully adjusted to the diet and longed for the familiar: 'When I get back home to Hong Kong I'm going to EAT A LOT! I miss the Chinese food: the rice (not Indian one), and all those steamed food' (sojourn survey, beginning of fifth week). 'After five weeks of this trip I really miss home. Now, whenever I see an aeroplane, I miss home' (diary, fifth week). Ada had not overcome her insecurities in this alien environment and still felt like a foreigner: 'I wanted to become independent but it is not so okay for security reasons. It may be better after going back to Hong Kong… In comparison, Hong Kong is a much safer, better place. Maybe because I'm not a local here?' (diary, fifth week).

According to Assumptions 2 and 3 of the INT, sojourners may suffer from 'emotional insecurity or vulnerability because of a perceived threat or fear in a culturally estranged environment' (Ting-Toomey, 1999), and this was certainly true for Ada. As a consequence, she was anxious and unable to fully relax. Five weeks in the host culture is not a long time. Would she have been able to make a breakthrough if the sojourn had been longer?

5.2.12   Reflection on linguistic, cultural, and personal gains

On the eve of departure, Ada's moods fluctuated wildly and, at times, she was more positive than she had been in the last month. When asked how she felt about leaving, in her last survey she wrote: 'Really a bit sad. I want to stay more with the host. I want to look more around here…' In a similar vein, in one of her last diary entries she expressed enthusiasm for the sojourn:

```
I have experienced disappointment, annoyance, love, happiness,
```

```
etc. The sojourn was really so abundant and full. This
experience helped me to be more confident in myself and gave me
a chance to know more about different people and learn to get
along with them. Very worthwhile to open my eyes, to see more,
and know something that seemed very far away from me.
```

She had become more self-reliant and a bit more willing to express her ideas, even if they differed from what others expected:

```
I start to ask for what I want instead of keeping quiet, and I
learn to express my opinion, even though it is opposite to what
others thought and they may not accept my views. But my
confidence level is a bit fluctuating: sometimes I am bold but
sometimes, I just keep quiet. (diary, fifth week)
```

As the departure date drew nearer, Ada reassessed the state of her English-language skills. While she felt 'more natural speaking English in all occasions' and 'responded more quickly in conversations', her perception of her overall proficiency was still largely negative. She had become more comfortable expressing her ideas in English but still considered it a foreign language that was 'quite hard to live in'. She had not internalized it. It is also important to note that Ada expressed concern about the potential loss of her mother tongue, even though she had only been away from Hong Kong for five weeks and had been in the company of other Cantonese-speakers. In her writing, she again linked her views to 'most' of her peers, although she appeared to experience more difficulty than most.

```
I don't think my English has improved. I think it in fact
worsened pronunciation-wise and grammar-wise. Sometimes, I'm
still hindered by accent for me to comprehend correctly what's
been said. Maybe because it is just a foreign language to me? I
don't think I can think in English. Translation is still there.
Maybe more code-switching? Sometimes I think my skills at code
switching is better than the one language skill. And most of us
start to have the feeling that when we speak Cantonese it is a
foreign tongue to us now. (sojourn survey, beginning of fifth
week)
```

For me, one of the most interesting comments in Ada's diary was written in the last week of the sojourn: 'Actually, we don't have lots of chances to interact with foreigners.' While she was living with an English family in an English-speaking country, she did not consider herself to be surrounded by opportunities to use the language and interact with people from the host culture. Even in her homestay, until fairly late in the trip, she made less of an effort to interact with her hosts than many of her peers: 'The time when I was at peace is whenever I was alone in my room I can write journals or do nothing there' (diary, fifth week). This avoidance strategy helped her to 'survive' but hampered relations with her host family. It also limited her exposure to new CoP and informal, social English. As Gibson (1979) and van Lier (2000, 2004) have pointed out, some language learners may only see obstacles in their environment and withdraw, reducing opportunities for linguistic and cultural enhancement.

This is only part of the picture, however. Ada's host family had not validated her preferred identity or feelings; they had failed to understand her insecurities and this had hampered her adjustment and willingness to bond with them. If she had been placed with more mindful, empathetic hosts, would the outcome have been different, as suggested by Lave and Wenger (1991) and Ting-Toomey (2005)?

5.3   Post-sojourn

Back in Hong Kong, Ada completed a post-sojourn survey and was interviewed about her experiences in England as well as her reactions to being back on home soil. Similar to the pre-sojourn interviews, she opted to reveal her thoughts and feelings in her mother tongue. Therefore, all of the interview excerpts are translations, as in the previous sections.

Throughout her stay in England, Ada found it difficult to develop a 'sense of belonging' in new CoP (Corder and Meyerhoff, 2007). She never felt completely at ease and suffered from disorientation in this foreign environment. In response, she became more nationalistic, with a heightened awareness of her attachment to Hong Kong and her family. In her post-sojourn interview, she explained: 'Hong Kong is my home. Although I know that England is a very good place, it doesn't belong to me. I had to go back to where I belong… I missed home very much when I was in England… Perhaps because my family is here, I think Hong Kong is the best.'

Even so, on re-entry Ada experienced some disappointment as she looked at her homeland through a different lens, comparing it with what she had seen during the sojourn: 'I felt a little bit frustrated when I came back. I don't know whether it's the quality of the citizens or not but I found that Hong Kong is dirtier. Sometimes I think some places could be cleaner but people here don't really care. They might spit. But I didn't see this in England. This makes me feel disappointed.'

Ada's pre-sojourn perception of Hong Kong as a modern mix of East and West also changed somewhat: 'I thought Hong Kong was quite Westernized but when I came back…now I think it's still quite Chinese. People's thoughts and habits are actually very Chinese unless you go to Hong Kong Island where a lot of Westerners live but when you come to New Territories and to my home, it's quite a Chinese place' (interview).

While much of her discourse had been negative throughout the sojourn (e.g., critical of both Self and Other), after she was able to relax at home, she began to reflect on how she had changed during her stay in England. She was able to identify several areas of growth; she had become more self-confident, independent, and expressive. In her interview, she also commented that she had acquired a broader perspective: 'The trip was very important to me. It was the first time to be away from Hong Kong and a lot of things are different there. I saw many new things in England and when I came back to Hong Kong, I had one more angle to see the world.'

Prior to the sojourn Ada had set rather unrealistic goals for the enhancement of her English-language skills during a five-week stay in England. Back in Hong Kong, this impacted on her negative perception of her linguistic gains. I also noticed in her post-sojourn interview that her assessment of her English language skills was filtered through an academic lens; that is, she focused on grammatical accuracy rather than fluency, noting her deficiencies rather than her strengths:

```
I found my weakness. I don't know whether it [this awareness] is
a kind of improvement. It's quite serious. When I'm spontaneously
speaking English, I have many grammar mistakes. Sometimes the
's' is missing; sometimes the tense is misused but it's too late
to correct my speaking.
```

Her last comment left little room for optimism and her use of English quickly reverted back to the pre-sojourn phase. She did not speak the language at home or in her circle of friends. English was still largely a 'tool' for academic study not social interaction, and her investment in the language did not appear to have changed much.

Ada conceded that she had found it difficult to adjust to an 'English life' and had felt unsafe during much of the sojourn. In her interview, she explained: 'I think I lacked the feeling of security in England. I wish I could be more relaxed in different environments. Sometimes when I don't feel secure, I can't perform well. I want to train myself to be more confident.' Her insecurities had held her back from exploring the host community on her own and had made it more difficult for her to establish a close relationship with her hosts.

Cultural misunderstandings also meant that she often felt misunderstood and marginalized: 'Sometimes I think my host family really didn't understand me. Perhaps it's the cultural differences. I think the problem is the concept. You could use language to tell them and explain but it's really the concept that they don't understand. It's something that made me feel disappointed.' In Assumption 5 of the INT, Ting-Toomey theorized that sojourners may experience 'identity awkwardness or estrangement in interacting with unfamiliar others because unexpected behaviours occur frequently and intrusively' (Ting-Toomey, 2005: 220). This was certainly the case for Ada.

The resentment and frustration she felt about not having her identity validated in

England resurfaced during her interview: 'In terms of nationality, I'm a Chinese but I also want to emphasize that I'm a Hong Kong citizen. For the British, we're all Chinese. They won't care where you're from. For them, a Chinese or a Hong Kong citizen is the same but for me there's a difference.' Understandably, she was also upset that they had often mistaken her for Japanese: 'Sometimes they even asked me, "How is it in Japan?" Well, I'm not from Japan. Maybe the Japanese and the Chinese look alike to them. They just think we're Asians and they mix up all Asians.' This had a negative impact on her willingness to interact across cultures.

Even so, Ada expressed regret that she had not spent more time with her hosts: 'Sometimes I wasn't sure whether the two of them wanted to go out on their own so I didn't bother to ask and lost the chance to be with them.' Would she have been able to establish a warmer relationship with them if the sojourn had been longer? Would her adjustment and willingness to use English have differed if she'd been placed with a more empathetic host family?

Considering her difficult adjustment and lack of attachment to English, I was more than a little surprised when she expressed interest in furthering her studies in another English-speaking country. Exposure to the world outside Hong Kong had opened her eyes to other possibilities for her future. Her sojourn experiences had given her a bit of confidence to consider other options for her life, especially from the safety of home. In her survey, she wrote:

```
I want to see one more culture. I don't know whether I could
achieve it or not. I now want to do a postgraduate programme
overseas; I never thought of this before the trip. I might not
go back to England for this as I've seen it. If I take the
Diploma in Education Programme I could have a one-year immersion
in Australia. Then, I could see one more culture and come back
and see what my identity is.
```

A year later, after finishing her Bachelor's degree, Ada opted to continue her studies in Hong Kong.

5.4   Ada's journey in review

Prior to the sojourn, Ada preferred to be identified as a Hong Konger, emphasizing that her core values were Chinese. She 'lived in' Cantonese and her use of English was largely limited to formal, classroom situations. Recognizing the 'linguistic capital' (Bourdieu, 1977, 1991) of English, she suffered somewhat from the psychological impact of being pressured to learn the language to advance in Hong Kong society. She felt 'inferior' when speaking English with a native speaker and considered it 'unnatural' for Chinese to use the language with each other if they both knew

Cantonese. Her language choices (including code-mixing) were found to be strategic and context-dependent, similar to the findings of McKay (2005) and Meyers-Scotton (2006) in other bilingual contexts.

Ada was very anxious about her ability to cope in England. While she experienced a brief honeymoon period on arrival, she soon succumbed to the strains of living in an L2 in an alien environment. As Bourdieu (1991) warned can happen, Ada experienced communication and identity misalignments due to incompatibility between a 'habitus' (her linguistic and cultural socialization in Hong Kong) and 'a field' (e.g., English homestay). This 'lack of congruence', feelings of insecurity, and perceptions of discrimination led to a rather turbulent intercultural adjustment for Ada and resistance to the use of English in social situations (Clément et al., 2007; Pellegrino, 2005). She never felt 'authentically understood' by her hosts and her desired identity was sometimes 'mindlessly bypassed'. Experiencing a 'lack of mutuality and engagement' in her homestay (Wenger, 1998; Ting-Toomey, 1999; 2005), Ada found it difficult to build relationships with her hosts. While she made some gains in terms of her language and cultural development, she retained an ethnocentric mindset throughout her stay and never felt that English 'belonged' to her. Her self-efficacy in the language was low, and this also curtailed her willingness to use it in the host community. Still in the throes of culture shock, Ada returned home with a deeper appreciation of Hong Kong and Chinese culture.

6   Cori's journey

I do not possess an intense sense of belonging to my hometown or any group, as if I am like a piece of driftwood. I do not know where my destination is. (pre-sojourn cultural identity narrative, Cori)

6.1   Pre-sojourn

6.1.1   Profile and family background

Cori, an attractive, self-possessed twenty-year old, liked to be on her own and, while friendly, was a bit detached from her peers. She described herself as 'observant', 'persevering', and 'willing to take up responsibilities'. Like Ada, she was rather quiet and introverted: 'I seldom talk and love thinking. And, I love writing more than talking… Actually, I need to be more sociable and I would like to be more creative.' Her first interview provided further insight into her personality: 'I am an independent person who needs some private space… When people first meet me, they will find that I'm quite silent and seldom smile. They may think I'm rather cool in the beginning but later they will find me okay.'

In secondary school she served as the vice-chairlady of the St John's First Aid Society (Cadet Section); she was also a student tourist ambassador in a programme sponsored by her school and the Hong Kong Tourist Association. After entering university, she lived in a hostel and joined several extracurricular activities. At the time of the study, she was a member of an international exchange organization on campus and regularly joined English Tables (social events designed to provide students with the chance to use English with native speakers in an informal setting). Unlike Ada, she had travelled outside Hong Kong and had developed a wide range of interests:

As a sports lover, I go swimming, jogging and playing badminton or volleyball when I am free. Water sport is my favourite also.

On entry into the SES, Cori revealed that she hoped to do postgraduate studies abroad after working for a few years. Unlike Ada, she was adamant that she would not enter the teaching profession: 'I don't want to teach. Never. I want to have a job in journalism or business.'

Cori's family was 'fairly well off'. Her father, a university graduate, was employed as a civil servant, and her mother, a high school graduate, worked as an accountant. Her younger brother was a student in an English-medium secondary school. All of her family members spoke English but primarily used Cantonese in their social/ family life. Her father used some English in his place of work (e.g., for public speaking, processing documents), while her mother rarely spoke the language. The couple's knowledge of English, education level, and economic status were higher than those of the parents of the other case participants.

In Hong Kong, the family's intercultural contact was primarily with their domestic helper, a Filipina; however, they loved to travel and were exposed to cultures outside Hong Kong. Most of their trips, which ranged from a few days to two weeks, were organized tours for Cantonese speakers. Three of the trips were to Australia, Canada, and the United States; the rest were to non-English speaking Asian or European countries. While Cori had much more travel experience than the other women, she had never been to England and had never travelled independently.

6.1.2   Identity

6.1.2.1   Relational self-construal

Like Ada, Cori's feelings about Mainland China were quite complex, emotive, and changeable; her perceptions were closely linked to the historical, political, linguistic, and social context of Hong Kong (Hall, 2002). Early on, I also discovered that she was preoccupied with 'ingroup identification' (Ting-Toomey and Chung, 2005). All of these factors affected how she saw herself and others.

> have prejudice or stereotypes towards them but the 'ingroup-
> outgroup' does exist when we recognize our differences, such as
> our mother tongue and our values. Undeniably, I would be a bit
> proud of being Chinese whenever I hear good news about China,
> for example, the first time for Chinese astronaut to go to the
> space successfully or Beijing will be the host country of the
> Olympic games in 2008. Still, I feel more ashamed of facing the
> dark side of Mainland China. Odd and distant feelings overwhelm
> me when I listen to the national anthem. (cultural identity
> narrative)

Like Ada, at this stage, she wished to be differentiated from Mainlanders. While she did not admit to being prejudiced, she was 'ashamed' of some aspects of Chinese culture and viewed Hong Kong culture as different due to the colonial period and Western influences.

6.1.2.2   Encapsulated cultural marginality

As a teenager, Cori became confused about her identity when her parents applied for official travel documents for her. This event triggered reflection on her place in society and her relationship with Britain and Mainland China. She was reluctant to fully embrace a Chinese or British identity and felt somewhat lost and in-between, 'like a piece of driftwood.' Janet Bennett (1993) referred to this as 'encapsulated marginality'; in this state, individuals who are exposed to several cultures are 'buffeted by conflicting cultural loyalties' and, as a consequence, feel aimless and unsure of who they are.

> I have a small degree of confusion towards my cultural identity.
> My parents, my brother and I hold a British passport, but we do
> not choose the HKSAR one or the BN(O).[1] It is just for the sake
> of convenience so we need not apply for a visa whenever and
> wherever we travel. As a person who has not been to the UK and
> only received colonial education in Hong Kong, I have felt very
> strange to write British as my nationality in any formal
> documents since I was small, but I am not reluctant to do it. I
> would be more reluctant to declare myself as Chinese because I
> mind if others think that I come from Mainland China instead of
> Hong Kong. Therefore, I will be relatively more comfortable to
> label myself as Hong Konger. To me, Hong Kong is a unique place
> where many cultures are mixed. I have connected myself to where
> I have been brought up with delicate sentiment. At the same
> time, Hong Kong does not have deep roots in my eyes. It is like
> a piece of driftwood floating on the Victoria Harbour without a
> permanent anchor. And I do not possess an intense sense of

> belonging to my hometown or any group, as if I am like a piece
> of driftwood. I do not know where my destination is. (cultural
> identity narrative)

In her narrative, Cori described the 'push and pull' of Western and Chinese cultures on her sense of self and the resulting confusion and turmoil that enveloped her. She rebelled against these pressures and resisted anything that would label her a 'traditional Chinese'; like Ada, she preferred to be identified as a Hong Konger.

> Another interesting phenomenon is that I avoid buying or wearing
> clothes with the 'made in China' label. Though I know many
> clothes of good quality are now produced in the Mainland, I just
> psychologically do not feel comfortable with them. Nevertheless,
> if I were asked to put on 'Shanghai Tang' or 'Vivienne Tam', the
> clothes famous for its Chinese styles aimed at the foreign
> market, it is my pleasure to do so. The other example is my own
> experience with school uniforms. In my secondary school, I wore
> a 'Cheung Sam' instead of a dress or skirts in western styles.
> To be frank, I hated being forced to wear a Cheung Sam, as I did
> feel that I belonged to the 'traditional category'. Sometimes,
> for the sake of convenience, I matched my Cheung Sam with sport
> shoes, which was a very ugly and discourteous 'mix and match'.
> These two exemplars show how I revealed my discontent or
> confusion about my cultural identity to others.

At this stage of her life, Cori was more confused about her cultural identity than Ada and much more resistant to traditional Chinese culture. Feeling marginalized and lost, Cori envied people from other cultures who were more certain of their place in the world. In the following excerpt from her narrative, she seemed to feel inferior to others, not believing that her own culture was 'worth being introduced'. At this juncture, she exhibited a high level of what Ting-Toomey (2005) defined as 'identity insecurity'.

> According to my observation, one of the major differences
> between westerners or Mainland students and us is that in most
> cases they have a strong sense of belonging to their home
> country and I do not. Whenever we talk about our own cultures,
> they are quite proud of themselves and become more and more
> talkative and confident. This also applies to those shy people.
> Looking at myself, although I try to take a more balanced role
> in this kind of conversation, I am still relatively more passive
> as I fail to recognize that my own culture is worth being
> introduced. Others can feel that we express our ideas and mind
> with insufficient enthusiasm or patriotism from our gestures and
> tone.

How would her identity insecurity and low self-esteem impact on her intercultural encounters in England (the homeland of the colonizers)? Would she fear 'outgroups or unfamiliar strangers' as predicted by the INT (Identity Negotiation Theory)?

6.1.3   Languages

6.1.3.1   Language ability and usage

Cori spoke four languages: Cantonese, English, Putonghua, and a little French. She was most confident about her proficiency in her mother tongue: 'My Cantonese is very fluent and my English is okay. Putonghua is okay. I can only say one or two sentences in French.' She received a 'B' on her A-level examination in English and considered her overall proficiency in the language to be 'good'. Nonetheless, she only rated the individual skills (reading, writing, listening, and speaking) as 'fairly fluent'. She was least confident when using English with native speakers who were not familiar to her; similar to Ada, she was afraid of making mistakes and losing face.

Although her family members knew English, they seldom spoke it at home, preferring to use Cantonese. Occasionally, Cori helped her younger brother practice his oral skills in English or tutored schoolchildren in the language. The only other time she spoke in English in this context was when she interacted with the family's domestic helper. She sometimes read English newspapers or watched the news in English if her family happened to be doing so but did not make an effort to turn to an English channel. Like Ada, she did not seem to be heavily invested in the language on a personal level, largely limiting its use to formal CoP (communities of practice, such as academic settings).

Cori received her primary and secondary education in local grammar schools. While Cantonese was used as the language of instruction in her primary school, her co-educational secondary school had an English-medium policy and a few teachers were native speakers of English. In an interview she revealed that this school had placed 'a great emphasis' on the language and, unlike many other schools in Hong Kong, her classmates had not been 'very afraid of speaking it'. Her use of English did not change after entering university. Like most of her peers, she primarily used it to communicate with teachers and classmates in formal academic settings and rarely used it in her personal life. When conversing with friends at the university she frequently code-mixed as did Ada.

In the community, Cori used Cantonese (or code-mixing) to communicate with other Hong Kongers. She did not feel comfortable using English in situations where it was not required and did not seek out opportunities to use it in informal situations.

6.1.3.2   Attitude towards languages

Cori found speaking Cantonese much more 'natural' than English because of her fluency and ability to freely express her ideas. Even so, in an interview she revealed that she harboured some negative feelings about her mother tongue: 'I think there are more rude words in Cantonese than in Putonghua so I don't like Cantonese in that way. And I will listen to Mandarin songs more because I think their lyrics are more refined.' Her comments illustrate the complex, multifaceted, and deeply personal relationship that bilingual (multilingual) speakers may have with the languages that they speak. It is also important to recognize that these views may shift over time as circumstances change (e.g., proficiency level, exposure to an environment where the additional language is used in everyday life).

Cori's parents encouraged her to master English and had a very positive influence on her learning. While she described her attitude toward the language as 'quite positive', she preferred to use Cantonese as she was more comfortable conversing in her mother tongue. This is also the language she chose for her interview.

```
RA:     How do you feel when you use English with a native
        speaker of the language?
Cori:   In general, I feel comfortable but it also depends
        whom I speak to. If I am close to that person, I will
        speak well. Otherwise, I may become nervous and make
        many grammatical mistakes.
RA:     If you are talking to a Chinese in English?
Cori:   No problem.
RA:     How do you feel?
Cori:   Comfortable.
RA:     Does it vary depending on the context?
Cori:   Yes. For example, when I am having the English
        Department's courses and everyone knows that we have
        to use English in the class, I feel comfortable. But
        when I meet my friends and they speak Cantonese, I
        feel strange if I use English with them. It would feel
        as if I am outgrouped... For friends whose mother tongue
        is Cantonese, I won't use English with them.
```

Her attitudes towards the languages she spoke were closely tied to the context of the interaction (e.g., informal vs. formal situations) and the ethnicity and proficiency level of her interlocutors. In the above excerpt, her preoccupation with 'ingroup' affiliation resurfaced, illustrating the strategic and relational nature of her language choices. This was in line with Zuengler's (1989) finding that learners may choose to use a language according to 'solidarity' criteria.

In Hong Kong, Cantonese serves as a powerful linguistic force to bind Chinese speakers together. For Cori, the use of English in informal situations in this context could result in being branded an 'outgroup' member – something she wished to avoid. Following a collectivist orientation, the desire to maintain close interpersonal bonds with those in her 'ingroup' was paramount.

```
RA:     Many Hong Kong Chinese students who are English majors
        use Cantonese when talking with each other outside of
        class. Why do you think there is a reluctance to use
        English outside situations in which it is required?
Cori:   I think it is due to the atmosphere among this group
        of people. If someone does not speak English first,
        others won't follow. So, we all wait. And we all,
        being English majors, know that speaking in English
        outside class is good but we don't want to be the
        outgrouped ones. No one is willing to take a step
        forward and so the situation will continue.
```

While Cori felt that it was acceptable to use English with her peers in academic situations, she considered it 'strange' for Hong Kongers to converse in the language in informal situations: 'Their mother tongue is Cantonese and so they will leave me with the impression that they are showing off.' Her candid revelations have implications for foreign-language students and teachers in other contexts, raising our awareness of the affective, sociocultural, and psychological factors that may curtail a learner's language choices at any given point in time.

How would Cori feel about using English with her peers in England? Would these reservations persist or would her views change in an English-speaking environment?

6.1.3.3　Code-mixing

Cori sometimes felt 'superior' when peppering her Cantonese discourse with English words, believing that it linked her with her 'ingroup', young bilingual, well-educated Hong Kong Chinese. Her strategic use of code-mixing may be explained by Edwards' observation that 'the strong preferences for given varieties [languages or dialects], which have always existed, are based upon sociopolitical considerations; central here are the dominance and prestige of speakers' (Edwards, 1994: 206). In other words, Cori's choice of code-mixing extended well beyond her desire to express herself more easily; she used it in certain sociocultural settings to present a particular image and status in front of her interlocutor(s). In Hong Kong, she was aware of the 'linguistic capital' of code-mixing.

Nonetheless, in an interview, Cori revealed that she, too, had reservations about this practice, feeling that it disrespected both languages: 'I don't think it's good to do it. If you speak Cantonese, why do you add some unnecessary English vocabularies? I think it is not good. I think it is not respectful to either of the languages.'

```
Like other Hong Kong students, as a bilingual who can speak
Chinese (Cantonese and Mandarin) and English, code-mixing has
become my habitual way of talking on informal occasions. Code-
```

mixing refers to a condition when a speaker who is fluent in two or more languages or varieties uses them in the same conversation. In my case, I subconsciously code-mix Cantonese and English when chatting with family members or Hong Kong friends. Personally, I don't regard such code-mixing as a proper way of expressing myself. Not only do I disrespect either Cantonese or English, but also both of my language skills are prone to deterioration. Still, I feel more superior and natural when using some English words in my Cantonese speaking. If I use Cantonese in every line, it sounds strange and awkward to me. To a certain extent, I resist to change this habit when my friends sharing a similar cultural background also code-mix in such a way. (cultural identity narrative)

In an interview that took place four months later, Cori talked further about code-mixing and her fruitless attempts to eliminate 'this habit'. Her frank comments helped me to better understand the depth of the 'unwritten rules' that governed some of her linguistic beliefs and behaviour.

RA: In which situations do you use code-mixing most often? Why?

Cori: Code-mixing is a part of my speech. It is difficult to get rid of now. I tried to get rid of this habit but I failed.

RA: Why did you want to get rid of it?

Cori: I think it's not good. In some formal occasions, like having a job interview or public speaking, you cannot use code-mixing. This habit may turn out to be very natural and hard to get rid of so I think it is not good.

RA: How do you feel when you are code-mixing?

Cori: It depends on the situation. For example, If I say 'Today I went to have 'aan' [lunch in Cantonese], I think it is okay. But, if I am saying a sentence in Cantonese, in which more than 50% of the words are in English, then this is not good.

RA: How do you feel when you listen to others code-mixing?

Cori: It depends on the extent of code-mixing. If someone is speaking in Cantonese and the use of English is more than 50%, I will think I don't know what he is talking about. Especially when I hear the speech of some American-born Chinese; they speak in Cantonese and then they speak more and more English. I don't like this.

RA: Have you always felt this way?

Cori: Yes. I don't like code-mixing but I cannot get rid of it. I think it is due to the influence of my peers.

> When the group of people around you does it, if you
> don't do it, it will be strange.

Similar to Ada, I noticed that Cori judged Chinese speakers (e.g., American-born Chinese) by the amount of English that they inserted into their Cantonese discourse. She had a very definite idea about how much English was appropriate in various contexts. Her comments further emphasized her susceptibility to peer pressure. While she wished to reduce or even eliminate code-mixing from her speech, she did not want to appear 'strange' when interacting with her friends. She claimed that this was what held her back from breaking this 'habit'. I was again struck by her tendency to spend a lot of time alone and yet be quite preoccupied with how others regarded her.

6.1.3.4   Language, culture, and identity

Like Ada, Cori reflected on how her communication style had been influenced by her cultural background and, in doing so, disclosed feelings of inadequacy that she attributed to 'a sense of being nowhere'. Her tone was very negative, critical of herself and other members of her self-defined 'ingroup'.

> My manners when interacting with people are unconsciously
> influenced by my cultural background. Most Hong Kong students
> are less expressive in terms of facial expression and body
> movements than people of other cultures. Most Hong Kong students
> fail to have good eye contact with their listeners, especially
> when giving a speech or interviews. Sometimes, during a serious
> discussion, Hong Kong students take a longer time to break the
> silence. I am one of these typical Hong Kong students. That
> Chinese is culturally more introverted than westerners is not
> the only excuse. I cannot blame that I am not trained to be more
> presentable under our spoon-feeding oriented education. For my
> part, lack of self-confidence resulted from a sense of being
> nowhere contributes to these fatal weaknesses in speech.

Cori again displayed a 'low cultural identity salience', which Ting-Toomey and Chung (2005) defined as a weak association or membership affiliation with her cultural group. Would this remain the same in England or, in an unfamiliar, alien environment, would she reassess her identity and cling more tightly to her Chinese self? Or, alternatively, would she develop more affinity with the host culture?

Cori's dissatisfaction with her code-mixing habit and her need for the approval of her peers became more apparent in the following excerpt. In her narrative, she drew a linkage between her hybrid Hong Kong identity and her use of 'impure Cantonese'. Her bewilderment and confusion about her place in the world was palpable. She lacked confidence in both her Chinese and English language skills and had doubts about her language choices:

Apart from code-mixing, in specific situations like lessons for my major, I code-switch between English and Cantonese. English is the only medium of instruction in the classroom and is also encouraged outside the classroom. However, when we students are asked to hold a discussion among ourselves during class or we are outside of class, we may code-switch back to Cantonese. I conform to speak Cantonese during class discussion under peer pressure. That is, when others code-switch back to Cantonese, I can't keep using English or I would appear an outgroup member. Just like our identity as Hong Kongers, we are standing in the middle of the continuum of Chinese and western cultures. We are not 100% confident in English so we stick to our 'impure Cantonese' (Cantonese with a lot of English) whenever we can. This kind of impure Cantonese acts as a mirror of my cultural background in that I cannot decide which single variety to use in daily conversation. It also shows our inability to properly communicate with others. Not only do I suffer from this problem, it is also a problem shared by my social circle. (cultural identity narrative)

According to the INT, 'individuals in all cultures or ethnic groups have the basic motivation needs for identity security, inclusion, predictability, connection, and consistency on both group-based and person-based identity levels...too much emotional insecurity (or vulnerability) will lead to fear of outgroups or unfamiliar strangers' (Ting-Toomey, 2005:218). Would Cori's deep-rooted feelings of linguistic and cultural inferiority and identity insecurity lead her to experience 'identity chaos' during the sojourn?

6.1.4   Pre-departure aspirations, expectations, and anxieties

Prior to the sojourn, Cori set a long list of goals for her stay in England, including cultural, linguistic, and personal enhancement. It is important to note her desire to learn some idiomatic expressions in English and make friends across cultures. Would these socio-emotional aims motivate her to actively participate in the host culture? Would she spend more time cultivating a relationship with her hosts than Ada? If yes, would she enjoy a smoother transition to English life?

To gain more from the sojourn, it is important to set personal goals for it beforehand. First, I would like to further enrich my literature and linguistics studies by situating myself in the place where English language is 'originated'. Second, my sensitivity to cultural difference can be sharpened. I can grasp the essence of British culture through personal experience, such as interacting with local people there, feeling or touching a place, reading their newspapers. Third, it is nice to improve my

Cori's journal entry provided further evidence that she was more self-confident about her ability to cope in England than many of her peers. While several divulged their fears about getting lost, she was dreaming of exploring on her own. At this stage there was a marked contrast in anxiety levels among the students. When asked if she adapted easily to change, Cori's survey response differed dramatically from that of Ada: 'I think my ability to adapt is rather strong. If I encounter some problems, I'll try to solve them on my own first and I won't evade them.' In the months leading up to the sojourn, she appeared to be quite excited about the trip and less anxious than most of her peers about what lay ahead.

In an interview, Cori also expressed support for the language policy that would be in place for the sojourn and was generally confident about her ability to follow it: 'I don't think it will be very difficult to follow except for some specific terms that I think I cannot express in English. Perhaps we will change the channel then... There won't be so many people speaking Cantonese in England and it'll be more comfortable to use English there.' Had she underestimated the potential psychological toll of functioning in an L2 on a daily basis?

Although quite self-assured, Cori did express some misgivings about her lack of cultural awareness shortly before our departure: 'My concern is related to my sensitivity or ability to experience the difference between British culture and Hong Kong culture as culture is subtle and abstract...I may fail to interpret the underlying cultural meaning' (intercultural reflections journal). Would her perceived lack of sensitivity hamper the development of relationships across cultures?

6.2   The sojourn

6.2.1   The psychological impact of 'switching channels'

Cori began her diary by writing about her language use at Hong Kong's airport, just before we left for England. While most of her classmates readily 'switched channels' after passing through immigration, she felt uncomfortable expressing herself in English, due, in part, to perceived weaknesses in her oral skills. As an English major she believed that others had high expectations of her and she felt under pressure to perform well. Her low self-efficacy, that is, her expectations of poor results when speaking the language, decreased her willingness to take risks. This contrasted sharply with the optimism and self-confidence she had expressed in class a short time earlier.

On the plane, she was concerned about what other Chinese might think of her if she spoke in a foreign tongue. Her social identity was closely tied to Cantonese. Cori's worries again evoked Byram's (2003) warning that it is important to acknowledge the psychological impact of being pressured to function in another language.

```
Meeting my SES mates at the airport, we remained speaking
Cantonese as most of our family members saw us off at the
departure hall. After going through the screening of the
immigration, we really had to switch our 'channel' to English.
Some started chatting in English; some kept chatting in
Cantonese. At that moment, I felt quite strange. As a not very
talkative girl, I remained silent initially. Then, I started
talking in English. It seemed that I was not used to this
expected but abrupt change but I did not want to be an outgroup
member. At the trough of my alertness, I spoke English poorly,
as if my tongue was being knotted. I was ashamed of being an
English major, too. We expect ourselves and are expected by
others to speak and write good English. This 'subconscious
pressure' haunted me again.

When many more outsiders on the flight surrounded us, my
uneasiness was intensified. I have never tried to chat with Hong
Kong Chinese in English 'casually' in such a crowded place. To
relieve myself from the self-perceived social pressure, I
automatically switched back to Cantonese and chose to sleep at
once. When I woke up for the meal, my reflex urged me to speak
Cantonese. I immediately felt embarrassed as I could hear other
team mates chatted in English. It seemed that I was still far
away from the ultimate goal of 'tuning my mind into English
channel'. (diary, first week)
```

A few days after her arrival in England, however, she was encouraged by her success in communicating in the host language: 'Today was the third day of our sojourn and we all observed the "English Only" policy. I am quite comfortable with speaking English all the time. Though making silly mistakes in my oral English, I treasure this opportunity to think and present myself in English effectively' (diary, first week). I wondered if her optimism would continue in the weeks ahead.

6.2.2   Struggling to live in English

As the sojourn progressed, similar to Ada, Cori began to miss Cantonese and found it a struggle to live in English. She realized how much she 'cherished' her Chinese identity, which, to her great surprise, was tightly linked to her mother tongue. This was a dramatic turn of events. Before the sojourn, she had felt 'like a piece of driftwood,' lacking 'an intense sense of belonging to any group.' Living in an alien English-speaking environment had made her more self-aware not only of her identity, but also of the strong link between language and selfhood (identity). Similar to the other women, it served as a powerful identity trigger:

```
I have never imagined that I would miss my Cantonese. The
following experience was really weird. On the third day I woke
up early due to jetlag. Not being able to sleep again, I
listened to some Cantonese and Mandarin songs. As the music went
on, gradually I realized that my lips moved. I followed the
lyrics naturally, which meant I sang in Chinese and I spoke
Chinese! At once, I froze the lip movement. Then, I felt that my
tongue was very itchy as if I was tempted to utter some
Cantonese words. The more I suppressed myself, the itchier my
tongue was. To resist this temptation, I grinded my tongue with
my teeth. I did not violate our policy. The whole experience
just lasted for ten minutes but I think I would never forget
this strange symbolic behaviour. Did I miss my Cantonese? I
think so, but the feeling was not intense as no relapse
happened. Still, after that morning, I discovered that I
cherished my Chinese identity in the deepest part of my heart. I
have never imagined that my national identity is that important
to me. Bizarre, but it is a good sign of loving my own culture.
(diary, first week)
```

Would this new-found sense of pride and nationalism provide her with more confidence to interact across cultures? Or, would it impact negatively on her degree of openness towards the host culture?

Like Ada, Cori believed that her English was substandard in comparison with native speakers of the language, and, at times, she too was overwhelmed with self-doubts and low self-efficacy: 'I always feel that my English is not good enough. This fear is intensified when I chat with the locals. I should brush up my language proficiency because I am still far way from the English major standard.' By this stage, she was code-mixing more, slipping in Cantonese words when she could not find equivalent expressions in English or needed to make 'urgent requests' and 'express her emotions immediately' (sojourn survey, beginning of second week). While she had been convinced that the language policy would be easy to follow, in truth, she struggled to function in English. She was experiencing firsthand the difference between the restricted use of the language in primarily academic settings and informal, social English discourse in daily life.

As Cori did not have the habit of taking an active role in conversations, in either Cantonese or English, she found it exhausting to try to build a relationship through dialogue with her hosts: 'Frankly speaking, I am not that talkative and sociable… I am weak in initiating a relaxing casual chat and drawing others' attention to my speech. The intermittent emergences of silence make me embarrassed.' Like Ada, she often sought refuge in her room to escape the pressure she felt to talk.

Part of the stress Cori experienced was due to unfamiliar scripts ('habitus') in the new culture ('field') (Bourdieu, 1991) and the pressure she felt to assume the role of 'foreign ambassador', presenting a good image of her culture to her English hosts (Ward et al., 2001). She struggled to find a voice in this social arena; her communication style was out of sync with the 'dispositions' of her host family (e.g., humour), and she was unsure how she fitted in to their existing social network. As Thompson explained, in this challenging situation 'an individual may not know how to act and may literally be lost for words' (Thompson, 1991: 17).

```
'To speak, or not to speak', I choose the latter. Usually, I
prefer remaining silent and observing what is around me. Maybe I
don't have much confidence in my oratory power; thinking of
something interesting to talk about makes me nervous. Lest being
misunderstood as impolite or indifferent by my host parents, I
tried my best to talk as much as I could. As Tessa and David
[host parents] love laughter and enjoy the sense of humour, I
have a greater pressure to give immediate responses. What I
don't want to happen is to be labelled as a dull and cold
Chinese girl from the very beginning of my stay. During these
two days, I found speaking and moving my jaws up and down
continuously very exhausting and torturing. This 'non-stop'
talking drove me to bed as early as 9 pm. Going back to my room,
I felt much more relieved and relaxed. It was very comfortable
to let my mouth and brain rest for a while. My face muscles
could rest for I need not smile that intensely every minute.
(dairy, first week)
```

As well as being a self-proclaimed introvert, Cori was raised in a high-context culture where it is not necessary to communicate every idea and emotion, especially in the home environment (Lustig and Koester, 2006; Ting-Toomey and Chung, 2005). She was not familiar with the 'speech genres' of her English hosts and also found 'non-stop talking' exhausting. Nonetheless, on a positive note, she expressed the desire to persevere:

```
Back home in Hong Kong, I can keep quiet after acknowledging my
family. They understand that I am not used to speaking. Inside
```

```
my family, conversations are brief but everyone understands each
other. No one would be regarded as rude for being quiet.
Obviously, the current situation does not allow me to escape
from this personal problem. I have been improving my social
skills in recent years and now the progress should be speeded
up. Despite the tiredness, I know that I came here to speak more
English and grasp chances to interact with my host parents. I am
ready to overcome this challenge. (diary, first week)
```

Would she be able to sustain this determination and spend more time with her host family? Or would she soon grow weary of English and escape to the comfort of her L1 and the confines of her bedroom as Ada had done?

6.2.3   An abrupt end to a 'dreamlike state'

In the first week, similar to Ada, Cori's diary revealed that she was full of enthusiasm about her new surroundings: 'I have been very excited and mentally energized since my arrival. Every experience here is novel. Every day is enriching… I could visit the shops and the spots of interests according to my own pace. To me, it was like having a sweet dream for six days since everything including the fickle weather went on perfectly.'

Similar to Ada, however, this 'dreamlike state' ended rather abruptly. Cori expected to be discriminated against and, like Ada, she was on guard for signs of maltreatment (e.g., being overcharged in transactions, not being treated as well as locals). Her experiences and perceptions of England were shaped by her race, L2 status, and gender. When intercultural encounters did not go as smoothly as expected or situations differed from what she was used to in Hong Kong, her first reaction was to consider the interlocutor a racist. At the end of her first week in England, she wrote a lengthy entry in her diary about some upsetting intercultural incidents that she had experienced:

```
This free afternoon, I went to Coventry on my own… I
deliberately did not find a companion to see how people treated
me as an individual Chinese. As a result, I experienced both
exceptionally good and bad treatment from others… First, while
entering the university sports centre, I felt being looked down
on by the young staff there when I asked politely how I should
pass through the entrance gate. I could still remember the way
one young lady stared at me after she helped me to solve the
problem. Actually, I did not understand why she behaved like
that. This was just the appetizer. The main course arrived when
I went into an Irish café in Coventry. The shop assistant in
front of the cashier did not look like a friendly young lady
either. Anyway, I acknowledged her, then read the menu.
Suddenly, she asked me annoyingly, 'Have you made up your mind?'
```

> Her face also expressed her impatience towards my hesitation about the choice of food. At that moment, my anger grew and grew in my heart...I dare to say she would be fired if she held such an attitude towards customers in Hong Kong...
>
> Not trusting the online ticket system, I decided to seek information on the best way of going to London next weekend. It was my first time to handle transport matter on my own outside Hong Kong. I was a bit nervous. For one thing, the transport system in England was an alien to me... For another thing, I did not want to make mistakes like paying a higher price for a slower service. I got into the travel agency, the bus company and the train station in order to buy the ticket. The staff usually treated me indifferently as if they were reluctant to speak to me. All of them requested me to repeat my questions with a very bothersome look. This made me even more nervous as I lost the confidence in speaking English after being challenged. These series of terrible incidents drove me mad when I saw these nasty people greet the local customers more politely. Did I deserve all these because of my black hair, my yellow skin or my Chinese accent English? I feel as inferior as a second class citizen. (diary, end of first week)

In the same diary entry, Cori recounted a more satisfactory encounter that took place shortly after the unpleasant incidents:

> Fortunately, throughout the afternoon, I met some really nice English people. For example, the staff in the tourist centre was very helpful. He patiently taught me how to walk to the faraway train station... On the way back home, these upsetting moments kept haunting me. I did not understand why people talked to me differently. After evaluating my behaviour, the following reason might justify all my misfortunes. I am always regarded as too polite in Hong Kong. I never miss 'hello', 'excuse me', 'thank you' and 'please' in Cantonese. Looking back on how I greet others in English, I miss these courteous terms quite often. Perhaps getting things done becomes more significant when I speak English. Besides I came up with another reason for my negative emotions... There are both bright and dark sides in any country, in any cultures, just like I faced people from two extreme ends in one afternoon.

After she had cooled down a bit, through the process of writing, Cori began to reflect more deeply on these intercultural encounters and to consider how her communication style might have played a role. She recognized that she had used few 'courteous terms' (discourse markers of politeness) during these transactions and may have broken some social norms in this context. Bakhtin (1986) cautioned that miscommunication and misunderstandings are apt to occur in intercultural encounters due to differences in speech genres. Moreover, when the event does not go well it can threaten the identity of the L2 speaker, and the individual may become less willing to interact further. In Cori's case she was aware of the culturally appropriate way to communicate in transactions, but as she had had very limited exposure to the use of English in these situations, she had not put her knowledge into practice.

In the 'critical incidents' that she recounted it is also possible that the clerks did not catch her accent when she first spoke or, due to her lack of confidence, she might not have spoken loudly enough for them to hear. What I found significant about her reflective journal entry is that it provided evidence of cultural awareness and personal growth early in the sojourn. Would this continue?

A few days later, her belief that Chinese were not highly regarded by 'whites' resurfaced. In a survey at the beginning of the second week, she made no mention of the impact of her communication style on unsatisfactory intercultural encounters: 'After meeting with some locals, so far I feel that the whites have a strong sense of pride when they meet non-white people... I've experienced the feeling of a 2nd-class "citizen" in a foreign place.' Similar to Ada, when encountering dissimilar Others in the majority culture, she perceived prejudice and discrimination. 'The correlates of perceived discrimination', according to Ward et al., are 'almost exclusively negative and include increased stress, more identity conflict and greater psychological and sociocultural adjustment problems' (Ward et al., 2001: 153). Both women felt a power imbalance when interacting with people in the host community; they resisted their positioning as non-native speakers of English and minority members in a predominantly white community. Would her fellow sojourners experience similar conflicts and adjustment issues? Would they respond in a similar manner?

Like Ada, Cori also discovered that her views about health and wellness did not match those of her hosts, and she too had difficulty accepting the food provided in her homestay: 'I'm quite sensitive to the temperature of food and I'm quite picky in maintaining the "yin" and "yang" of food...Chinese theories. The food tasted good but they are quite "hot" in Chinese sense. This makes me feel not too comfortable' (sojourn survey, beginning of second week).

Not surprisingly, with these unsatisfactory experiences, she became homesick, although she did not seem to suffer as much as Ada due to some effective coping strategies: 'I missed my friends in Hong Kong the first few days, which was not expected. This kind of homesickness was not intense, which could be handled by planning more new activities and chatting with new and old faces around me' (sojourn survey, beginning of second week). She expressed optimism about the rest of her stay, indicating that she was looking forward to 'more in-depth communication' with her host family. She hoped 'to change and to be changed', giving the impression that she was open to new ideas and a possible broadening of her identity while making an impact on those around her.

Every Monday morning, the SES students and I met with a cultural studies specialist from the host institution for an hour-long debriefing session. In the first session, at the beginning of the second week, Cori talked about several of the critical incidents that she had described in her diary. In my field notes, I observed that our English host listened patiently to all complaints and offered expressions of empathy (e.g., 'I'm sorry this happened to you') as well as encouragement. This gave the students, including Cori, a chance to release the tension that had been building up. His reassurance also prompted many to take a more active, albeit tentative, role in their new environment. Later, as I was reviewing the diaries, I discovered that Cori had written about our first sharing session, which had had a significant impact on her:

> It was our first time to have the weekly Q & A session with Roger and Jane. To my amazement, the fantastic atmosphere was filled with energy and productivity. Almost everyone was very excited to share with others their new discoveries and personal perception. The situation today was totally different from our usual tutorial classes in Hong Kong. There was much less dead air. We were more willing to express our own thoughts. It was just the eighth day, yet I was impressed by the distinctive improvement in fluency and rate of response of my classmates. At least I could also feel that the new environment triggers these positive changes. The sense of satisfaction refreshes and encourages me to keep up my progress. I am much more confident in speaking English and articulating my opinion in a group. Another reason I enjoy this short Q & A session is that I could learn from others' perspective. Each of us has our own story with the host family and 'adventures'. I should be more observant and analytical in the coming weeks, as I did not see what my classmates could view. It would be great if we could keep this high spirit in our new academic year. (diary, second week)

She was markedly more positive after this cathartic session. Would her optimism continue? Would she take a more active role in new CoP?

6.2.1   Language choice and ingroup linkage

The second weekend was free for the students and Cori opted to travel on her own to London to meet a friend from Hong Kong who had been studying there for several years. Unfortunately, the reunion did not go as expected and the encounter was somewhat disturbing for her. A lengthy diary entry about the encounter disclosed her deeply rooted beliefs about the inappropriacy of English as a language of intimacy among Chinese friends: 'I was really shocked as it was the first time she talked to me in English. As I replied to her in Cantonese, she tried to code-switch back to Cantonese, but after uttering a few words, she failed. I felt strange and uneasy. "Is she my friend?" I doubted. She suddenly became very unfamiliar.'

Cori's comments bring to mind Ting-Toomey and Chung's explanation of the linkage between language, culture, and identity: 'In speaking a common tongue members signal equal ingroup linkage' (Ting-Toomey and Chung's, 2005: 158); conversely, the use of a foreign tongue can seem like an intrusion or challenge to their ingroup affiliation. In a similar vein, Meyers-Scotton (1993, 2006) and Zuengler (1988, 1989) discovered that the strength of an individual's cultural identity and ethnicity may impact on language choice. In this case, Cori's interlocutor did not use the expected language, the one she associated with her ingroup and cultural identity. This affected Cori's social psychological state, leading her to feel a lack of solidarity and affiliation with her friend.

Around the same time, Cori experienced further frustration and embarrassment when more people from the host community did not understand her. While she acknowledged the need to improve her English, she emphasized that this should not happen at the expense of her Chinese. She seemed to believe that enhanced proficiency in English could threaten her mother tongue unless she took steps to protect it. I also noted that Cori still held a very strong instrumental orientation towards the learning of English, focusing on how she would position herself in the job market back home:

```
I felt ashamed when the locals could not figure out what I said.
Much more effort is needed to brush up my standard to others'
expectation... Outside Hong Kong, I should speak much slower if my
audience is not accustomed to a foreign accent. I should learn
the way people construct their sentences and the choice of words
in other countries. This could not be learnt from books but
through cultural exposure... Not only should I work hard on my
English, but also I should not neglect my Chinese. It is
impossible to speak or write English as well as British or
Americans do since it is not my mother tongue. Writing style
needs time to build up too. Therefore, I should self-position
myself as a degree holder who is proficient in both Chinese
(Cantonese and Mandarin) and English. (diary, second week)
```

Finding life in English highly challenging, Cori reflected on her positioning and shifted her language-learning goals accordingly. Her comments raise our awareness of the agency of L2 learners. As Pavlenko and Piller (2001) and other socioculturalists have discovered, individuals continually make choices that influence their language and cultural learning. We must also recognize that environmental factors can play a role in their decision-making at any given time.

6.2.5   The impact of identity misalignments

Similar to Ada, Cori felt that her attempts to assert her desired self-image were not recognized or respected by locals. She was upset when 'foreigners' lumped her in with all Chinese, even though she had not felt strongly about her unique 'Hong Konger' identity before the sojourn: 'Foreigners often think that Hong Kong is very similar to China but we often emphasize that we are from Hong Kong, not Mainland. Our culture is totally different from the Mainlander's way of life' (diary, second week). In my field notes I had noted that we had discussed this possibility before the sojourn but actually experiencing it had had a strong, emotional impact on many of the women, including Cori.

It is also interesting to note her use of the label 'foreigner' to refer to people in the host culture. 'Intercultural frictions' can occur due to an individual's broad categorizations of people (e.g., 'foreigners, outsiders') (Ting-Toomey, 1999). This way of thinking can perpetuate the polarized 'us' vs. 'them' discourse, as in the previous case chapter. When *both* parties are mindless of the other person's preferred identity, some miscommunication and lack of mutuality are inevitable.

Cori experienced difficulty adapting to English life and found making connections across cultures problematic. As a consequence, much to her surprise, she developed 'a stronger sense of belonging' to her Chinese identity, as predicted by the INT. Similar to Ada, under threat, her 'cultural identity salience' became stronger (Ting-Toomey, 2005) and she began to see Hong Kong (and China) in a more positive light:

```
The indifferent responses from the locals makes me recognize the
importance of respecting my own identity as Chinese and my
mother tongue. Hong Kong is not as bad as I perceived before.
Perhaps my experience here makes me more patriotic and possess a
stronger sense of belonging to Hong Kong or even Mainland China.
(sojourn survey, beginning of fourth week)
```

In this context Cori also became more tightly connected to her mother tongue. This discovery supports Zuengler's (1989) contention that an interlocutor's perceived degree of empathy towards the L2 speaker's ethnicity and culture may impact on that individual's interlanguage performance and willingness to use the L2. In Cori's eyes, locals ('foreigners') did not respect her preferred identity; this made her more resistant to the use of social English and, simultaneously, strengthened her desire to improve her first language.

6.2.6   Malaise, resistance, and the desire to change others

Cori's personality and difficult adjustment in an unfamiliar culture made her less open to personal expansion than some of her peers:

> We undergo changes when encountering something new. The most important point is that we don't lose our original good self and we don't blindly adapt to a new culture. I am figuring out how to change others and make others learn from our culture when we are changing ourselves. (sojourn survey, beginning of fourth week)

Cori resisted being positioned as a passive 'apprentice' in new CoP (e.g., homestay). Instead of 'blindly' adopting the values and norms of behaviour that are prevalent in the local culture, she was determined to make an impact on those around her. Her comments provide further evidence of the role that agency can play in sojourn outcomes.

Basically, Cori did not agree with the following advice given to sojourners by Kim: 'We need to recognize, further, that we, not the local people, are the ones who are expected to make adaptive self-corrections. This simple understanding echoes the time-honored folk wisdom, "When in Rome, do as the Romans do"' (Kim, 2001: 226). Cori rejected Kim's belief that newcomers need to recognize 'this common-sense principle as part and parcel of living in an alien milieu' (2001: 226). Cori wished to chart her own course and not align herself too closely with the dominant culture. Issues of power, status, and agency permeated her discourse, which was more defiant than some of her peers.

At this stage of the sojourn Cori had become more negative and easily frustrated: 'England is not as perfect as I think before, not as clean and civilized as I think before; English people are not as well-cultured or friendly as I expected' (sojourn survey, beginning of fourth week). According to Ting-Toomey and Chung (2005) and Ward et al. (2001), sojourners with unrealistic expectations may have a negative reaction to their environment and become disappointed and disillusioned. This appears to partially account for Cori's woes.

Like Ada, Cori suffered from culture shock and often longed for the familiar comforts of home (e.g., 'the nourishing Chinese food like sweet soup and savoury soup'). While the other women had been afraid that this would happen, she had been very self-confident prior to the sojourn perhaps due to her frequent travels with her parents. Consequently, she may have put less effort into her pre-sojourn preparation. In England, to her surprise, she discovered that living with people from another culture was a totally different experience, and she was not emotionally prepared for the waves of homesickness that washed over her. Her experiences support Ting-Toomey and Chung's (2005) and Ward et al.'s (2001) belief that pre-sojourn preparation and personal expectations are crucial factors in the 'culture shock management process'. It helps explain Cori's malaise and difficult transition to English life.

> I have never imagined I would experience homesickness. However, my sickness made me mentally fragile. Lying in the bed, I could

```
not sleep. My stomach remained painful even after I took
panadol. It was my first time to feel entirely helpless and
lonely. I would like to phone back to Hong Kong at that moment
though my family cannot help me but I cannot due to the time
lag. During the insomnia, I missed home. I missed my own bed
though it was a smaller one. I could relieve my pain by the
Chinese herbal remedies or at least I could refresh myself by
congee or Chinese soup. (diary, third week)
```

After reading her diary entry, I wondered if she would have benefited from taking a break from the strains of adjustment by enjoying a relaxing, familiar Cantonese meal with some SES friends. This may have helped to alleviate her stress and get her back on course.

6.2.7   Linguistic and cultural gains and limitations

Despite her malaise, Cori was convinced that her understanding of English culture had become 'undeniably much deeper'. She had become more aware of the situated nature of discourse and the speech genres that are prevalent in this context. Further, she believed that she understood 'the behaviour of English people more… For example, why English people like entering a conversation by weather and why they need to create humour when interacting with others' (sojourn survey, beginning of fourth week). Even so, she did not feel that she had established a warm rapport with her hosts: 'I feel more natural to engage in conversations with them and I understand what they speak to me; however, we are not as close as I thought we could be' (sojourn survey, beginning of fourth week).

In the last week, Cori identified further gains in both her language and social skills:

```
Undeniably, I speak more fluent English… I am more comfortable
and feel much less tired of speaking and socializing. I'm now
able to initiate and maintain conversations without feeling
tired. I am more aware of my weaknesses in English proficiency,
especially speaking. Less mistakes in tense or in complex
sentences. Less redundancy. Some improvements in pronunciation
and clarity. I have not learnt much local expressions and
slangs. (sojourn survey, beginning of fifth week)
```

In her diary she wrote at length about her enhanced fluency in the language, but noted that she had not paid much attention to 'those colloquial or slang'. During her stay, this had not been a 'priority' for her, even though it had been one of her pre-sojourn goals. Her lack of interest contrasted with the women whose stories are presented in the next two chapters. Since this discourse is common in informal social interactions, it provides another indication that Cori was not as invested in developing close interpersonal bonds with her hosts as Elsa and Niki:

> In respect of language reinforcement, undoubtedly I speak more fluently. Since my host parents kept pointing out my mistakes when I spoke, like tense, sentence structure, they made me more aware of speaking proper English. I paid attention to the intonation, pronunciation and the words used in British English too… I have paid almost no effort in learning those colloquial or slang. Perhaps my subconscious has already informed me that this was not my priority. I have had no background of it and I could not find them relevant to me. (diary, fifth week)

Similar to Ada, Cori complained about the lack of opportunity to use English in England: 'The English policy is, of course, a good idea but it'd be better if we speak English more with the locals rather than being confined to our group' (sojourn survey, beginning of fifth week). Later, the same week, in her diary she wrote: 'I did not have enough chance to engage in a longer and deeper conversation with locals.' While the students were in classes together on weekdays and went on excursions together, on most afternoons and Sundays they were free to explore and talk with people in and outside their homestay situations. The next two chapters provide examples of students who seized the opportunity to break from the group and interact with locals in their homestays and wider community.

6.2.8   Lack of mutuality and heightened awareness of her 'Chineseness'

Like Ada, Cori was sometimes disturbed about not using Cantonese for daily life and even expressed the fear that she might be losing her language and Chinese identity. Again, Byram's admonition about the psychological impact of foreign language use on 'an individual's existing social identities' (Byram, 2003: 53) came to mind. In the following excerpt, similar to the day of departure from Hong Kong, she was anxious about what other Chinese would think of her if she used English in their presence:

> I am a bit scared now. I could not code-switch back to Cantonese or Mandarin immediately when I met the Chinese in shops. I struggled and could not utter a word. It was quite impolite for me to respond them in English when they greeted me in Chinese. I don't want to be misunderstood to lose my identity. (sojourn survey, beginning of fifth week)

She continued to demonstrate a heightened awareness and appreciation of her Chinese identity and began to reject her link to Britain through her official identity documents. Like Ada, she believed that she would never be fully accepted by locals:

'I am a Hong Kong Chinese although I hold a British passport. I feel more reluctant to claim myself as British. Although I can speak good English, I know I will be treated as an outsider of the language and their country' (sojourn survey, beginning of fifth week). At the end of her stay she still felt that she was being discriminated against and did not believe that she had been well received by the community: 'My host family thinks that I can live in England. They think I can communicate with the locals well and adapt to the new environment quickly but I don't feel very comfortable when people treat me slightly different because of my identity' (sojourn survey, beginning of fifth week). In Cori's view, existing social networks, hierarchies, and racism restricted her access and positioning in the host culture.

In her last sojourn survey as well as in her diary, Cori disclosed that she had not built up a close relationship with her host family members; rather, she perceived herself to be 'a passer-by in their life' or 'just one Asian out of many' who had stayed with them. She believed that she had expressed interest in their culture but did not feel that it had been reciprocated:

There was always a gap between my hosts and me… For one thing, it seems to me that I am just a passer-by in their life. They are really very used to having guests of different cultures at their home, so they prefer watching TV all night long to taking the initiative to chat with me. Even when I chatted with them and talked about my culture, they just listened to what I said without remembering my words. They replied to me out of courtesy, but not mainly because they are interested in my character or what I am saying. To them, I guess I was just a normal Chinese student from Hong Kong (not Mainland), who can speak good English without strong Chinese accent. Or I was a well-organized individual but at the same time an absent-minded girl who was always late even I woke up early. Visitors kept moving in and out throughout 24 years. And I was just one Asian out of many. For another thing, I am not out-going and caring enough so I am insensitive to understand others, especially we do not share many common interests and we are from different age groups. Though I could see my own improvement and my own effort in these weeks, communication cannot be one-sided all the time. While I was very eager to explore the British culture and practise my English, they show no motivation to learn more about China, Hong Kong or Chinese language. Mutual deep understanding cannot be achieved when there is a great difference in the curiosity to know each other. (diary, fifth week)

In Cori's mind, her cultural identity had not been valued or respected by her hosts, leaving her feeling empty and unfulfilled. She perceived a lack of empathy towards her ethnicity and culture, and this impacted on her willingness to use English and interact with locals, especially her host family. Cori's revelations caution us not to assume that homestay placements will lead to frequent and positive host–sojourner interactions and mutual identity reconstruction. In Cori's case, she resisted her positioning on the periphery of new CoP (e.g., homestay) and felt disempowered and resentful. As a consequence, she had less exposure to the sociocultural practices of her hosts and picked up fewer colloquial expressions in English. Would she have been able to establish a closer relationship with different hosts? Or would her self-presentation (e.g., limited social skills), unrealistic expectations, and lack of focused pre-sojourn preparation have resulted in a similar outcome?

6.2.9   Enhanced awareness of identity, culture, and language

Similar to Ada, being outside Asia for more than a month heightened her awareness of her ethnicity and cultural identity. Never feeling completely at ease in England, she rather suddenly became quite nationalistic, developing a much stronger attachment to her Hong Kong identity. This is significant, as prior to the sojourn she had failed to recognize that her own culture was 'worthy of being introduced'. In response to a difficult adjustment in an alien environment, she acquired a much deeper appreciation and love of both her cultural roots and mother tongue:

```
Before the travel experience, I did not think deeply about the
relationship of nationality and identity though we have studied
many literary works concerning this issue. However, noticing how
people treat me differently because of my accent, my hair colour
or my skin colour, I become more and more aware of the
significance of recognizing our self-identity. I am a Chinese
girl who has been brought up in Hong Kong, but I hold both
British passport and HKSAR passport for the sake of travelling
convenience. I did not find uneasy with this situation. Now, I
have a stronger sense of being Hong Kong Chinese. All of a
sudden, I have a much stronger sense of belonging to Hong Kong.
Hong Kong is always my home. It comforts me. It recognizes me.
No matter how long and how far I travel in the future, Hong Kong
should be my final and my favourite destination. In terms of the
environment, Hong Kong is definitely not a perfect place of
living, but what is more important is that I would not be
discriminated or be looked down on.

No matter how proficient one's English is, one is very often
labelled as the outsider of the language when one does not look
like British or speak like British. Others cannot look down on
me only when I respect my own identity and the uniqueness of my
home culture. It is similar to the case that why some people
dislike those American-born-Chinese who refuse learning Chinese
```

```
or deliberately keep speaking English even they know that using
Chinese would be more appropriate in certain occasions.
Sometimes, I find that I unnecessarily code-mix English with my
Cantonese. Now, I have a drive to get rid of this hard-to-
reverse bad habit. Respecting my mother tongue is also a sign of
respecting my own identity. (diary, fifth week)
```

While Cori was surprised by this shift in her identity and enhanced appreciation of her L1, sociolinguists (e.g., Block, 2007; Kinginger, 2004) have observed a similar occurrence in other border crossers who have experienced a turbulent transition to another culture.

6.2.10   Intercultural adjustment and personal expansion

While Cori had considerably more travel experience than the other students, it had been limited to short, organized tours with her parents and other Chinese Hong Kongers. For the first time, she was in a new environment without her parents by her side. The sojourn also marked the first time that she would need to interact with someone from another culture in English for a sustained period. Prior to the sojourn, she had commented that she possessed well-developed problem-solving skills and was quite confident that she could handle difficulties; however, she did not have an easy adjustment in part due to her weak social skills and the choices she made. She also appeared to have paid less attention during the pre-sojourn preparation phase. In survival mode, she spent much of her free time taking photographs (hiding behind the lens) before withdrawing to the haven of her room. In effect, she was less open to new experiences than many of the sojourners who were venturing outside Hong Kong for the first time. Perhaps due to her self-assurance and independent personality, she did not draw on her SES groupmates or hosts for socio-emotional support, and this may also have hampered her adjustment. Considering her expressed need for ingroup approval this may appear contradictory, but none of her closest friends in Hong Kong were on the trip. As she had mentioned when she first joined the programme, it takes her more time than most to warm up to people, and this, no doubt, also impacted on her sojourn experiences.

Interestingly, Cori regretted some of the choices she had made during the sojourn: 'It is a pity that I was not outgoing enough to interact more with the local people... I wish I had spent more time with my host family and established a much more closer friendship with them' (diary, fifth week). If the sojourn had been longer, would she have altered her behaviour or would this realization have dawned on her only on the eve of departure no matter the length of the sojourn? Her storied experiences may also illustrate the benefits of taking a breather during the sojourn (e.g., having a Chinese meal with friends). Most of her peers supported each other and this helped them face adjustment challenges. If Cori had been more open to others, would her adjustment have been smoother?

In spite of these disappointments, Cori felt that she had made gains during the sojourn and penned the following in her diary on the eve of departure: 'I have never imagined a 35-day study tour could be so powerful… Undoubtedly, I have changed. Luckily, I realize what I should change and what I should not change, so I guess all my changes are positive' (diary, fifth week).

Like Ada, she felt that she had become more self-confident, outspoken, and culturally aware.

```
I feel easier talking: to voice out my opinion, initiate or
maintain conversation… Apart from the progress in language, my
understanding of host culture has been boosted… I think I am
more culturally sensitive through my exposure and curiosity to a
new environment. (diary, fifth week)
```

This had been one of her pre-sojourn goals and she felt that she had made some progress in this area.

6.3   Post-sojourn

In her post-sojourn interview, similar to Ada, Cori elected to use her mother tongue. She also shared her thoughts about her re-entry in her diary and in the post-sojourn survey.

Cori acknowledged that she had spent very little time interacting with her hosts. While some of her classmates set this as a priority, she had used much of her free time to explore on her own. Even so, she attributed the rather distant relationship with her hosts to their lack of interest in her and her culture, seemingly unaware that she may have appeared very detached and disinterested in them. This may also partially explain why she still 'felt like an outsider' in her homestay and the host community at the end of the sojourn.

```
My host family found that I was always out and came back half an
hour before dinner. I would not trap myself in the house during
the afternoon… It seemed that we seldom engaged in in-depth
conversation… I didn't fully understand them and they didn't
understand me thoroughly either. They saw me as a foreigner and
I always thought of myself as a foreigner, too. I always felt
like an outsider. (interview)
```

Without a collaborative effort, Ting-Toomey warned that sojourners and their hosts may end up with 'great frustrations, miscommunications, and identity misalignments' (Ting-Toomey, 2005: 221), strengthening ethnocentric tendencies and inter-group stereotypes. Lack of mutuality and engagement, as Cori's story reveals, can have a significant impact on intercultural relations and personal growth.

Cori discussed some of the difficulties she had faced in building relationships across cultures in English. Similar to the pre-sojourn phase, she expressed reservations about her grasp of intercultural pragmatics: '[S]ometimes I still find it difficult to judge what questions I could ask so they won't feel offended, or what topics I could talk about so they're interested in the conversation. I know it takes a long time to improve' (survey). Her lack of understanding of the speech genre that was appropriate in certain situations (e.g., an informal conversation with her hosts) likely contributed to the miscommunication and misunderstandings that she experienced. These negative encounters, in turn, threatened her self-image and made her more resistant to engaging in new CoP.

In particular, Cori had difficulty understanding and accepting communication styles that differed from what she was used to: 'When the English talk to everyone on the phone, they call them "sweet heart" or "darling" but when they use this so frequently, you don't know what exactly they are thinking of you. I doubt their sincerity and don't like this' (interview). Similar to Ada, in this liminal state, she displayed personal inflexibility in an unfamiliar cultural environment and was not as open to differences as the women whose stories are recounted in the next two chapters.

Cori's lack of understanding of new CoP, coupled with inflated, unrealistic expectations, contributed to her dislike and distrust of the host culture, in general. In the post-sojourn survey, she wrote:

> I used to think that all English were polite and gentle. Some are gentlemen but a lot are not... From reading books, I think all the British people are very cultured, going to the theatre and reading literature but I'm too naïve. That makes me a little bit disappointed as I expected that the whole country was very cultured.

Conversely, while in England, Cori developed a deeper love and appreciation of Hong Kong. In her post-sojourn interview, she said:

> I used to think Hong Kongers liked to complain and complain. After coming back, I started appreciating what we have. In the past, we might think that Western countries are good... Now that I've come back I realize that many things in Hong Kong should be appreciated.

She had been ambivalent about her homeland before the sojourn and very confused 'about her place in the world'. This was a dramatic shift in orientation.

Cori now embraced her Chinese identity and was more reluctant to declare herself British: 'I now treasure myself as a Chinese and I like my country and Hong Kong more. I have a British passport and, in the past, when I filled in the forms "British" for my nationality, I felt okay. But now, I don't want to declare myself British' (interview). According to Ward et al. (2001), a significant life event such as moving from one's home culture to another culture may evoke both cognitive and affective components of identity. Those who were members of the privileged majority in their home culture, like Cori, may 'experience a stronger need for ingroup identification' when repositioned as members of a minority group in the new culture. She felt threatened in the host culture and responded accordingly.

The trip to England also increased her desire to improve her Chinese. Her motivation to learn English remained largely instrumental, focusing on the 'linguistic capital' she would gain in the competitive job market in Hong Kong:

```
I need to spend more time and effort to master my language… not
only English. I mean I need to master both English and Chinese.
In the job market, why would people employ me just because of my
English ability when they could employ a native speaker? I need
to be unique with strong English skills as well as Chinese
skills so a native speaker couldn't replace me. (interview)
```

A bit later in the same interview, she expressed the desire to enhance her English and planned to practice it more in order to 'speak and write better'. She added: 'I want to have my own writing style. It's not only about the vocabulary you use. Although you could use beautiful vocabulary from the dictionary, it's not powerful. I think I need to express my own opinions well with the language in my own style.' She largely resisted appropriating the discourse of Others, preferring to chart her own course. While very 'ingroup' oriented at times, Ada was rather distant from her peers. Her views about language and identity issues were very complex, somewhat contradictory, and largely context-specific. Her stories lend support to the poststructuralist depiction of identity as 'diverse, contradictory, dynamic and changing over historical time and space' (Norton and Toohey, 2002: 121).

Cori went on to talk at some length about code-mixing. Prior to the sojourn, she had sometimes felt 'superior' when doing it. During her stay in England, she became convinced that this habit 'disrespected her culture'. She was more determined than ever to eliminate it from her speech:

```
I want to use English only or Chinese only with less code-
mixing. I want to speak English properly. Some people might
think it's superior to code-mix (perhaps I also thought that
before) but I think it disrespects your own culture. I want to
```

While Cori did not seem to make great strides in terms of her linguistic and intercultural communication skills, her desire to improve her proficiency in both English and Chinese was strengthened and, on occasion, she displayed awareness of the role that her behaviour (e.g., communication style, word choice) might have played in critical incidents. She had become more aware of cultural differences and the need to enhance her intercultural pragmatics skills. This was a positive, albeit tentative, step forward.

Cori ended her interview on a positive note: 'I feel very happy and feel that I've changed. I'll forget some trips that I took with my parents but I won't forget these five weeks.' Like Ada, she was considering new possibilities for her future: 'After this trip I found that I'm more interested in linguistics. I'm now considering going further to a postgraduate programme in linguistics, which I never thought of before.' Before the sojourn, she had been adamant that she would never enter the teaching profession. To my great surprise, she now expressed interest in 'being a teacher or working in the field of language education to help children develop a curiosity about English'.

Two months later, Cori joined an academic year-abroad programme that placed her in a non-English-speaking European environment.

6.4   Cori's journey in review

Before the trip to England, Cori tended to reject traditional Chinese culture and felt inferior to 'Westerners'. In J. Bennett's (1993) terms, at times, she appeared to be in a state of 'encapsulated marginality', feeling lost and uncertain of her identity. Like Ada, she lacked confidence in her oral English, and did not seem to be invested in the language on a personal level. She preferred to converse in Cantonese, although using English in some contexts made her feel superior. Similar to Ada, she was very aware of the 'linguistic capital' of English and was instrumentally motivated to learn it.

Cori was generally self-confident about her ability to cope with English life, in part due to her frequent travels with her family and her independent nature. She was caught off guard when she found it difficult to 'switch channels' and function in an L2 in an alien environment. Her lack of familiarity with the 'habitus' in the new environment ('field') (Bourdieu, 1991) and her resistance to new 'ways of being' (Bakhtin, 1986) led to a turbulent stay and the gradual intensification of her attachment to a Hong Kong Chinese identity.

Unmet expectations (Ward et al., 2001) and agency (Ahearn, 2001; Pavlenko and Piller, 2001) played important roles in shaping the outcome of her sojourn. While many of her peers opted to spend much of their free time interacting with locals, Cori explored on her own. She did not feel understood by her hosts and did not build a close relationship with them. This had a negative impact on her attitude towards the host culture and her willingness to use social English and experiment with local sociopragmatic norms. Rather, she exhibited the desire to change others and chart her own course. Whereas many of her peers recognized linguistic affordances, she tended to see obstacles and a lack of opportunity to use English (Gibson, 1979; van Lier, 2000, 2004). While she believed that she had experienced personal growth in England, she had always felt 'like an outsider' and was relieved to be back in Hong Kong. The sojourn awakened a desire to enhance her Chineseness (language and identity), while her motivation to improve her English remained largely pragmatic, focusing on the linguistic capital of the language.

Notes

1   After more than 150 years of British colonial rule, in July 1997 Hong Kong became a Special Administrative region of the People's Republic of China (PRC). Since then it is referred to as the HKSAR. To allow Hong Kong residents who were born during colonial rule to retain the status of British nationals, the UK created a new nationality category, British National (Overseas). Holders of BN(O) passports have no right of abode in the UK. Eligible residents who did not register for this status prior to the Handover and were eligible to become PRC citizens became solely PRC citizens on 1 July 1997.

7 Elsa's journey

Each language and every culture is like a room with an abundance of treasures. Once you are willing to open the door yourself and step into the room, you can discover its unique and lovely aspects…(pre-sojourn cultural identity narrative, Elsa)

7.1 Pre-sojourn

7.1.1 Profile and family background

Elsa, a petite twenty-year old, was a very soft-spoken young woman with a ready smile. In her opinion, most people would describe her as 'very serious, quiet and genteel'. Her closest friends, however, would realize that she could relax enough to tell jokes. In her first interview she divulged more personal traits and revealed that, like Cori, she had a wide range of interests:

> Regarding my personality, I'm very self-demanding. You may say that I'm a perfectionist. My friends think that I am very serious. They also think that I look genteel and quiet but, in fact, I'm not very much like that, however, I have interests in different areas, including sports such as ball games and swimming. Although I'm self-demanding, I give myself considerable freedom. For example, if I get bored with my homework, I will give myself some time to relax. But when I do my assignments, I must do them well.

On the homestay placement form, she provided more insight into her identity, hobbies, and upbeat personality:

> I am a Christian. In leisure time, I usually listen to classical music and English songs. I enjoy singing and playing the piano. I love watching the ballet very much. I am crazy for lovely dogs

> and cats (I long to keep one but I never have this chance
> before). I can stay indoors quietly without getting bored by
> myself but hiking and fishing are definitely my favourites! All
> in all, I am an easygoing person.

In her secondary school, she was a House Official and chair of the English club. She also edited the school magazine and joined English poetry recitals. At the time of the study, Elsa had not taken part in any extracurricular activities at the university. Like Ada, she preferred to focus on her academic studies. Her lack of independence may also have been a contributing factor: 'I'm not a very independent person because my mother and elder sister always take good care of me. I'm very attached to my family. I don't live in a hostel so that I can spend more time with them.' Like most of her peers, she had led a very sheltered life. While she had made a few short trips (less than a week each time) to the Mainland with her family when very young, she had not ventured outside the Chinese-speaking world. She had had very limited intercultural contact in informal situations. Similar to Ada, Elsa expressed interest in entering the teaching profession after graduation.

Elsa's mother, a housewife, had left school at the end of Form 5 (Grade 11); her father was employed as a civil servant, after taking adult education courses: 'When he was young, he had no money to go to school. I'm not sure if he went to secondary school or not but…I remember he studied in night school. I think his education level is quite good actually because he likes reading the newspaper.' A middle child, Elsa had an elder sister who was a university student, and a younger brother in secondary school. All of Elsa's family members could speak some English, and her father used it at work (e.g., to provide directions to foreigners); however, none of them used the language in their social life. They preferred to use their first language, Cantonese, at home.

Elsa was very proud of the closeness of her family members, describing their relationship as 'healthy' and 'harmonious,' with 'a strong sense of unity.' In an interview, she declared how much she loved her parents and her family. She was very dependent on them.

7.1.2   Identity

7.1.2.1   A dual, relational self-construal

Like the other women whose stories have been told so far, Elsa wished to be referred to as a 'Hong Konger' rather than Chinese, embracing an identity which she believed encompassed both Chinese and Western elements and gave her a more international persona. In her narrative, she engaged in what Bakhtin referred to as 'outsideness' (Section 2.1.2). He advocated that individuals 'simultaneously enter the other culture and remain outside it, developing their own unique perspectives' (Bakhtin, 1986: 6).

In her cultural identity narrative, Elsa explained this process in her own words:

```
A Hong Konger or A Chinese?
To be frank, I do not feel a sense of root towards my own
nation. This may be due to Hong Kong's colonial background,
giving me the space to look back at my own nation from the
perspective like a foreigner. I really adore, however, the
western cultures under the influence of its films, books, and
music. Therefore, to identify myself to a particular
geographical area, I would choose 'Hong Konger' instead of
'Chinese', as I see a 'Hong Konger' as someone internationalized,
with the western cultures which I adore incorporated inside.
```

Elsa displayed awareness of the relational nature of identity (Bakhtin, 1981, 1986; Hall, 2002), noting wryly that other peoples' labels of you were impossible to ignore. In the last sentence of the following excerpt from her narrative, she mused about her possible reception in England. This would be her first trip outside a Chinese environment, and she was concerned about being a visible minority and a 'Cantonese speaker' of English in that context. A short story about a Chinese woman in a bicultural marriage prompted her to begin preparing herself mentally for how she might be positioned in a country outside Asia:

```
Identity is something not totally under your own control:
identity, of course, is part of who you think you are but other
people also have the power to determine who you are. Let me
verify this point by a story I have studied about identity... Mary
Loh's (1991) 'Rice' is a story about a Chinese girl who dislikes
her own culture but is inclined to western cultures. In order
not to be associated with Chinese customs, she marries an
Englishman, thinking this as a fulfilment for her to be
identified as a westerner. To her astonishment, after marriage,
her English husband asked her to cook Chinese food, rice, for
him. This shows the irony that this Englishman married her
because he wants an 'oriental woman'. Her Chinese identity is
born with her, and therefore is an indivisible part of her, not
up to her own choice. Coming back to my case, I find myself very
similar to the girl in 'Rice' so now I am reminded of my inborn
identity as a Chinese, as I bear black hair, yellow skin. I am
seen as a Cantonese speaker in all foreigners' eyes. Even if I
walk in the streets of UK speaking very fluent English, I am
still an Asian to British people. I have to accept this innate
fact.
```

Elsa was convinced that, even if she became socialized into a new identity in England, she would still be 'perceived, interpreted, and measured' by locals in the host culture in terms of her ethnicity and L2 status (Bourdieu, 1991; Joseph, 2004). How would her belief that 'others have the power to determine who you are' impact on her identity reconstruction in England?

7.1.2.2   Ingroup affiliation and identity reconstruction

Religion played an important role in Elsa's life, impacting on her sense of self and her relationships with others. In her writing, she revealed how she used this aspect of her identity to categorize people. At this stage, she narrowly defined her 'ingroup' and did not display openness to people who did not share her religious beliefs. Like Cori, her comments illustrated her observance of the 'ingroup favouritism principle' (Ting-Toomey and Chung, 2005).

```
The Most Important Identity to Me
There is still another cultural community that I really belong
to and I strongly recognize myself as belonging to a religion
group, and I find my particular religion a concrete and absolute
thing in culture that conspicuously differentiates me from non-
believers… The way I choose friends and socialize with other
people is very much based on my religion too. I see non-
believers as human beings belonging to their flesh. Thus, I
share no common points with them in spiritual aspects, and I
should not adopt their thoughts and behaviours. (cultural
identity narrative)
```

When I first read this excerpt I wondered how Elsa's seemingly strict 'ingroup' orientation would impact on her interaction with others. Would she be able to make connections across cultures with people who did not share her religious beliefs? I also discovered that her notions of identity were rather complex and, at times, contradictory. Later in her cultural identity narrative, she made use of metaphorical language to vividly depict her perception that her sense of self was quite fragile. Over time, she had become aware of the fluid nature of her identity and the impact of interactions with others in defining herself.

```
If I am asked to describe my cultural identity with a metaphor,
I will choose to use 'a cloud floating free'. A cloud is only a
very little and indeterminate piece in the unlimited broadness
in the sky. This is like the way I see myself in this big world
with all my current, different identities adding up. I am still
an anonym in the universe. This is also similar to the unlimited
nature of knowledge, in which I remain extremely poor; I can
never grasp all of it with effort throughout my life. Truly,
every time I think of my own identity, I am reminded of the
broadness of the world and my need to develop a modest and
broad-gauge quality within myself. Besides, for a free floating
```

cloud, even the lightest wind can blow it and carry it away. So,
this free floating cloud very well reflects the unshaped nature
of my different identities; whereas the wind is like any
(sudden) occasions which determine and shift my identity. This
is because my identity can change all the time, depending on the
situation.

While Elsa's earlier comments about 'non-believers' had been quite judgmental,
the excerpt above conveyed openness to personal expansion. In line with other poststructuralists, Ting-Toomey claimed that an individual's motivation to change 'can
propel an identity transformation process in multiple directions' (Ting-Toomey,
2005: 214). Would Elsa open herself up to a broadening of her identity during the
sojourn? If yes, how would she change?

7.1.3   Language

7.1.3.1   Language ability and usage

Like Cori, Elsa spoke Cantonese, English, some Putonghua and a little French:

For Cantonese, I'm very fluent, since it is my mother tongue. In
terms of my spoken English, I'm of average standard. My
proficiency level in Putonghua is similar to that of English. I
don't usually use the language actually. Regarding French, I'm
very poor indeed because I'm only a beginner.

She received a 'B' on her A-level exam in English. After entering the SES she
rated her overall proficiency in English as 'good'. In terms of the various skills, she
perceived her reading, writing, and listening skills to be 'very fluent' but was less
confident about her speaking skills, rating them as 'fairly fluent'. Overall, she was
more assured of her English language proficiency than the other women.

English did not play a role in Elsa's social life, and there were strong social
sanctions against its use in family interactions: 'My parents do not speak English at
home as they consider it unnecessary and strange for us to talk to each other in
English. It would be a violation of naturalness in a family context.' Their mother
tongue served as a powerful symbol of their affiliation with each other and the larger
Hong Kong Chinese community, illustrating Norton and Toohey's (2002) observation
that, a language is not merely a 'linguistic system of signs and symbols', it is 'a
complex social practice' that binds people together.

Although her home environment did not encourage the use of English, Elsa made
a concerted effort to practise all four English language skills:

I read the newspaper and search for things on the internet. As
for listening, I watch the news on the English TV channel and

```
often listen to English songs. I also sometimes practice English
speaking at home and do writing assignments. Sometimes when I
write little notes at home, I use English. I also watch some
television programs, like 'Amazing Race', in English on a
regular basis because I can learn some daily English from them.
```

She demonstrated a much higher level of investment in the language than many of her peers.

Elsa attended a Chinese-medium primary school, where she began learning English in formal language lessons with Chinese teachers. From Forms 1 to 5 (Grades 7 to 11) she studied in a 'famous' English-medium secondary school that emphasized academic results:

```
The students there were all very diligent. Since I was in the
elite class at that time, my classmates were very good at their
studies. They did not often go out to enjoy themselves but spent
most of their time studying… I think they were outstanding
students but, generally, they only had an instrumental
orientation to their studies.
```

For the last two years of her secondary education, Elsa moved to a Chinese-medium school where 'the students were very kind, friendly, and willing to help each other. Their academic results were not that good but they built up close relationships with each other.'

Prior to the sojourn, like Ada and Cori, Elsa lacked confidence in her oral English and was more nervous interacting with native speakers of the language. Her low self-efficacy (lack of confidence in her ability to perform) limited her use of the language in Hong Kong. In her interview, which she opted to do in Cantonese, she explained:

```
RA:     How do you feel when you use English with a native
        speaker of the language?
Elsa:   I'll feel a bit nervous. I'll try to be careful in
        order not to make any grammatical mistake.
RA:     Does your feeling vary depending on the context?
Elsa:   Yes. For instance, if I need to speak with a native
        speaker in the classroom where a lot of people are
        present, I'll feel even more nervous. If there are
        fewer people around, or even only the two of us
        present, I'll feel more natural so it depends on the
        situation.
```

When discussing the reluctance of English majors to use English with each other outside of class, Elsa offered several explanations for this phenomenon, including 'resistance' to the language and the fear of making mistakes. Her insights provide useful information for foreign language teachers who are frustrated by their students' reluctance to practice the language outside of class.

```
I think for everyone, the mother tongue is their most familiar
language and thus they prefer to use it. In addition, there may
be some resistance to foreign languages. In fact, it is not
really true that they don't have an interest in English. Most of
us chose English as our major because of our own interest in it…
I don't really understand why English majors don't like using
English. Perhaps they think that it's strange. Also, it is not
that easy to express your meaning in English, especially some
subtle meanings. At the same time, you'll be afraid of making
mistakes because it's not your mother tongue.
```

I also noticed that her feelings about speaking English with a non-native speaker from her culture were context-dependent. In the same interview, she explained: 'I think who that Chinese speaker is matters. If he is very fluent, I may feel a little bit worried. If my English is clearly better than his, I won't worry at all because he won't be able to point out my mistakes.' Her comments illustrate some of the psychological factors that may impact on a speaker's willingness to use the target language in a particular situation (Clément et al., 2007; Dörnyei, 2005). Elsa's self-image was closely linked to her perception of her proficiency level and her views about how she might be judged by others. In England, would these concerns about her self-presentation hold her back from using English with peers who were more proficient in the language? Would her lack of self-confidence and low self-efficacy impact on her willingness to interact with native speakers?

Like Ada and Cori, Elsa did not use English in her social life and did not seek out opportunities to gain exposure to the language in informal settings outside of the academic setting. All of her friends were Hong Kong Chinese, and they preferred to converse in Cantonese or code-mix with each other.

7.1.3.2   Attitude towards languages

While most at ease when communicating in Cantonese, her mother tongue, Elsa tended to take it for granted. She was more concerned about the enhancement of her English proficiency to be successful in her studies and society. Central in her thinking was the perceived pragmatic value of the various languages she spoke. Although 'the embodied cultural capital' (Bourdieu, 1991) of Putonghua, the official language of Mainland China, had increased in post-colonial Hong Kong, she had little interest in it. She had not internalized this political change:

```
As Cantonese is the language that I have been speaking since I
was young, I don't have much feeling towards it. I'm not very
sensitive towards it. For example, I don't know why we should
```

use some terms in a particular way or what the exact meaning of
certain words is. I don't pay explicit attention to those
things. By contrast, English is the language that I pay most
attention to because of my study in school and university. This
is the language that I need for my academic study and also one
that is important in society so I make a special effort to
maintain the standard of my English. I'm not very interested in
Putonghua, just that it has a role in our society, especially
after the 1997 handover when Hong Kong became part of China.
Therefore, I think we should learn this language. (cultural
identity narrative)

Similar to Ada and Cori, Elsa recognized the benefits of learning English to acquire 'a wider range of symbolic and material resources' (e.g., a better paying job, more status in local society) or what Bourdieu (1991) referred to as 'linguistic capital'. Later, in the same interview, her comments again revealed that her drive to learn the language was stronger than the other women whose stories have been explored so far. She wished to make English 'become part of herself' and appeared to be more invested in the language:

RA: Do you feel differently when you speak Cantonese?
        English? Putonghua?
Elsa: I feel very natural when speaking Cantonese. I'm even
        unaware of any special things about it. When speaking
        English, depending on the situation… I may feel
        unnatural but I would like to integrate this language
        into myself, to make it become part of myself. For
        Putonghua, there is nothing special… I'm very
        conscious when speaking this language.

Elsa discovered that her attitudes towards English had changed after she became an English major. She no longer viewed the language as just another academic subject to master. Her comments lend support to Norton and Toohey's (2002) contention that an individual's drive can change as one becomes more proficient in the language. In Elsa's case, she had begun to broaden her perception of its value and place in her life.

When I entered the university, I began to attach more importance
to the English language and really wanted to improve my English
language skills. Before that, I merely treated English as a
subject that I had to take in the A-level exam. Now I realize
that English is much more than the four basic skills (reading,
writing, listening and speaking). I am now studying literature
and linguistics in English. I also notice English more in
different domains of my daily life.

Would Elsa's broader perception of English, accompanied by a deeper level of investment, result in more linguistic gains during the sojourn?

7.1.3.3   Language, imagination, and identity

In her narrative, Elsa professed her love of English, believing that it offered the key to a wider universe and the chance to explore other worldviews. In her mind, the language provided a way to extend herself beyond her immediate experience and cultural context. Her comments evoke Wenger's description of imagination as a 'process of expanding oneself by transcending our time and space and creating new images of the world and ourselves' (Wenger, 1998: 176). While immersed in a Cantonese-speaking community, Elsa envisaged developing a sense of belonging to an international language that linked her to the outside world.

Hence, her motivation to learn English was much more complex than a simple instrumental desire to gain access to the material benefits associated with proficiency in the language (Ryan, 2006). Her comments revealed some underlying 'psychological and emotional identification' with the language (Meinhof and Galasiński, 2005). 'As the value of their cultural capital increases', Norton and Toohey have argued, 'learners' sense of themselves and their desires for the future are reassessed' (Norton and Toohey, 2002: 12). Elsa's expanding vision clearly illustrates 'the integral relationship between investment and identity'.

```
My Love for Studying English
It is an inescapable truth that the experience of reading and
writing changed me a lot: I have fallen in love with the
language aspects since I realized the importance of reading and
writing in society is something that can broaden my views and
allow 'invisible' intercultural communication (the perception
and expression of distinctive ideas and thoughts) throughout the
world and between mankind. Chinese and English, and even other
languages, can bring to me the same degree of appreciation.
However, as I already had a good and natural command of Chinese/
Cantonese, I develop a strong desire to master English, and I
have set my target to learn this language well, although it is
not my first acquired language. There is no denying that I need
to make a lot of effort in overcoming the language obstacles,
especially my lack of confidence and naturalness in it. However,
once I see Chinese news reporters speaking fluent and native
English in the English TV channel, I am encouraged and get back
on track again. Nowadays, there is the great demand of English
in this internationalized society... As an English major, English
gives me a sense of self. I believe nothing can make my affinity
for English, or languages, die out. (cultural identity narrative)
```

Through the use of metaphorical language, Elsa revealed another side of herself, one that longed to be free to explore. She imagined herself to be 'stepping half-way' though the doorway of a room (a language and culture) that was full of 'an abundance of treasures'. Her love of languages permeated her discourse and she again displayed a willingness to open herself up to new experiences. This attitude helped cultivate a fertile environment for the enhancement of her language and intercultural communication skills.

> Through personal past experiences, I figured out the surest way to learning and success is 'to try'. I strongly believe that languages or any 'cultural' barriers cannot be an obstacle to being successful. Each language and every culture is like a room with an abundance of treasures. Once you are willing to open the door yourself and step into the room, you can discover its unique and lovely aspects and get benefits from its great values; but if you are reluctant to step in, you will never 'experience' joys and its advantages through intercultural communication although you always hear about them from other people. To 'look into' different cultures is to 'step into' this room of treasures and I believe I have progressed from standing outside the door to stepping half-way into it. Yet I still need more self-initiations and improvements and there are so many new and valuable things for me to explore in the future. (cultural identity narrative)

After reading Elsa's cultural identity narrative, I was somewhat surprised to discover that her views about the use of English among Hong Kongers in informal situations were similar to those of Ada and Cori. She, too, felt that it was 'really strange', revealing the strength of this unwritten social norm in this context and the close linkage between social identity and language use:

> RA: You've just said that it's strange for two Hong Kong people to speak English. If you really see two Hong Kong Chinese people speaking English with each other when there are no native speakers of English present, do you have any other reaction, besides feeling strange, towards this scene?
>
> Elsa: Then they must not be local Hong Kong people. They should be 'ABC' (American-born Chinese).
>
> RA: What if they are really local people who can speak Cantonese?
>
> Elsa: Then I'll feel quite strange. But I'll think that they may be practising English because I do this myself as well. I think this is acceptable but I know that, to other people, this is really strange.

```
RA:     In your opinion, what is so strange about this? What
        is the problem?
Elsa:   There is no need to use English actually. Both of them
        know how to speak Cantonese. Then why do they use
        English without a purpose?
```

For Elsa, Ada, and Cori the use of Cantonese increased their connections to their 'ingroup', while English made them feel somewhat detached.

7.1.3.4   Code-mixing

In casual conversations Elsa frequently code-mixed. It had become such a habit that she was no longer aware of it and 'couldn't control it' as this translated excerpt reveals:

```
RA:     Are there contexts in which you use code-mixing?
Elsa:   I always do this. I use it most when I talk casually
        or naturally.
RA:     Why?
Elsa:   I think this is affected by the cultural context of
        Hong Kong. I'm not the only one who does this. Many
        other Hong Kong people do it, too. We don't really
        realize when we are code-mixing. Perhaps I do it much
        more often than others, but I don't do it
        intentionally. I can't control myself.
RA:     How do you feel when you are code-mixing?
Elsa:   I don't have any special feeling because I'm not aware
        of my code-mixing.
RA:     When you listen to others code-mixing, how do you
        feel?
Elsa:   I think this is a very common phenomenon. When we say
        something like 'nin' (very trendy) or 'nout' (very
        outdated)), these are already some examples of code-
        mixing. I think most Hong Kong people have accepted
        this kind of usage so I don't have any special feeling
        towards it but if someone keeps using code-mixing in
        the same sentence, I'll think that he is too
        artificial and pretentious. It will be unnatural if he
        keeps using some difficult English words.
```

In her interview Elsa labelled speakers 'pretentious' if they code-mixed more than was acceptable in her eyes. Again, similar to Ada and Cori, this revealed a tendency to categorize or judge people.

7.1.4   Pre-departure aspirations, expectations, and anxieties

When Elsa first learned of the 'English only' policy for the sojourn she was not in favour of it, which was somewhat surprising, as she seemed more invested in the language than many of her peers. Similar to Ada, when discussing her limitations, she preferred to use 'we' instead of 'I'.

```
Elsa:    I don't really think that the language policy's a good
         idea. When we talk to the local people in England, we
         have to use English but if we also have to use English
         among ourselves, there may be some problems. For
         example, we may not communicate well.
RA:      You think that you can't communicate well with each
         other in English?
Elsa:    I think it's quite hard to express ourselves. We may
         have a lot to say to each other, but due to our
         limited English we can't freely express ourselves.
RA:      Do you think it will be difficult to follow this
         policy?
Elsa:    Not really difficult. To speak in English is not
         really a problem. However, in terms of expressing
         ourselves… I'll be willing to speak English as
         required but there is certain degree of difficulty to
         speak English all the time.
```

When she better understood the reasons for the policy, a few months later, her attitude changed. In the following survey, she still had reservations about using English with her peers but thought that she should make an effort to use it as much as possible in England to maximize the sojourn experience:

```
The policy is kind of necessary. I can follow it if I push
myself (always bear in mind/force myself); because I am not very
good at oral English I tend to speak Cantonese once I cannot
convey my ideas. I agree that if this policy is not enforced, it
will be kind of useless for us to experience a total foreign
setting when we keep talking in Cantonese with each other… I
hope I will be able to follow the policy! This is the only way
to learn and experience in an English-speaking country.
```

As this would be her first trip outside China, Elsa was keen to improve her English by 'coming into contact with English culture and the people who speak that language'. In her intercultural communications journal she wrote: 'I have heard how interesting and fresh it is to get along with people from another culture, speaking another language. I would very much like to practise my English with them, as well as look into the lives of English people, and how the English society runs every day.'

When interviewed a few months before the trip, she again chose to give her views in Cantonese. She commented that she hoped to become more self-confident when

communicating in English and develop a British accent. She also restated some of
the socio-emotional goals that she had set earlier (e.g., to build relationships across
cultures):

> On the sojourn I want to become more independent and mature,
> which, I think, is very important. Although I get along well
> with others, I would like to be more active in building
> friendships or interacting with others, even strangers. With
> regard to language, I don't think my spoken English is good
> enough. I can write very well but speaking in English seems to
> be an obstacle to my communication. If someone suddenly asks me
> to speak in English, I cannot speak fluently so I would most
> like to improve my oral English as well as my intonation and
> pronunciation. Actually, I'd really like to develop a British
> accent.

Further, she aimed to enhance her interpersonal skills, develop herself 'psychologically and intellectually', and become more outgoing and interactive. By undergoing personal change, she wished to open herself up to 'a meaningful, colourful
life' (intercultural reflective journal). In a survey, she added: 'I hope to become an
extrovert, exploring more new things through the program.'

While very excited about the trip, similar to Ada, she had reservations about her
ability to connect with her hosts. She seemed to be in awe of 'foreigners', especially
'native speakers of English', and was not confident of interacting with them on a
personal level. In a pre-sojourn survey she explained:

> I have already imagined the trip in England. In my mind, I
> always think about living in host family and the issue of 'how
> to get along with the foreigners'. Personally, I like native
> speakers very, very much (because of their cultures, their self-
> confidence, the way they walk out is very different from
> Asians). However, I am not confident of coming into 'close'
> contact with them. There still lays a spoken language obstacle
> between them and me (I don't know why) so I hope I'll be able to
> get on with the host family a lot.

Elsa did not adapt easily to change and this caused her some stress as the departure
date drew closer. 'If there are lots of changes and I can't get used to them, I'll think
a lot and feel unhappy. I guess I'll have culture shock, something that we discussed
in class. I can't easily adapt to change' (interview).

Overall, she was insecure about her level of preparedness and concerned about
the length of time that she would be away from home: 'Somehow I don't think that
I'm prepared for the trip – psychologically speaking. I think the professors have
done all they can for us. For myself, I'm still a bit nervous. This is a trip for five

weeks! I don't know why but I'm nervous' (interview). Similar to Ada, would her negative expectations about her adjustment result in a difficult transition to life in England?

7.2   The sojourn

7.2.1   Changing language channels

On the day of departure, Elsa wrote a lengthy diary entry about shifting languages at the Hong Kong airport. Unlike Cori, she embraced this 'golden chance' to use English and did not feel peer pressure to revert to her mother tongue. Her writing revealed some rather high expectations for the sojourn and additional pressure from her siblings to 'attain a beautiful British accent':

```
Tonight was an important turning point in my use of language.
The departure zone of the Hong Kong Airport marked my shift from
speaking Cantonese to English… This sojourn must be the golden
chance for me to accomplish some improvements in my English oral
(and listening) abilities. I assumed no one could understand how
seriously I held this language aspect of the sojourn as my
biggest personal goal. On top of my high expectation, my sister
and brother even wished that I could attain a beautiful British
accent after the trip. Anyway, I was very happy about the
'English-only policy', which allowed us no excuse to speak
Cantonese so there should no longer be any 'teacher pets' or
'show-offs' under such rule. Besides, it was fantastic to have
companions who carried the same view as I to strictly follow the
policy. In this way, I need not worry about being discriminated
by the others. So I started speaking English, with my classmates
enthusiastically joining in as well. The feeling was completely
strange and new. Only at that point did I notice that we had
never chatted with each other so completely in English in any
non-class situation (actually even in class situation, e.g.,
during a break!).
```

Through the act of writing about her experiences, Elsa discovered that her level of confidence when using English depended on her perception of the proficiency level of her interlocutor(s). She was less secure when her conversation partner(s) had a better command of the language and was particularly apprehensive about interacting with native speakers:

```
Despite the good start, I really experienced some difficulties.
I found that my expression was greatly hindered under the use of
English. I must think before I spoke the whole sentence;
```

otherwise I would end up making grammatical mistakes or
hesitating frequently for finding the right words. I also
noticed an interesting phenomenon: if I spoke to those
classmates whose oral English skill I considered as similar to
mine (not that excellent), I would feel more open to talk to
them, thereby forgetting/feeling easy at the mistakes I made
occasionally; yet, before those who were good English speakers,
I recoiled a little and cared more about my English expressions,
e.g., pronunciation, grammar, fluency, use of words… I felt much
less natural. But the greatest fear and pressure came
automatically when I came across native English speakers… I
minded too much. It was me who formed all these images of my
weaknesses and others' superiority, thinking how people thought
of me and judge my language skill. What an unproductive and
silly thought! I longed for a change of attitude in myself; I
wanted an open mind without all those unnecessary misgivings.
Hopefully, these upcoming five weeks can not only improve my
English speaking skill, but also lead me to self-reflection in
all aspects such as my personality and ways of thinking.

Elsa hoped to overcome these inhibitions to make the most of the sojourn. Would
she be able to develop an 'open mind' and acquire a higher level of self-understanding?

7.2.2   Heightened awareness of race and L2 status

On arrival in England, a wide range of emotions engulfed her as she entered the
airport terminal: excitement and happiness mixed with pangs of self-doubt and
trepidation. As this was her first experience in a non-Asian setting, she noticed that
she was visibly different from most of the people around her. This intense awareness
of her race and L2 status made her anxious about intercultural encounters, but she
was determined to muster 'the courage to face the new'.

The scene in the Heathrow Airport, when I was suddenly
surrounded only by foreigners (mostly 'giant' Westerners whose
skin, eye and hair colours were different from mine; speaking
English or other foreign languages), struck me a great deal. And
due to these intrinsic differences between them and me,
psychologically I felt distanced from them though all of us were
now under the same roof. Still, I was happy as I knew a
fantastic challenge was just ahead: I was to live in this
foreign land with such a diversity of people and particularly,
the Westerners whom I had always admired. And the challenge
definitely involved communication with them: 'Will I be able to
hear all what they say when they speak too fast?'; 'Can I
express myself clearly to them?'; 'What should I do to
facilitate effective communication?'; 'What are considered by

```
them as appropriate/inappropriate responses?'; 'How can I assume
a pleasing manner in their eyes?' All the way my mind was
occupied by uncertainty, curiosity and my effort to force out
the courage to face the new, a courageous belief in my own
upcoming experience rather than merely the words/knowledge of my
friends about foreign countries.
```

Similar to Ada, in spite of the pre-sojourn preparation, she was nearly overcome with panic and fear of the unknown by the time she arrived at the host institution to meet her English family. This was partly due to her reverence of Westerners:

```
Once the coach stopped at the university, I felt very nervous.
My heart beat fast and my hands got cold. I was too excited
about which homestay I would be assigned to. As I entered the
university hall, I was shivering. And when I saw all those
foreign-looking host families, I was nearly scared away.
Spontaneously, I felt the impossibility for me to live in
strangers' house, not to mention my intrinsic mindset of holding
Westerners in awe. This feeling was so sudden, powerful and
suffocating, attacking me and totally out of my prediction
beforehand. I found that any information sheets on homestay I
had read, or thorough preparation in the past on how to get
along with the host family members, were unable to stop that
instantaneous panic feeling of being sent away with someone from
another culture; I had underestimated the significance of living
in a homestay but then all I could do was to take some deep
breaths, gather my courage, and went away with my host mother.
(diary, first week)
```

Cori had also been in awe of Westerners and this had negatively impacted on her interaction with locals. Would Elsa suffer the same fate or would she develop more self-confidence and be willing to take risks to forge bonds across cultures?

7.2.3   Adjusting to a new linguistic environment

Once she settled into her homestay and had a bit of rest, she entered a rather euphoric state, seeing everyone and everything around her through rose-coloured glasses, with 'a sense of satisfaction' running through her heart:

```
Waking up this morning, I could hardly believe I was in England.
It was all like a dream, a dream that came true finally (after
the long preparation over a year). I looked around my bedroom
and then viewed through the window: the air was still and quiet
amidst birds' chatter, everything was clear like a framed
picture, too rarely/artificially clear with no sign of impurities
```

> or pollution which very often surrounded my living place in Hong
> Kong. The colours of my room, the neighbouring houses, the trees
> and the sky, were plain, fresh and lively. A sense of
> satisfaction ran through my heart. (diary, first week)

Her comments reminded me of Ada's and Cori's enthusiasm during the first few days of the sojourn. Their euphoria had been short-lived. Would Elsa's story unfold in the same way? This blissful 'honeymoon' state was still present early in the second week when she wrote the following in her first sojourn survey: 'The beauty of England exceeds my predictions. And I also didn't expect to have such a large bedroom of my own! The magnificent buildings here are stunning and gave me a very big surprise.'

Similar to Ada, in her first survey Elsa admitted that she was having difficulty understanding 'local people's quick discourse with lots of linkages and colloquial words'. In her diary, during the same time period, she provided insight into the frustrations she felt when trying to get her ideas across in English:

> Sometimes, it is difficult to switch into proper English, I may
> have reversed phrases, missing 's', tenses and articles. I see
> my English is bad. Really bad! The time when I felt confused or
> embarrassed is when I don't know how to express an idea in
> English and need more time to think and search for the right
> word.

Despite these initial hiccups, Elsa was keen to stick to English and religiously filled in the 'daily language log' to keep track of her progress and sustain her motivation to use it throughout her stay:

> I evaluate my English speaking behaviour every night and I am
> then most enthusiastic to correct/improve myself each time.
> Usually my failure in speaking English is due to carelessness
> (especially when I woke up from sleep, forgetting I have to
> speak English!). (survey, beginning of second week)

7.2.4   Mutuality and engagement: heightened awareness of Self and Other

Unlike the women whose stories were told in the previous chapters, very early in the sojourn, Elsa felt that her host, a single mother of one adult son, was genuinely interested in her and her culture. In her diary, she wrote: 'Talking with my host mom has developed my confidence in contacting English people. I believe that she is willing to listen to our culture and our living environment. I feel more natural for my use of English, too.' As she perceived 'host receptivity' to be high, she was more willing to use her L2 and overcome her fears of interacting with native speakers/ Westerners as predicted by the INT (Identity Negotiation Theory) (Ting-Toomey, 1999). Would she also be more open to personal expansion and identity reconstruction?

For the first time, Elsa experienced what it was like to be a visible minority. As suggested by Bakhtin (1981) and Ting-Toomey and Chung (2005), she developed a heightened awareness of Self and Other and her racial/ethnic identity. She recognized that she was positioned on the periphery of the host community and, instead of viewing this negatively, considered it an opportunity to learn more about both cultures. Initially, like Ada and Cori, she focused on 'surface-level' differences that caught her attention (e.g., food, appearance):

> Through living in a foreign country and with my host family I am more aware of my own differences from the locals here (even trivial differences as skin colour, my hair colour, eye colour, body size/height — something I've always known but never felt about!) And I am definitely more aware of my own culture: food and life style I have all these years. Truly, I think I'm always doing a compare and contrast between things I have in Hong Kong and in here. And I certainly know more about England and British culture through an 'outsider' perspective. (diary, first week)

While a bit apprehensive about being different from most of the people around her, she was 'excited' about her new environment and keen to explore:

> A foreigner is someone who catch the locals' attention most of the time/easily: a stranger to locals. As a foreigner, I felt a bit nervous to things that I am unfamiliar with but most often I am excited about the newness of everything around me. (survey, first week)

Her tone was less negative than Ada and Cori, even though she too had felt out of place and apprehensive in her new surroundings.

7.2.5   Sociopragmatic failures and perceptions of discrimination

On her first weekend in Kenilworth, her host invited Elsa and Lara, one of her SES friends, to join a family gathering. In her diary, Elsa provided a detailed description of the event, focusing on their disappointing attempts to interact across cultures. This was partly due to their lack of familiarity with the speech genre in this context and subsequent sociopragmatic failures.

At the barbecue, Elsa plucked up enough courage to introduce herself to two local teenage girls; however, when they largely ignored her, she attributed this to prejudice against Chinese: 'I was too insignificant or different (owing to my Chinese identity) for them to interact with.' Unfortunately, as the following diary excerpt revealed, her attempts to 'break the dead air' might have seemed rather judgmental, stereotypical, and intrusive to the English teenagers. The use of the more American expression, 'you gals', might have further distanced her from them. It is also conceivable that the teenagers were simply engrossed in their own world and lacking in social skills.

> Frustration was part of my new experiences in this gathering. First, once the host was not there talking to me, I found myself neglected by the others. It was normal that the women were busy preparing for meals. But for the two teenage girls (just a little younger than me), they were not showing any signs of interest to socialize with me. I did approach the garden table where they were sitting in, took my seat, waited for the right moment, leaned forward and introduced myself to them. But they just smiled a little and talked no further with me, not even telling me their names. Their resumption to their own chat at once made me feel that I was alienated. Another time I broke the dead air by saying to them 'you gals drink a lot of beer, don't you… I am not used to alcohol' 'We do' was all their responses. Feeling as if I was dismissed, I asked no further. Later even when the girl's mother was with us at the table, I was disappointed to find her talking JUST to them, not with Lara and me. I had used to think all British were chatty, very elegant and composed, mature and proper in socializing, and ready to respond to and communicate with new faces, but now I saw that either this impression was not always true, or I was too insignificant, or different (owing to my Chinese identity), for them to interact with. From the blonde girls, I also learnt that teenagers over here might be just the same as those in Hong Kong: they formed and were absorbed in their own social bubble, not quite having interest in other people or matters

The situation did not seem to improve when some older guests joined the gathering. Elsa and Lara did not understand their discourse, and from Elsa's perspective the locals did not make much of an effort to draw them into the conversation or make them feel welcome. Her frustration and disappointment grew as she realized that they were 'clearly outsiders', and cast in a very passive peripheral role due to their lack of familiarity with the topics of conversation and mode of discourse. In this event she felt 'a lack of mutuality in the course of engagement', which Wenger warned can 'create relations of marginality that can reach deeply into our identities' (Wenger, 1998: 193).

> When all the adults were out in the garden, they started talking. At one point, Everett [the host] suddenly turned to Lara and I (who were standing quietly near them) and asked if we

```
could understand their natural discourse. I answered 'not all,
not really when you speak so fast'. Then they laughed a little
and resumed to their quick talk, though now being conscious of
our ignorance in their speech content. Of course, they were
never to blame as they were just interacting normally.
Nonetheless, from my perspective, Lara and I were clearly an
outsider. We had no idea of the topics they were talking, and we
could not find any space to join into their conversation either.
All of a sudden I realized we were in a passive role, impotent
in facilitating communication across culture except waiting for
their occasional questions/words to us which were like an
invitation to us to speak, a golden chance for us to weed out
the uneasiness deep within. (diary, first week)
```

Elsa continued to write about this incident in the survey that she filled in at the beginning of the next week: 'English people should be very civilized in my past imagination but it turns out that NOT all of them are; in fact, many teenagers here are not culturally civilized but rude, impolite and discriminate against Chinese!' She had rather idealistic expectations about the behaviour of people in the host community. Like Ada and Cori, she also attributed miscommunication across cultures to racism rather than a lack of understanding of the 'habitus' (Bourdieu, 1991). As Ward et al. (2001) warned, perceived discrimination by sojourners may result in the following negative outcomes: elevated stress, depression, identity conflict, communication problems, and resistance to the host culture. How would Elsa's negative perceptions impact on her attitude towards the host culture and her use of English in the remainder of the sojourn? Would her adjustment difficulties mirror those of Ada and Cori?

7.2.6   From insecurity to a desire to fit in

Elsa initially felt quite insecure in her new surroundings and, like Ada, worried about her personal safety, especially since the adult son of her host was living at home. Elsa was not used to being around males in an informal environment and felt uncomfortable in his presence; she was also apprehensive in the community after dark: 'I have learnt to always bear an alarming mindset to follow every safety precaution (e.g., not walking on the street too late alone; putting my luggage behind my bedroom door when I sleep at night as I don't have a door lock)' (survey, beginning of second week). Her revelations brought to mind Ting-Toomey's (2005) admonition that 'too much emotional insecurity (or vulnerability) will lead to fear of outgroups or unfamiliar strangers'. Not surprisingly, some symptoms of homesickness crept in, and, similar to the women in the previous chapters, she began to long for Chinese dishes prepared by her mother. Would Elsa's fears curtail her involvement in new CoP?

Elsa did not let this malaise hold her back for long. From the onset, she closely observed the world around her to discover what made the culture 'tick'. In essence, she sought to unlock the mysteries of the 'durable motivations, perceptions, and forms of knowledge' that the locals carry around in their heads as a result of their socialization in England (Bourdieu, 1991):

```
I started to ask myself, 'What things did not the locals do?' I
thought if I tried to observe whether our group was doing
anything that I had never found the locals did, maybe I could
locate our 'faults', i.e. for those of our behaviours that had
never been found to be done the same by the locals, they were
most probably considered strange/inappropriate here, and we must
take steps to avoid them. So I was searching for 'taboos' for
prevention. One thing I inferred by this method was that we
might sometimes be very loud on the street/in public transport.
(This was because I had not heard the same noisiness produced by
the people here so far, especially in the morning bus.) We might
be too excited seeing each other on the same bus, or too amazed
to find new things around us, that we probably had disturbed the
serenity and orderly atmosphere nearby. Indeed, such sensitivity
in cultural differences had been in my mind since my arrival.
That was why Mira and I had better not hold our hands in the
Heathrow Airport! (diary, end of first week)
```

Elsa's habit of reflection and desire to enhance her intercultural communication skills distanced her from some of her peers who appeared to be locked in an ethnocentric mindset at this stage of the sojourn. While she acknowledged that she was still on the periphery of the host culture, she was keen to 'fit in' and make the most of her stay. This spurred her on.

7.2.7   Fears and perceptions of discrimination

Living in public housing estates in Hong Kong, surrounded by a large number of people, most of the student sojourners felt like fish out of water in their spacious, quiet surroundings. While the small town where their homestays were located had a very low crime rate, many of the women felt vulnerable. Like Ada, Elsa had nightmares and a very vivid imagination that centred around her insecurities in an alien environment. In the following diary entry, she described her fears and perception that she was being discriminated against because of her ethnicity:

```
We had a wonderful time in Lily's house and it was already 10
p.m. when we departed. The sky started to get dark. Lily gave me
a torch when she learnt the distance I needed to get home. It
might sound silly but once I was walking along that long, quiet
and shadowy footpath, I suddenly thought of the Goosebumps, a
```

```
scary/horror story series I used to read a lot. Immediately I
felt unsafe, and started to run… It was completely dark by that
time. As I passed a pub, some men in the open area were looking
at me, someone who was 'jogging' with a big sack on her back,
holding a map in her left hand and an illuminated torch in her
right hand. Once I passed, they burst out loud laughter. 'What's
going on?' I could not help accelerating ahead. When I turned my
head and glanced back, however, I found that the men (tall and
strong, in a gang) had come out of the pub, and were heading
towards my direction! I was frightened to death and all I could
do was to run desperately, until I finally arrived home, safely…
Thank God! I really felt that discrimination was an experience
Chinese students could not avoid here. (diary, first week)
```

As her emotions were running high when she described what had happened, she was not able to step back and consider how she must have appeared to onlookers as she rushed past with a torch in hand. With some distance would she be able to reflect more deeply on critical incidents like this? Would she be able to laugh at herself and recognize that her behaviour and elevated level of fear might have played a role in this unfortunate episode?

7.2.8   Cultivating an open mindset

While her intercultural adjustment was far from smooth, her response to differences gradually became more positive than some of her fellow sojourners. She worked through difficulties and, early on, was more amenable to trying new things. In essence, she had begun to demonstrate personal flexibility, a key attribute of successful border crossers, according to interculturalists Kim (2001, 2005) and Ting-Toomey (2005).

```
I tried half a glass of beer today. Though it tasted awful to
me, I was very happy that at least I had tried it. As I had
always responded to my host mom (every time she worried about
what food suited me best, for instance) that I came here to try
new things, and to live in the way the locals did. Yes… I wanted
to experience everything of the English living style; be it good
or strange or bad (like the bitter beer), it was always
interesting and worth trying. (diary, first week)
```

While initially fearful in her new surroundings, she was keen to more fully experience the English way of life: 'I am looking forward to having more outings with my host mother and to walk my host dog. I hope to bear a settle-down mind and enjoy life totally here… Most importantly, I want to increase my English usage to 100%' (sojourn, beginning of second week). While some of her classmates were preoccupied with news from home, Elsa decided to maximize the opportunity that the sojourn afforded her by concentrating on her new life. She was working hard to nurture a positive, more open mindset:

> Instead of focusing on Hong Kong/my family members who are far apart from me, I look forward to enjoying the upcoming programme in the following weeks, which I persuade myself to believe is passing very quickly. In this way I'll value the remaining time to be here but not be overwhelmed with homesickness/culture shock. (survey, beginning of second week)

Early in the second week, Elsa discussed with me her fears about living with an adult male in her homestay. Since she had started to build up a positive relationship with her host mother, I encouraged her to talk openly with the woman about her concerns. Later that evening, her host listened as Elsa poured out her anxieties. As I had hoped, the woman was empathetic and reassuring. Elsa was buoyed by their 'heart-to-heart' talk and much more satisfied than Ada had been when she had divulged her security concerns to her hosts. In my field notes a few days later I commented on the significant difference that I had noticed in Elsa's demeanour. She seemed much more relaxed, cheerful, and self-confident on outings and had become more talkative.

The 'mutuality' that she experienced when confiding in her host had provided her with much-needed support and a deeper sense of belonging in her homestay situation. Her experience clearly illustrated the potential benefits of having a supportive, understanding host. As Wenger explained: 'the mutuality of this process of giving and receiving can be very fulfilling. It can make a community of practice the source of great social energy' (Wenger, 1998: 193).

7.2.9   Socio-emotional support and L2 acquisition

Elsa had had reservations about her ability to use English during the sojourn. By the beginning of the third week, however, she described a 'positive cycle' in which SES groupmates encouraged each other's use of the language. Her friends also supported her, easing her cultural and linguistic adjustment. By this time, she had also become more attuned to the English used by locals. While Ada and Cori had shown little or no interest in colloquial expressions, Elsa was determined to pick up as many as possible.

> It was interesting that regardless of my identity as a student majoring in English, I had to be very prudent in using the language before the locals and my host members (i.e. native English speakers). After all, compared to them, I was an outsider of the language – of their language system with so many colloquial expressions. Anyway, I did make some effort in

```
acquiring the proper way of giving responses. In other words, I
wanted to respond in a way that the locals would consider as
normal. I found out (by watching the local TV) that the normal
response to some amazing facts was: 'Really?' And when I heard
my host son's answer to his mother's question, 'How are you?'
was 'Fine', or 'Not bad', I realized that such a greeting phrase
really meant asking if the person was alright, i.e. I should
answer that real question. (diary, second week)
```

Elsa engaged in what Bakhtin (1981) termed 'ventriloquation', that is, she appropriated the discourse of locals to forge a closer bond with her hosts and be seen as a member of the community. While some of the other sojourners remained fixated on themselves and their adjustment difficulties, Elsa displayed a growing cultural awareness and sensitivity to her hosts and their culture:

```
Thinking back, I must have offended my host mom when I kept
addressing her beloved dog, Puddles, with the pronoun 'it'
instead of 'she' on the first few days of my arrival when I
could not get used to addressing animals according to their sex,
like addressing human beings. (diary, second week)
```

Instead of becoming upset and insulted when her English was not understood, Elsa recognized that some miscommunication was inevitable. She was also less fearful of making mistakes in front of native speakers. More receptive to being 'a language child' than some of her peers, she openly displayed curiosity and interest in the linguistic and cultural world around her:

```
So many trivial things in communication drew my interest. Was
not that like a baby learning to speak? When I uttered a
sentence word by word, or when my expression was all broken with
my hesitations, or as I asked for my host members' verifications
upon any certainties (e.g., 'Is it called…?', 'Am I right to
say…?') in the middle of my speech, I must be like a 'language
child' who was funny yet enthusiastic in their eyes. (diary,
second week)
```

Elsa chose to take an active role in shaping her own learning. At this point in the sojourn, she appeared to be a 'willing-to-learn guest' (Ting-Toomey, 2005), accepting her peripheral position as a social 'apprentice' in new CoP (Lave and Wenger, 1991).

7.2.10   Coping with adjustment strains

Nonetheless, a short time later, at the beginning of the third week, Elsa remarked that her 'appearance and accent' differentiated her from locals and she was growing unhappy and impatient with her status as 'an outsider in the community'. Disappointed with 'not totally fitting in', Elsa began to exhibit more signs of stress. Unable to sleep, she phoned her parents for some soothing words in Cantonese. Reassured, she again focused on making the most of the sojourn by building a good relationship with her host family: 'So far, I regret that I was worrying about my personal safety in my homestay so much that I was living in fear all the time before. I used to spend more time outside my house but now I enjoy going back to watch TV and stay with my host members' (survey, beginning of third week). Her comments highlight the potential benefits for L2 sojourners to take a short break from the stresses of being immersed in the host language and culture; support from family and friends, in Elsa's case, helped to ease her adjustment and keep her on course for further personal expansion.

In the same survey, she revealed that she was trying to 'accept cultural differences' and 'minimize frustration owing to shocking cultural practices'. Her aim was to develop 'the attitude of learning/exploring/understanding more of the new culture' in order to 'broaden her view and capacity'. While more open to different sets of dispositions ('habitus') than Ada and Cori, she emphasized that she would not compromise her core values:

```
For me, when my host mom initially asked what I'd like for
meals, or whether I want to add milk and sugar to tea, etc. I'd
simply say, 'just do the way you always do, I'd like to try and
experience what you have in your culture'. But while coping with
a new culture and adopting different cultural practice, I'd
still keep my own principles of life and certain ways of doing
things that I strongly stick to, i.e. I won't abandon them.
(survey, beginning of third week)
```

Elsa's stance is in line with Kim's view that, 'in accepting change, we may also recognize that our basic cultural programming endures even as it is changed by new experiences' (Kim, 2001: 226).

Elsa took an active role in her homestay and this greatly enhanced her confidence when using English in other contexts, including our debriefing sessions on Monday mornings: 'I am more confident of myself in speaking up in the class. Maybe because I interact so much with the local English people, I have broken the barriers I always had in expressing myself in English' (survey, beginning of third week).

Interestingly, the euphoria that Elsa had experienced early in the sojourn resurfaced once she felt more secure; she described herself as being in a 'dreamlike' state: 'I am very happy now. I feel like everything is in a progress all this time, e.g., my adaptability at home and at school, my familiarization with England.'

```
This is the first time in my life to travel outside China. I am
```

> extremely excited about it and up to now, I still wonder if I am
> dreaming: I am now in the other end of the world, a place where
> English literature flourishes, the country I've longed to go to
> for a long time… How unbelievable! How fantastic and wonderful!
> Every day, sometimes in early morning, I'd like to look outside
> the window of my bedroom and experience everything here in
> England (e.g., the neighbouring houses, the British trees), and
> I still have that exotic feeling. England is a poetic place to
> me! (survey, beginning of third week)

She even felt overcome by a 'sudden, passionate flow of thoughts' which inspired her to write a poem to express her love of England and Kenilworth. Despite her initial fears about going abroad, she now felt reluctant to return home.

> I don't want to go back to Hong Kong. I don't think I'll be able
> to accept the fact that I have to go back and live there
> Back to reality.
> Back to a world of haste and burden.
> Back to the concrete high-rise buildings, and
> Leave this little village of naturalness and peace –
> A land simple enough to be framed as a picture
> With vivid life and cheerful colours of harmony,
> Which is just like a dream. (diary, third week)

Would these romantic, idealized images of the host culture endure through the natural ebbs and flows of intercultural adjustment? Or would she replace them with more realistic images and a more balanced view?

7.2.11   Identity misalignments: feeling betwixt and between

A short time later, this magical spell was broken. Like most of the SES sojourners, Elsa discovered that some English people mindlessly bypassed her preferred identity. This was very troubling to her, as her self-image was emotionally attached to her self-construal. They simply did not grasp why she felt compelled to make a distinction between Hong Kongers, Mainland Chinese, and, indeed, other Asians:

> I used to think my Hong Kong identity, which I was proud of, is
> unique to others (e.g., Chinese identity, Japanese identity,
> Korean identity) because Hong Kong is an international city and
> is influenced by the Western culture (which I like), which is
> different from the Mainland. (Indeed I'd prefer being called a
> Hong Konger instead of a Chinese). But I have the feeling now,
> that Asians are seen as the same (probably an outsider, and of
> nearly the same origin) by Westerners here. (survey, beginning
> of fourth week)

As she had predicted before the sojourn, she believed that locals regarded her as an 'outsider' even though she was making a lot of effort to fit in. Would this lack of recognition distance her further from the host culture as Ting-Toomey's (1999, 2005) INT predicted would be the case? Would Elsa withdraw or make an effort to assert her desired self-image?

Near the end of the third week, Elsa was caught off guard by another bout of homesickness. In a lengthy diary entry she described a fitful night in which she dreamt of home. As she had been cultivating a close relationship with her host mother and leading 'a Westerner's lifestyle', she suddenly felt disloyal to her own mother and first language. Both were beginning to seem distant to her, and this alarmed her. It is important to remember that her own mother considered the use of English at home to be 'a violation of naturalness in a family context'. It is conceivable that Elsa was experiencing what Ting-Toomey (2005) described as 'identity threats or frustrations' and, in the face of change in a new environment, craved 'old, familiar identity habits' and the safety of home.

```
Having longed for a chance to stay in England, and enjoying a
wonderful time here, how could I ever predict that even I, who
had not been very dependent on my Hong Kong family, would be
haunted by the yearning for home just after I had had great fun
watching an excited film with my host family? Over the last two
weeks, I had been proud of my independence and quick
adaptability to the new environment. I had been telling my
buddies that I did not miss my family, and that I had not even
thought of them when I was busy experiencing new things here.
Now I believe that the homesick feeling attacks you only when
your mind was free and at rest, and when you were not prepared.

Two o'clock. I still could not fall asleep. When my thoughts
were hanging around randomly, they suddenly reached my home at
the other end of the earth. At once, I saw the images of my
parents and sister and brother but they were so far away from
me, and I felt so distanced from them. This feeling was hard to
describe, but it was associated with the concrete facts that I
was now in a Westerner's house, leading a Western lifestyle…
'Oh! How much I miss the Chinese dishes my mother cooks',
thought I; and the Cantonese seemed weird and unnatural to me
when I thought of how they spoke. Finally I came up with a
strong sense of belonging to my Hong Kong parents: 'It was they
who gave birth to me…not my host mom, although she is now so
close to me and is part of my daily life.' Spontaneously I found
I missed my family, and I desperately missed the intimate
relationship we shared, the warmth and care they gave me, as
well as the easiness, freedom, and informality I enjoyed before
them when there was not the need for me to make effort and rack
```

```
my brain just to get along with them. (diary, third week)
```

Elsa's discomfort also evokes Ryan's warning that 'L2 learners may be faced with a conflict between their aspirations of membership to the external [host] community and existing loyalty to the local [home] community' (Ryan, 2006: 32). This lends further support to the poststructuralist notion of identity as context-dependent and 'a site of struggle'. As Giroux (2002) and Guilherme (2002) explained, L2 sojourners may fuse feelings of belonging with a sense of detachment through the process of intercultural mediation. In this liminal state, Elsa was disoriented and homesick. It was as if her identity and sense of security had temporarily dissolved. Would she weather this turbulence and resume her journey of personal expansion?

7.2.12   Self-disclosure and risk-taking: pathways to intercultural friendships

Her malaise was again short lived. At the beginning of the fourth week, Elsa expressed pride in the warm relationship that she had developed with her hosts, especially her host mother. In contrast to Ada and Cori, she seized every opportunity to participate in homestay activities. Instead of considering TV viewing a barrier, she saw it as a chance to interact with her hosts. As the weeks wore on, she enhanced her social communication skills in English, growing in self-confidence:

```
I get along well with both my host mom and her son. Now I feel
natural and easy before them and we often watch TV together. I
think I spend quite a large proportion of time with them at
home. Sometimes I think the most important thing to build up a
relationship is not to talk non-stop; it can help if one just
exposes oneself to the family simply by sitting with them
together, watching the same TV programme or having the same
snacks. This is also my process of learning to adapt. Then
naturally, we will have topics to talk with one another about.
We can really talk about anything (especially the TV programme
we're watching). My relationship with them (especially my host
mother) has been very good... (survey, beginning of fourth week)
```

The building of a trusting intercultural friendship, according to Ting-Toomey and Chung, requires 'both the willingness to reveal something about yourself and the willingness to pay attention to the other person's feedback' (Ting-Toomey and Chung, 2005: 182). This involves some risk-taking. Elsa took the plunge and found that self-disclosure helped her to bond with her host mother. Significantly, she felt that this sharing of personal details had been reciprocal: 'I have the unexpected development of truthfulness and honesty between my host mom and I. We talk of things that absolutely require trust between us. I feel excited and happy about this. And this certainly strengthens our relationship.' This contrasted sharply with the experiences of Ada and Cori who had not felt a strong 'sense of belonging' in their host family and did not believe that their hosts were truly interested in them or their culture. Feeling understood and supported, Elsa was much more positive about the host culture. This, in turn, impacted on her willingness to use English to deepen her friendship with her hosts. Her narratives lent further support to Ting-Toomey's contention that 'the more help the newcomers receive during the initial cultural adaptation stages, the more positive are their perceptions of their new environment' (Ting-Toomey, 2005: 221).

In the survey that was administered in the same week, Elsa was asked: 'To what extent do you now want to experiment with English cultural norms?' Her response revealed a willingness to 'converge' and try new modes of behaviour and discourse (Bourhis et al., 2007). It provided evidence that she had again begun to 'appropriate other voices', trying out local expressions and patterns of speech that were new to her (Bakhtin, 1986). Her personal expansion was still underway.

```
I greatly want to experiment with them [English cultural norms]
at this point, because I realize (strongly) that time is running
short and I know I am here to experiment with them no matter
they suit me or not; after all, I gain invaluable experience and
understanding through different tryings. And I am willing to
try. For example, I try to initiate a greeting with someone I
don't know I meet on the streets; I keep saying the 'magic word'
'Thank you' to the locals once they do me any favour; and upon
any invitation my host mom/other host moms made to me, I'd try
my best to attend it despite how busy I am, because I want to
seize any chance I have to experience local activities. (survey,
beginning of fourth week)
```

In the fourth week, all of the women were asked if they had had any sojourn experiences that they would always remember and Elsa provided a long list. Interestingly, most items focused on social encounters with locals, in and outside her homestay (e.g., attending a church service and reception, having tea in a garden with English people). She had made a genuine effort to participate in 'activity settings' in the community (Vygotsky, 1987; Lantolf and Thorne, 2006), in stark contrast with Ada and Cori. Her choices reflected a much higher level of investment in learning social English. As she began to experience successful encounters across cultures, she became more motivated to enhance her understanding of the norms of social discourse in England. A positive cycle had been established.

7.2.13 Adjusting to life in English

In the same survey, Elsa disclosed her enthusiasm for the 'English only' policy. While she had had reservations about it before the trip, most of her 'SES buddies' used English with each other and she did not feel peer pressure to slip into Cantonese:

> I'm following the language policy. The main reason is my strong
> intention to improve my oral English. That pushes me to follow
> this great rule (I love this rule very much, which give me NO
> excuse to utter any Cantonese, whether it be much or just a
> little). The whole team's effort to speak English also backs me
> up. I think it is an excellent, absolutely correct idea.
> Speaking English and getting immersed fully in the language is
> what the trip is supposed to benefit us. It should thus be
> enforced!… The great satisfaction I have is from using 100%
> English in a day. It is unforgettable! (survey, fourth week)

Nonetheless, like Ada and Cori, using English on a daily basis had not been easy for Elsa: 'I've encountered lots of problems to adjust to "living" only in this language (e.g., sometimes it's difficult for me to express certain subtle ideas and personal thoughts).' Instead of giving up, she persisted and, as the weeks passed, she became 'much more comfortable with using English all the time' and 'more courageous to speak it' (survey, beginning of fifth week). She was somewhat disappointed, however, that her oral skills had not improved as much as she had expected they would: 'My fluency still has great room for improvement and I realize (disappointedly) that I may probably never be able to sound like a native English speaker. Aspects in pronunciation are too hard to capture/acquire' (survey, beginning of fifth week). Elsa also wrote a lengthy diary entry in which she bemoaned her limited vocabulary in English, especially for common, everyday objects and again emphasized the importance of learning colloquial language:

> I used to be proud of my knowledge in the English language, and
> my ability to write with a variety of vocabularies. However, it
> was not until I had been here when I started to realize how
> narrow my vocabulary capacity had been! I felt irritated and
> frustrated when as an English major, I did not even know the
> English of some common things in everyday life – words that must
> consider to be very simple and basic by native speakers of
> English… In an all-English environment as England, I found that
> many expressions were new and interesting to our group, e.g.,
> 'cheesy', 'cheeky', 'perky', 'a scamp' were also often heard
> around, but I found it difficult to memorize their meanings, and
> I was not able to adapt them into my own speech so quickly and
> naturally. I understood that living in an English-speaking
> country, one certainly needed to master the colloquial way of
> speaking. (diary, end of fourth week)

Like her peers, Elsa's use of English prior to the sojourn had largely been limited to academic settings. In an English-speaking environment for the first time, she was intrigued by informal, social discourse. Interestingly, in her pre-sojourn goals she had not mentioned the need to 'master the colloquial way of speaking'; however, she recognized that this could enhance her communication with people from the host culture and, therefore, help her achieve some of her socio-emotional goals (Ward et al., 2001).

By the last week, Elsa revealed in her survey that she felt much more at ease in her surroundings:

```
Even the scene with just British/Westerners, which I once found
unfamiliar and eccentric in the early stage of my trip, now
seems normal to me. I am very comfortable with the local culture
and people in most ways, except in cases of discrimination
occasionally and sometimes the food culture here.
```

She had become more familiar with the 'habitus' and no longer felt like a fish out of water.

7.2.14   Enhanced awareness of Self and Other: mutuality and engagement

Similar to the women whose stories were told in the previous chapter, Elsa had developed a heightened awareness of Self and Other (Bakhtin, 1986). Being in a foreign environment had provided a significant identity trigger for her: 'In England I am always aware of my identity because the people here make me distinct. Many locals notify me that I am different with their glance/special attention to me as I walk past them' (diary, fifth week). Feeling different increased her appreciation of her own cultural roots and ethnic identity and gradually, much to her surprise, she developed a more balanced, positive view of her home culture:

```
Amazingly, I now learn to treasure my Hong Kong Chinese identity
far more than before. At the beginning, I was very one-sided,
only adore everything of the western culture. One factor may be
that I realize that I am 'stuck to' my inborn identity, and I
have to accept it, and make the best of it. But also, living for
quite a long time here, I start to miss my home culture, and I
can discover valuable points in the oriental culture. (survey,
beginning of fifth week)
```

In contrast with Ada and Cori, Elsa developed a warm rapport with her host mother, early on, in part due to their mutual willingness to self-disclose and share their thoughts and feelings with each other. Wenger's (1998) notion of 'mutuality and engagement' in CoP suggested that newcomers who perceive their hosts receptive may find their stays more fulfilling, and this appears to have been the case for Elsa.

> Revealing myself more to my host mother had made her treat me like a close fellow so that we started to go beyond the many cultural limitations we were supposed to beware of overstepping. She told me how she thought about religion; I talked of what I felt about the way the locals behaved towards me. I told her things about my mother; she did talk more about herself (e.g., her age), her big family, and some health problems. At the same time, she showed more interest in my background and started asking me about more personal things as my parents' occupation and my own goal/ambition. My host mother is someone I will never forget, as our acquaintance was under such a valuable chance and in such a special context. (diary, fifth week)

Vygotsky (1978) maintained that 'participation, collaboration, and social interaction' are essential elements in the learning process and it is in this developmental stage that learning is dialogical. Extending this notion to the informal learning of L2 sojourners, we can see that Elsa took an active role in social situations in her homestay. In doing so, she learned a great deal from her host mother, who was more knowledgeable about the host environment and 'habitus'. In the final sojourn survey, Elsa described her communication with this woman as 'superb' and identified, with pride, very specific gains in her interpersonal communication skills in English:

> My intention to develop a good relationship with my homestay family increased from the beginning and persisted throughout the sojourn, i.e. I spend more time with them in the sitting room and less time in my bedroom. I feel much easier to communicate with them now... My interaction with my host mom is superb... Different from my past self, I am more comfortable with dead air, and I no longer force out any topics to discuss just for the sake of creating some noise. At the same time, I can initiate a topic to talk naturally. In fact, with my host mom, we can talk about anything, from some general topics like TV programmes and food to deeper issues like her family and dating. Now I feel like I am one of the family members in the house. I am very satisfied. (diary, fifth week)

Did Elsa also have an impact on her host mother? Bakhtin (1981, 1986) and Lave and Wenger (2001) have argued that this engagement offers the opportunity for both parties to broaden themselves. From Elsa's accounts, one might speculate that the mutuality they experienced may also have had a personal impact on her host mother.

7.2.15   Enhanced intercultural communication skills and personal growth

By investing a lot of time and energy in social relationships across cultures, Elsa realized her goal of improving her intercultural communication skills. Her socio-pragmatic awareness had increased and, as the following excerpt illustrates, she recognized the benefits of adjusting her communication style to make her conversation partners feel at ease. She displayed empathy and personal growth. Instead of criticizing and rejecting different ways of communicating, she was open to adjusting her own style:

```
Conversing with local people in different social contexts (e.g.,
shopping) and gatherings (e.g., in barbeque, charity walk) also
equipped me with the skills to communicate with people across
cultures. For instance, I am now more ready and courageous to
interact with a foreigner/any stranger… I think I've learnt the
key to interact with people, saying what is appropriate, giving
suitable responses for politeness, smiling and staying natural
as signs of friendliness… I am still learning the way to strike
a balance between a too active and a too passive role in
communication. Making others feel comfortable (and even
delighted) to talk to me is my goal. (survey, beginning of fifth
week)
```

This theme of openness continued when Elsa reflected on what she had gained from spending five weeks in an English-speaking country: personal expansion and a growing interest in the social world around her. 'The trip has enlarged my little world, giving me space for self-reflection and imagination… I learnt the importance of being more open to experience new things and the need for me to appreciate and enjoy things out of the academic boundaries' (diary, fifth week).

```
I've gained a lot, learnt a lot. Indeed, the sojourn's benefits
to me are, I believe, not yet fully revealed, but will certainly
affect and contribute to my values/ways of thinking in the rest
of my life. I think I am more independent and also more mature
(in my ways of seeing things) especially when I encounter
building up a relationship, adapting to new things, and finally
departing from my own culture. In this trip, I came across so
many different people and my horizons are much broadened. I've
learned to accept differences and learn from the strength of
others. And I am now more curious about the world. (survey,
beginning of fifth week)
```

Elsa mediated between two cultures and in the process began to open herself up to new ideas and 'ways of being'. Her expansion is congruent with contemporary poststructuralist notions of identity as socially constructed and fluid.

7.2.16   Perceptions of language policy and use of English

Elsa described herself as 'a loyal supporter' of the 'English only' policy and, in the last week, wrote at length about the process of adjusting to life in English. Like Ada and Cori, she had struggled, but by the second week had begun to feel more 'natural' when using the language:

```
As a loyal supporter to the English-only policy, my goal was to
immerse myself totally in English in the four basic language
areas as reading, writing, listening and speaking. However, in
the first half of my trip, it had not been very successful: I
always had difficulty in getting rid of my Cantonese
exclamations. Sometimes I used Cantonese carelessly (e.g., when
I met my buddies in the bus stop early in the morning), which
proved that I had not yet internalized the language into my
mind, and I had the natural tendency to switch back to
Cantonese. However, after the first week, I could already feel a
shift of my language-speaking tendency. To begin with, my spoken
English was much more fluent than at the beginning. Besides, I
felt more natural and easy (and I was more ready to respond to
someone in English), which showed that I was getting used to the
language. Most importantly, when I called back home on phone
(since week two) and spoke to my family in Cantonese, I was
feeling weird and unnatural in using Cantonese too! So I could
conclude at the point that I was in the middle position between
two languages. I knew I was in the process of shifting away from
Cantonese, yet I had not reached the English end. This was
because my spoken English had not reached an excellent level. I
believed it took a long time for me to see the full reward of
continuously immersing in an English environment. (diary, fifth
week)
```

Elsa was convinced that the language policy had made her more aware of the differences between English and her mother tongue. In her diary she provided further evidence of her attention to detail and reflective nature:

```
This English-only policy increased my awareness of the language
issue, which usually involved the differences between the
Cantonese and English language system. For example, I could see
certain ideas/words just exist in Cantonese, while other just in
English. Any conversion in between would need wordy elaboration.
I also noticed interesting language issues, e.g., the opposite
```

```
way in the Cantonese and English use of question tags and my
Cantonese framework of mind in counting numbers.
```

While Cori had found it awkward and unhelpful to use English with other SES students, Elsa had drawn strength from their support of the language policy and picked up many new expressions from their speech. As Gibson (1979) and van Lier (2000, 2004) observed, individual L2 learners may perceive a similar environment quite differently. Elsa was more receptive to the world around her and took greater advantage of linguistic affordances:

```
Another great advantage of this policy was that I did not only
learn   new   English   vocabularies   from   the   local   people/
environment, I also learnt them from my classmates. When we
spoke English all the time, we actually learnt from each other:
it was an exchange of the things we knew. In our group, many of
the   classmates   spoke   excellently.   'Tactic'   and   'reciprocal'
were,  for  example,  words  I  learnt  from  my  classmates'  speech.
(diary, fifth week)
```

Elsa was of the opinion that speaking English throughout the sojourn had been 'incredibly valuable', noting that 'such practice is not possible in Hong Kong since there are more restraints and even inappropriateness to use English in my social setting, given my Chinese identity' (diary, fifth week). Her 'love for English' and her investment in the language had deepened due to 'real contact with beautiful England and its language's speakers'. 'Truly, English has now become an indivisible part of me. I am just not willing to abandon English in my life' (diary, fifth week).

Shortly before her return to Hong Kong, Elsa revisited her language goals for the sojourn and assessed her progress:

```
Expectations Unfulfilled: I could not adopt the British accent.
I had already compromised my belief that one day I could sound
completely  like  a  native  English  speaker.  This  was  quite
impossible for me. Interestingly, it was not that sad to me. I
had  rather  concentrated  more  on  how  to  learn  to  speak  more
fluently  and  without  grammatical  mistakes.  Clarity  of  my
meanings  and  grammatical  accuracy  became  my  concerns.  I  am
pleased with my progress overall. (diary, fifth week)
```

While thrilled with her closer connection to English, Elsa had not acquired a 'beautiful British accent'. Rather than dwell on this, she had refocused her aims and appreciated the strides she had made in improving her fluency. Her diary entry revealed that she had become more realistic about what could be accomplished during a short-term sojourn. Her comments left optimism for further linguistic enhancement.

7.3   Post-sojourn

Back on home soil, in contrast with Ada and Cori, Elsa opted to be interviewed in English about her sojourn experiences and reactions to being back in Hong Kong. She had become more comfortable using English and felt more confident about her ability to express her thoughts and emotions in the language.

While elated to see her family and friends, she missed her English hosts and England, and experienced re-entry culture shock, a phenomenon that involves 'the realignment of one's new identity with a once familiar home environment' (Ting-Toomey and Chung, 2005: 134). Similar to Ada, Elsa saw Hong Kong in a new light and was initially dissatisfied with the environment. This malaise persisted for a week and then she gradually felt more settled: 'Slowly, I accepted my situation, my own identity and my own society so I think I feel better' (interview).

```
Since I've come back, I've felt that Hong Kong has more Chinese
people, Mainlanders and I feel that Hong Kong is not that
international at all. I used to think that it was a famous
international city and Hong Kong people were good at English but
now I think it's just a Chinese society, one of the Chinese
societies, especially when there are so many Mainlanders coming
to Hong Kong every day. And I also feel that Hong Kong students
or the general public are not very good at English. (interview)
```

Her discomfort on re-entry served as another identity trigger, forcing her to reflect further on her positioning in both England and Hong Kong. While she felt a part of both cultures, she did not feel that either had fully accepted her. In her mind she had entered a state of 'in-betweeness' (Yoshikawa, 1987). She recognized different cultural frames of reference and realized that she had been undergoing a process of transformation 'in which the ultimate outcome represents an identity that is not exclusively anchored in one culture/language or another' (Ricento, 2005: 904). Her comments clearly illustrate the potentially profound impact of a short-term sojourn:

```
I was part of the local culture because I was living there and I
was going to see plays like all the other British people but I
know I'm a foreigner in their eyes. It is very interesting. When
I was in England, I thought I was a foreigner in their eyes but
when I come back to Hong Kong, I think that I'm different from
other 'Hong Kongers' because I have been to part of England. Two
different perspectives. It's different. Sort of in-between.
(interview)
```

When reflecting on what she had gained during the sojourn, Elsa felt that she had 'become much more mature mentally', 'more independent', and 'much more self-confident' (survey). After living with people from another culture, she had broadened herself: 'I've grown quite a lot because I learned to accept cultural differences. In a foreign country I had to learn the merits of other people and other cultures.'

In her interview, Elsa also talked enthusiastically about a significant shift in her willingness to use English, even with 'native speakers'. She no longer avoided talking with them and realized that she was now more self-confident in their presence. She was especially proud of her ability to converse in informal social settings:

```
My English has improved but it's difficult to say how. I'm more
ready and confident to speak English and I accept my own English
language skills more. Isn't it interesting? I mean it's not in
terms of the language skill that I've gained the most. For
example, I still make grammatical mistakes. I can still point
out a lot of weaknesses in my language skills but I'm more ready
to speak English. This is great progress actually. And my
vocabulary capacity has increased because I came across many new
words there. It is also another language skill. I also picked up
some slang from my host family. I often asked my host mom to
explain words that she said that I didn't understand. Besides
the words, I also learned some appropriate ways of responding
and some phrases like, 'Oh, what a shame!' I learned a lot more
about the practical language usage in their daily life.
(interview)
```

Elsa reaffirmed her 'love of English' and expressed a strong desire to continue using it in Hong Kong. Her 'affinity' for the language had grown and she was more invested in it. She also revealed a shift in her attitude towards the use of English among Chinese. Even so, it is important to note that while she now deemed it acceptable for Chinese Hong Kongers to 'practise' the language with each other, she still did not view it as natural:

```
In Hong Kong because we're both Chinese we can communicate with
each other in Cantonese so one can argue that it's pointless for
us to communicate in English. There's not the need so the
feeling is that we are intentionally doing so if we use English.
But there's nothing wrong with it because we want to practise
more. After the journey, I feel, I'm more ready to use English
so I feel it's easier to switch from Cantonese to English.
Before the journey, I kept going back to Cantonese, once I
encountered an emotion or ideas that were difficult to express.
But now if I want to talk in English, I can stick to it more
firmly. My attitude has changed a little bit. I think I love
English even more after the journey, although I loved it
already. I just think that English is a beautiful language. I
```

```
love the pronunciation. And then when I was on the journey, I
heard different expressions that I liked. I mean, you know,
language is a very interesting thing. In different countries,
the different language systems are so distinct from each other.
There are certain ideas that are only possible in that country.
In Hong Kong, in the Cantonese system, there aren't equivalent
expressions. I like the English way of saying many things. They
have fewer words that are not graceful or insensitive. Maybe
it's a more polite language. I don't know. Anyway, now I like it
even more. My attitude towards English has changed because I
lived there for five weeks and came across English more. This
made my affinity for the language increase. (interview)
```

Similar to many of her peers, the sojourn also impacted on Elsa's views about her future. It had widened her horizons and, at the time of the interview, she was considering pursuing further studies in England. Her ties with English had been strengthened and opened her mind to other possibilities for her life:

```
After spending five weeks in England, my interest in English has
been strengthened. I don't want to let go of this language so
I'm not willing to, or reconciled to, just finishing the three
years of university study and going out to work. I want to
pursue further studies in English. After seeing the beautiful
landscape of England and knowing a little more about literature,
I want to study it in more depth. Before the journey, I'd never
thought about going overseas to do postgraduate studies. I just
wanted to do an MPhil in this department but now my horizon is
broadened and I'm now considering the University of Warwick.
```

Shortly after the sojourn, she joined a month-long study tour in Edinburgh and later pursued postgraduate studies in Hong Kong.

7.4   Elsa's journey in review

Prior to travelling outside the Chinese world for the first time, Elsa preferred to be identified as a Hong Konger rather than Chinese but was also receptive to identity expansion. English did not feature in her social life, but she made more of an effort to practise it at home and displayed a deeper investment in the language than Ada and Cori. Aware of the 'linguistic and cultural capital' of English (Bourdieu, 1991), Elsa wished to make the language 'part of herself' and develop a more international persona (Ryan, 2006). Even so, she lacked confidence in her oral English and was reluctant to use it with native speakers (Clément et al. 2007; Pellegrino, 2005). She also felt it was inappropriate for Chinese to use it with each other when not required.

During the sojourn, like Ada and Cori, she experienced miscommunication across cultures and sociopragmatic failures and, at times, believed that locals were discriminating against Chinese. Over time, however, she developed the habit of stepping back to reflect on how her own behaviour impacted on the communication process. In Bakhtin's (1986) words, she made more of an effort to appropriate the language and habits of locals and was more open to personal expansion. She took an active role in cultivating relationships across cultures and, as a consequence, gained more exposure to social English. By the end of her stay, she had picked up many colloquial expressions and felt more 'at home' in this environment than Ada and Cori. She had developed a deeper awareness of Self and Other, and her 'affinity' with English had deepened. She had also become more self-confident with speaking in the language in intercultural situations. Back in Hong Kong, she experienced re-entry culture shock (Ward et al, 2001) and entered a state of 'in-betweeness' (Yoshikawa, 1987), discovering that the sojourn had changed her in some profound ways.

8   Niki's journey

I do have a vision. It is about being a competent bilingual
person, a person who strides across the Eastern and Western
cultures and adopts the best of the two. (Sojourn diary, Niki)

8.1   Pre-sojourn

8.1.1   Profile and family background

Niki, a wistful twenty-year old, had a quirky sense of humour, an infectious laugh,
and a keen curiosity about the world around her. In an interview, she described herself
as an introvert who feared failure: 'When I want to do something and want to suc-
ceed, I will put all of my effort into it as I don't want to fail. Once I'm determined, I
will go ahead. I'm afraid of failure. Sometimes I regard success and failure as too
important.' She believed that her close friends would say that she was 'quite funny',
adding: 'I may bring much laughter but sometimes I am quite depressed. The change
is quite big.'

On the homestay placement form Niki provided further insight into her interests
and personality:

I love Literature and Music. I read a lot for leisure. Though an
amateur, I prefer a house with a piano, but this is not a
necessity. I also like to talk a lot. I'd like to chat with the
family I am going to stay with. I hope they would be friendly
and talkative. On the other hand, I definitely need some private
space and time when I feel like it. Personally, I am not much
interested in TV programs but I am a movie fan. Above all, it's
alright for me as long as the family is kind and friendly. I
think this is really important and essential.

In secondary school, she was a committee member in a current affairs club. At
university, she joined a college English society and helped to organize social activities,

a newsletter, and the orientation camp for freshmen. She also participated in the Rotary Club, the Strategic Investment Society, and the Astronomy Club. She opted to live on campus to take a more active role in university life.

Niki had made several short trips to Asian countries with her family, and near the end of secondary school she visited a friend in England for ten days along with some school friends and an adult chaperone. After graduation she aimed to 'do something academic' but, unlike the other women, she did not have any concrete plans or goals when she joined the SES.

Niki described her family as 'lower middle class to lower class', adding that they lived in a public housing estate and her parents' educational level was not high. Her father finished Form 5 (Grade 11) while her mother left school at the end of Form 2 or 3 (Grade 8 or 9). Her father worked in the transportation industry, and her mother was a housewife. Her sister, a university graduate who was four years older, had recently joined the workforce. Niki's family was not used to interacting with people from other cultures, as they were, in her words, 'rather traditional'. Her parents spoke Cantonese and did not understand English. Her sister occasionally used English at work but not in her social life. Cantonese was the language used at home.

8.1.2   Identity

8.1.2.1   A divided person with a core Chinese identity

Like Ada, Niki described herself as a 'divided person'. In her words, an internal struggle had 'nearly torn her apart' as she questioned her place in the world. Similar to Cori, feelings of cultural marginality had sometimes engulfed her, leaving her feeling lost, in search of a place to anchor and take root. Janet Bennett (1993) explained that people in this state might have difficulty making decisions or defining boundaries; they may feel alienated, angry, powerless, and believe that their life has no meaning or direction. In her narrative, Niki's revelations about her self-defined 'struggle' conveyed the depths of her inner turmoil and frustration:

```
A Divided Person
When it comes to cultural identity, the picture of a ship
without anchor drifting on the transcultural ocean, seeking a
safe and permanent harbour, inevitably crosses my mind. I am a
divided person in terms of cultural identity. On the one hand, I
am always restless, wanting to have a multi-faceted cultural
identity. It is only when travelling on board that the horizon
comes into view. In my opinion, the broadening of one's own
horizon is an essential part of an individual's growth. This can
be achieved through adopting a multi-faceted cultural identity.
On the other hand, as a human being, I also have the need to
identify with one single culture, to get a sense of belonging,
to seek refuge, security and support from that cultural group.
```

```
The internal struggle between cultural restlessness and the need
for stability nearly tears me apart.
```

Like most of the other women, she saw her 'complex' emerging identity as drawing from both Chinese and Western cultures, reflecting the hybrid nature of her environment and the impact of globalization on the world:

```
I am a hybrid of various values representative of different
cultures. Neither am I a pure Chinese nor an American. In fact,
since the contemporary world is becoming more international and
people are more physically mobile, there is hardly one person
who belongs to only one cultural group. Hybridity is so
prevalent that people's cultural identity becomes much more
complex than before. (cultural identity narrative)
```

When writing about the impact of globalization, Arnett claimed that, 'in addition to their local identity, young people develop a global identity that gives them a sense of belonging to a worldwide culture' (Arnett, 2002: 777). In Niki's case, she aspired to develop a global, hybrid, more complex identity that would give her a sense of belonging in the wider international community (Meinhof and Galasiński, 2005).

Like Elsa, Niki believed that her identity was subject to change as she encountered new experiences and cultures; however, she set clear boundaries for this expansion. Like Ada, she was firm in her belief that she was born with 'a core, central' Chinese identity, which could not be altered:

```
All in all, with globalization surging in full blaze,
intercultural encounters become more and more common. Like many
modern people, my own cultural identity is becoming more complex
as my experience accumulates. However, there should be one
cultural group that I primarily identify with among the others.
The importance of each cultural group, which constitutes my
identity, is not necessarily equal. While the identification
with other cultural groups helps me to get around easily, the
dominant one provides me with an anchor when I am tired and miss
home. I was born with this core identity upon which I have no
choice. Despite the opinion that cultural identity 'is not
static, fixed, and enduring; rather, it is dynamic and changes
with your ongoing life experiences', cultural identity is only
fluid up to a certain point. That is to say, no matter how our
'periphery identity' changes, our core, central identity is
permanent. I am a Chinese and a Chinese I will remain. (cultural
identity narrative)
```

Her comments reflect a 'high cultural salience', that is, a strong association of membership affiliation with her culture (Ting-Toomey and Chung, 2005). Nonetheless, her sense of self may change over time due to contact with Others and the desire to open up to new environments and ideas. Would Niki maintain this positioning in England or would she experience further identity reconstruction? Is a short-term sojourn long enough to impact on her sense of self?

8.1.2.2   Cultivating an ethnorelative mindset

Although she accepted her ethnic identity, Niki did not want to be confined by it. She was willing to open herself up to other cultures (e.g., 'adopt several essential western values'). In the following excerpt she candidly discussed her exposure to ideas and values ('habitus') that conflicted with traditional Chinese beliefs (Bourdieu, 1991). Instead of rejecting them out of hand, she made an effort to suspend judgment and tried to view the situation from the other person's point of view. In essence, she endeavoured to develop an 'ethnorelative mindset', which Ting-Toomey and Chung defined as 'understanding communication behaviour from another's cultural frame of reference and the ability to perceive from another's cultural lens' (Ting-Toomey and Chung, 2005: 378).

```
Though I accept myself as 'primarily Chinese', I do all my best
to avoid becoming habituated to one particular culture.
Habituation makes people inflexible. It tends to make adaptation
to other cultures difficult. To achieve this, I try not to take
culture for granted. This is really hard, as culture has
permeated so deeply into every part of our daily lives. For
example, the Chinese have reservations about pre-marital sex.
Personally, I don't think it is a wise choice because of the
responsibility it entails. When I first heard from my pen friend
(from Mexico) that she doesn't mind having sex with her
boyfriend, I am rather disturbed. What strikes me as odd is that
her parents agree with her also. In retrospect, this is not too
surprising. Different cultures tend to look at the same issue in
different ways, as is the case of pre-marital sex. Also, the
Chinese are becoming more open and liberal-minded to such
matters. So, I have to look at things from others' perspective.
Only till then did I really succeed to look at things in a
totally objective light. As Craig Storti puts it, 'the wiser
course in any cross-cultural situation is to suspend
interpretation on judgment, suspend the assigning of meaning
until you can find out what any given behaviour might signify in
the other person's culture'.
```

Would Niki be able to put this mindset into practice in a culturally different environment or would she find the transition too turbulent?

8.1.3   Language

8.1.3.1   Language ability and usage

Niki considered herself fluent in her mother tongue (Cantonese) and English but knew only a smattering of Putonghua (Mandarin) and French. Like the other women whose journeys are profiled, Niki earned a 'B' on her A-level examination in English; however, she was not confident in her overall English language proficiency, rating it as 'fair'. She described her reading, writing, and listening skills as 'fairly fluent' but only rated her speaking skills as 'fair'.

The other women had perceived their oral English to be inadequate in some contexts; in particular, they worried that interlocutors who were more proficient (e.g., native speakers) would notice their grammatical mistakes. When she became an English major, Niki, too, had been plagued with doubts about her ability to master the language, sensing a barrier between her and it. Early in the SES programme, however, she described how liberated she felt when realizing that she could be a successful communicator without 'perfect, native-like' English:

```
Oddly, when I first spoke English, my consciousness as a foreign
speaker surged. This was a totally different language experience
compared to speaking Cantonese. I often felt tongue-tied. Worse
still, I was overwhelmed by the feeling of incompetence. I would
avoid any grammatical mistakes at great length. In other words,
spoken English did not come to me naturally. Afterwards I could
not help blaming myself. Because of the failure to express
oneself in fluent English, I felt alienated from the English
culture. Ever since my liberation from the blind worship of
perfect, native English, I feel myself as a transformed person.
(cultural identity narrative)
```

In an interview three months later, however, much of her confidence had evaporated. She berated her oral skills, describing them as 'inadequate' and not sufficiently 'native-like'. A range of nagging self-doubts had crept back into her discourse.

```
RA:     How do you feel when you speak English?
Niki:   I sometimes feel inadequate as I cannot find the right
        words. I think my sentences, the syntax and
        expressions are not native-like enough.
RA:     How do you feel when you use English with a native
        speaker of the language?
Niki:   I feel I am inadequate.
RA:     What about when you use English with another Chinese
        speaker?
```

```
Niki:    I will also find my English inadequate although
         perhaps my confidence is higher in this situation.
```

Similar to Ada, Niki's parents did not speak English and she did not use the language with them. Even so, like Elsa, she made a concerted effort to practise her English language skills at home. In particular, she watched movies to enhance her linguistic and cultural understanding. As Niki said in an interview that took place in Cantonese:

```
I read and write a lot in English at home. When I watch movies,
I also use my listening skills. I love watching suspense movies.
I rely on the English subtitles not the Chinese ones. Sometimes
there is a chunk of English that I cannot understand well. I can
read the English subtitles and know how the native speakers
speak English. I never speak English at home.
```

At this stage, Niki and Elsa appeared to be more invested in learning English than the other two women. Although not forced to do so, they made more of an effort to practice the language at home and made better use of English media (e.g., TV channels, movies).

Similar to the other women, Niki attended a Chinese-medium primary school and was introduced to English in formal language lessons. For her secondary-level education, she attended an English-medium Catholic girls' school, where she also studied Putonghua. Her use of English in childhood was limited to formal, academic situations and practice sessions at home. While she communicated with her teachers and peers in English (or code-mixing) in the classroom, she switched to her mother tongue or code-mixed in informal settings. This situation continued when she entered university. As well as majoring in English, Niki elected to take a course in French.

In Hong Kong, Niki spoke Cantonese most of the time when not in school. English did not feature in her social life. Similar to the other women, she did not seek out opportunities to use the language in the community.

8.1.3.2   Attitude towards languages

Niki felt most confident and natural when speaking Cantonese: 'It is my mother tongue and I can speak fluently. I can speak it non-stop.' Like Cori, however, she was critical of the language, describing it as 'crude' and 'overly direct': 'After I have learned some other languages like English and French, I find that Cantonese does not sound very good. It is very blunt.'

Niki described English as 'a useful tool for public discourse', adding, 'if you know English you have the key to arts, culture, academic and business sectors because it is an international language'. Hence, similar to the other women, she recognized the 'linguistic capital' of English, noting that she could acquire 'a wider range of symbolic and material resources' by becoming proficient in the language. Nonetheless, at this stage, she was not invested in it on an emotional, affective level, attributing her perspective to the foreign language context of Hong Kong.

```
RA:     Do you consider English a language for public
        (academic) discourse instead of private/personal
        communication?
Niki:   I think it is for public discourse. For personal
        communication, it depends on the life of the person.
        If one lives abroad, e.g., in Canada or Britain, it
        must be lived in.
RA:     How about your opinion?
Niki:   It is a public discourse for me in Hong Kong rather
        than for personal communication. Though I also want to
        develop English for personal communication, the
        circumstances and the environment are not encouraging.
RA:     Why do you think it is a public discourse rather than
        personal communication?
Niki:   It is because we use English for lectures,
        presentations, discussions and tutorials. It is used
        in a classroom setting. English is seldom used in
        private life. For example, I do not speak English with
        my mother and father.
```

While she believed that the learning of English, 'an international language', had 'widened her horizons', she still fundamentally saw it as a tool for professional gain. She considered it an asset but was determined that it would 'serve' her and not dominate her life. Her writing disclosed some underlying psychological tension with the international language that she felt compelled to master to take advantage of its linguistic and cultural capital.

```
Though my command over English does not make me a British, it
does make me more international and widen my horizon. Before, I
saw English as the key to become a British (I admire British
culture). Now that my perceptions have changed, though my
enthusiasm over the language has not been dampened, I regard it
as a tool to get my messages across, especially to the
foreigners. Like playing the piano, it is simply another ability
or asset, another 'stock in trade'. Since everybody can use it
if they can master it, the language never belongs to any
cultural group, even the native speakers. I no longer adore the
English language as an isolated system from its social context.
I begin to focus on the practical use of the language in
everyday situation. The language is here to serve us, not we to
serve it. This is indeed a giant step in my language experience
```

and it gives me a kind of intercultural mobility. English is my
international passport.

As Czisér and Dörnyei have observed, English is 'turning into an increasingly
international language, rapidly losing its national cultural base and becoming associated with a global culture' (Czisér and Dörnyei, 2005: 30). This has profound implications for the way it is being perceived by EFL speakers today. Niki, for example,
argued that 'the language never belongs to any cultural group, even the native
speakers'. Rather than associate English exclusively with Britain and Hong Kong's
colonial past, she saw it as an international language that could be used by anyone.
She believed that it could open doors in her future and provide her with 'a kind of
intercultural mobility'.

Although she rarely used the language in her private life, she believed that it
should play a greater role since she was an English major. Because of the growing
number of exchange students on campus, she had become more aware of the benefits
of mastering the language to communicate with people outside her 'ingroup'. She
also expressed the desire to join an exchange programme to further her studies in an
English-speaking environment.

Up to now, English is still external to my sense of self,
although I would very much like to internalize it. However, due
to constraints of the environment, only Cantonese constitutes my
sense of self. Including English in my cultural identity is a
novel and fascinating idea. It also makes me savour the full
meaning of 'mother tongue'. In terms of intimacy, mother is the
one who is closest to us. So, our mother tongue is so deeply
embedded that it is in our flesh and bones. We speak it
spontaneously, without even noticing it. But speaking English is
quite different for me. First of all, I become aware that I am
not speaking my mother tongue. And my confidence dwindles. Then
I tell myself to be more cautious, only to find that the result
is worse still. There is always an unmistakable air of
artificial in it. Honestly, I seldom use English outside
classroom settings. Though a British colony in the past, the
day-to-day environment of Hong Kong is not conducive to the
acquisition of English. In terms of exposure and input, we can
easily gain access by means of TV broadcasting, radio and
newspaper, books etc. In terms of output, the chance to practise
spoken English is not enough, not to mention adopting English in
one's sense of identity. Nonetheless, the ultimate attainment of
this stage is being able to think in English. If English becomes
the 'voice' of our consciousness, English really constitutes our
sense of self. Then English really permeates into our bones.
Besides, it is fun to become a bilingual person. Sometimes I
felt like a serpent slipping from one layer of skin into another

> seamlessly when I am code-switching. With the switch in the
> 'thinking language', one's style of thinking will be altered,
> which eventually leads to an altered cultural identity.
> (cultural identity narrative)

While Niki's orientation to the language was largely instrumental and 'external to her sense of self', she hoped to broaden her usage and slip 'seamlessly' from 'one style of thinking' to another. Through the process of becoming bilingual, she hoped to 'eventually alter her cultural identity'. Would the sojourn change her perception of English and provide a stimulus for further personal expansion?

Like the other women, Niki found it 'strange' for two Hong Kong Chinese to speak English with each other when no native speakers of English were present: 'It seems that they speak English for the sake of speaking English, like they are showing off.' As in Elsa's case, her comments highlight the power of the unwritten linguistic code of behaviour in this context. If students wish to use English in social situations, they risk being ostracized, or in Cori's words, 'outgrouped' by their peers. Her comments are in line with Zuengler's (1989) and Meyers-Scotton's (2006) observations that L2 speakers may opt to use a language to demonstrate 'solidarity' with their 'ingroup'.

8.1.3.3 Code-mixing

In the same interview, Niki acknowledged that she, too, code-mixed frequently. Unlike the other women, however, she did not consider it a problem unless the English words she added to her Cantonese discourse were incorrect.

> RA: Are there contexts in which you use code-mixing (a
>   mixture of English and Cantonese)?
> Niki: Yes.
> RA: In which situations do you use this most often? Why?
> Niki: I use more code-mixing with English majors. We talk in
>   Cantonese but at the same we add a lot of English in
>   the conversation. It is because we all understand each
>   other.
> RA: How do you feel when code-mixing?
> Niki: Sometimes I am not conscious of it. For example, we
>   say 'inaug' for 'inauguration' in our department. My
>   friend who studies in the Chinese Department does not
>   know what 'inaug' is. They say 'inauguration' in
>   Chinese.
> RA: How do you feel when you are aware of code-mixing?
> Niki: I think it is good if the use of code-mixing is
>   appropriate. Of course, it is not good when you use
>   the English wrongly.

```
RA:     You think code-mixing is okay if the vocabulary is
        correct?
Niki:   Yes.
```

8.1.3.4 Language, culture, and identity

Shortly before the sojourn, Niki appeared to be more accepting of her proficiency level in English and her 'heavy, Cantonese' accent. She no longer seemed to feel the need to 'emulate the way the British speak'. In a positive frame of mind, she wrote that English allowed her to expand her identity and acquire a more international persona:

```
I began to feel more at ease with my grammatical mistakes and
foreign accent. I can see my horizon broadened before me. A lot
of possibilities also opened up. This is a delightful
experience, since my mastery over English liberates me from the
frame of being a Chinese exclusively. I can be an international
person. In fact, language experience is a kind of cultural
experience. Since I am an English major, I always sense my
obligation to polish my language skills. There is quite a lot of
room for improvement. The mastery over this language renders me
more attached to the British culture than others. But I will
never try to become a British through emulating the way they
speak again. Most parts of culture are deeply embedded within a
person. People's accent and behaviour are only overt
manifestations of their cultures. I began to accept myself as
inherently Chinese adopting several essential western values.
Meanwhile, I gradually came to terms with my heavy Cantonese
accent 'non-native' English.
```

Niki's comments disclosed her awareness of the inextricable link between language, identity, and culture. They also revealed that she harboured some concern about her positioning in England. Like Elsa, Niki had once longed to be accepted as British. Even if she fully mastered the language, she did not believe it would be possible due to discrimination. Bourdieu (1991) and Joseph (2004) have written about existing social networks, hierarchies, and attitudes that may not permit an individual to fully adopt a new position in a 'field' (e.g., the host community). Would Niki experience these barriers in a short-term sojourn? Would her fears be realized?

```
I once tried to speak with a British accent because in my
opinion, if I can speak 100% native English, I can become a
British. Of course, this is only a misconception. Culture is
more than the mastery over a language used by a particular
cultural group... Although many of us speak fluent English,
westerners are not likely to identify us with them. As
technology advances, physical distance between nations is
```

> reduced. But, the communication barriers and prejudice are yet
> to be removed. Communication gap is much more profound than
> physical distance. Cultural mobility should come along with
> physical mobility. (cultural identity narrative)

What is also noticeable in Niki's writing is the polarized 'us' vs. 'them' discourse that surfaced in the narratives of her peers. How would her views and expectations of 'communication barriers and prejudice' affect her sojourn in England?

8.1.4   Pre-departure aspirations, expectations, and anxieties

Like Elsa, Niki longed to study in England where she could use English 'in private life' (interview). 'We can have total immersion in the birthplace of English. Studying in England has been my dream since I was young. To pick up the language in a natural environment will be so much different from most of my learning environment in Hong Kong' (survey).

When asked her views about the 'English only' policy in an interview, her response was unequivocal: 'I think it's perfect; otherwise, what's the point of going to England?' After some more thought, she acknowledged that there might be difficulties in the beginning:

> We always speak Cantonese and suddenly we'll have to speak
> English completely. We'll need time to adjust to the situation
> but I think it will be better afterwards… Perseverance is
> important. We shouldn't be afraid of saying something wrong or
> speaking English badly and we should continue to speak English.

If a classmate addressed her in Cantonese during the sojourn, Niki thought that she would reply in her mother tongue as a matter of 'politeness' and 'solidarity' but 'gradually switch back to English'.

Similar to Ada and Elsa, she had high expectations for the improvement of her English language skills: 'I want to be able to speak and communicate as a native speaker does. I know it's a bit unrealistic in English but I hope I don't have to struggle or rack my mind to find the right word for what I want to say. I hope the language would come to me naturally' (survey).

She also aimed to become more positive about herself and the world around her:

> RA: What aspect of yourself would you like to improve?
> Niki: I think I always think in a negative way and find
>   myself good at nothing. For example, if I cannot do
>   some tiny things, I think I am too poor and deny all
>   the effort I have made. I hope I could become less
>   negative and more self-confident during the sojourn…

```
          When there is some little frustration, I tend to think
          the worst.
RA:       What efforts have you made to improve?
Niki:     I ask some classmates and friends how they would react
          if the same situation had happened to them. I try to
          get some other points of view.
```

Niki expected that the sojourn would 'widen her horizons' and change her in some ways: 'One cannot expect to be a totally transformed person in only five weeks but I still hope to have a few significant changes through the sojourn' (intercultural reflections journal). In a survey, she also wrote that she would like to make a British friend 'to break new ground'. By setting a range of socio-emotional goals, she revealed her desire to enhance her personal development during the sojourn.

Like many of her peers, Niki experienced some anxiety prior to departure. In a survey she wrote: 'I'm worried that I may get lost as I am totally unfamiliar with the environment there. I'm afraid that I may be so timid that I may lose this precious chance to improve my oral skills.' In her first interview she revealed that she did not adjust easily to change and was often nervous when confronted with a change in routine: 'I have to force myself to be more adaptive. I feel secure when I'm in a familiar environment where things are predictable but when I face uncertain things, I worry about what will happen.'

She was also anxious about whether she would be able to develop a good relationship with her host family. Niki conceded that she lacked the confidence to fully express her views and hoped this would improve during the sojourn: 'Sometimes I don't feel comfortable or at ease especially when there are strangers. I am quite self-conscious. I need to be more confident to voice out my opinion or suggestions regardless of what others think.' Would these anxieties have a negative impact on her adjustment?

8.2   The sojourn

8.2.1   Recognition and reassurance

Like Ada and Elsa, Niki wrote a detailed narrative about meeting her English hosts for the first time. As her name was called to join her host mother, she found herself gripped by fear and felt 'disorientated', as if she was 'being pulled asunder'. Her fears subsided when the woman greeted her with a reassuring smile.

```
The first day tends to be the most unforgettable day. The most
exciting moment is when we first met our host family. When I
first arrived and saw a bunch of English people waiting for us,
my heart started pounding and I desperately wanted to know which
```

was my host mum or dad. The homestay coordinator just matched
the host and the student one by one. It was just like being
adopted by a total stranger. Adjectives like 'nervous',
'anxious', and 'curious' all mingled together, which contributed
to my mood, with a tinge of suspense. One by one, my SES buddies
were leaving with their host parents. I became disorientated and
realized how much I clung to them whilst in an unknown
situation. We were just like being pulled asunder. I was afraid
we couldn't be in touch with each other anymore while away from
school. That was stupid, isn't it? But that was exactly how I
felt at that time.

Then it came to my go. Although I had not been waiting for long,
it seemed to me that I had waited for ages. I was so anxious and
kept wondering whether I will be in good hands. Eventually, here
came the moment of actuality. I met my host mum, Paulina. I can
tell from the way she looked she cannot be a mean person. She
was smiling all along. Now I finally understood why a warm smile
is so important. It is very reassuring, eases the tension and
breaks the ice. Paulina led me to her car and drove me home. Now
I was really relieved. We talked a lot during the ride. I was
impressed by the way she remembered what I had put down in the
home-stay form. The most impressive one was that she even
remembered my date of birth. She must have been reading my
profile for a long time. My confidence of mastering the English
language, especially the spoken, began to build up. (diary,
first week)

From their first meeting, Niki had felt that her host was genuinely interested in her
and this bolstered her self-esteem and desire to use English. Would the host–
sojourner bond continue to develop? Would Niki's language and cultural learning be
sustained throughout the sojourn?

8.2.2   Linguistic differences and pangs of inferiority

Similar to Elsa, what I noticed early in Niki's diary was far more attention to
linguistic details than the women who were featured in the previous chapters. Ada
and Cori struggled to cope with differences throughout their stay; by contrast, early
on, Niki was able to focus more on the enhancement of her English, even though
she, too, had bouts of homesickness and found speaking the language a challenge. In
the following excerpt, which was penned in the first week of the sojourn, she wrote
about the English expressions that had caught her attention and, like Elsa, disclosed
her feelings of inadequacy when interacting with native speakers in an unfamiliar
'field':

At first it took me quite an effort to speak in English all the
time since I had been speaking Cantonese in all daily settings.
Sometimes I felt self-conscious. I did not mind my Cantonese
accent very much, as long as it is intelligible to people from
other nations. I felt awkward for the way I spoke. It is not
authentic English. It seems to me that native speakers tend to
make shorter sentences. Most of them tend to have a short, but
clear style. Their communication style in English is more
effective, in general. Besides, they seem to use more nouns than
a second-language speaker does whereas we tend to use more verbs
and spin longer sentences. The other thing is Collocations.
During the whole trip, I learnt that the English use a lot of
phrasal verbs, while this is relatively rare for us. These are
all common expressions to them. For example, 'wave somebody off'
and 'stretch someone out'. I think this is partly a matter of
input. We simply do not have as much input as them. At first, I
felt clumsy and found difficulties in expressing more
complicated meanings, especially with my host family members.
Sometimes I panicked. It was like being flung into a deep and
vast ocean without any aid, left to one's own devices. However,
at the end, I always managed to express myself, although always
less than perfect. I think the greatest challenge for a second-
language learner to use English is psychological hindrance more
than realistic ones. As an adult, sometimes a pang of
incompetence and inferiority crops up when I was talking with
native speakers. (diary, first week)

Would she overcome these 'pangs of inferiority' and move towards fuller membership in new CoP (communities of practice)?

8.2.3   Aspirations of bilingualism and cultural expansion

In the first week, Niki became frustrated with her inability to follow the conversation
of native speakers of English. Rather than give up, she conveyed a willingness to
persevere with her language and cultural learning. In her diary, she restated her
vision of becoming a 'competent, bilingual person' who is able to adopt the best of
'the two Eastern and Western cultures'. While her statements do not reflect an
awareness of the broad nature of her categories (e.g., as if there are only two unitary
cultures represented), they reveal a desire to move closer towards intercultural
personhood (Kim, 2001, 2006) and a 'global identity' (Arnett, 2002; Kramsch,
1999b; Ryan, 2006). Would she remain on course for further personal expansion?

I was puzzled by my hosts' conversation because I missed most of
what they said. I guess it is because of my listening skills. I
just cannot pick up their spoken language. They talked rather

```
fast. This proved to be frustrating as I wondered when would I
fully understand their conversation and have a native command of
spoken English. Is this just an impalpable dream? Will it never
happen?… Given my Chinese background, it was understandable that
I cannot comprehend fully their conversation. I think the reason
being that I simply did not have enough English input in Hong
Kong. At first I was a bit embarrassed. On hindsight, there is
nothing to be ashamed of. I became totally at ease with that.
However, my Chinese background should not serve as a convenient
excuse for not trying my very best to pick up the language. I do
have a vision. It is about being a competent bilingual person, a
person who strides across the Eastern and Western cultures and
adopts the best of the two. (diary, first week)
```

Similar to Ada and Cori, Niki found it exhausting to live in English. I did, however, discover a significant difference in the way these three women reacted to this psychological pressure. Niki displayed more patience and resilience; she also seemed to be more realistic about what could be accomplished in the time available:

```
I know I am far from speaking in perfect English. Life of a
foreign language speaker is much more difficult than a native
speaker. We have to put in conscious effort constantly. It is a
long and thorny way, and we are staggering through. I think the
key is confidence and more importantly, perseverance… A
linguistic breakthrough does not happen overnight (diary, first
week)
```

Niki was more willing to 'make a conscious effort' to become competent in the language, reflecting a higher level of investment in English than Ada and Cori. She revised her language enhancement goals while in the host environment and seemed determined to persevere. As the weeks unfolded, would she experience more success than the other women?

8.2.4   Perceptions of racism and identity misalignments

Like many of her peers, Niki felt like an 'outsider' in England due to her physical appearance and the reactions of locals. At the end of the first week, she recounted an unpleasant encounter with a local teenage girl and her boyfriend in a grocery store. The girl gave her a 'dirty look', which Niki interpreted as racist. While upset, she expressed the desire to 'accept people for who they are' and not dwell on the negative: 'I always remind myself that it's a unique experience. No matter it is good or bad, it's part of the experience and growing process' (survey, beginning of second week).

> I am Chinese. You can tell it straight away from my appearance.
> I have black hair, dark eyes and yellow skin. This encounter
> with the teenagers was a life lesson: One should not be blindly
> pro-western, which was the attitude I had before. Although I had
> tried my very best to integrate into the English community, I
> was still regarded as an outsider in some people's eyes. It is
> hard to change the way people think. Racist attitude, once it
> was inculcated, is hard to eradicate… This encounter, though
> unpleasant, reminded me of my identity as a Chinese. Upon
> reflection, there are many values in Chinese culture that the
> new generation should treasure and preserve. There is a
> Confucian saying, 'Harmony in Diversity'. Differences across
> cultures are existential. It does not make sense to eliminate
> the differences… Accepting people for what they are is really
> essential to world peace. (diary, first week)

At this early stage of the sojourn, I noticed some similarities in her discourse and Cori's. Unpleasant experiences in England caused both women to reflect on Hong Kong's colonial past and its legacy. Both expressed resistance to 'the invasion' of the British and emphasized the need to 'treasure' certain elements of Chinese culture. When feeling threatened or disrespected in England, they clung more tightly to their Chinese identity. Nonetheless, Niki still expressed the desire to become a 'hybrid of the best of both cultures' and cultivate a bicultural identity (Arnett, 2002; Kramsch, 1999b):

> I do question the general attitude of most of the new generation
> in Hong Kong nowadays: In trying to pursue the Western ways, how
> much values of Chinese culture do they put into ruthless
> disregard? If one does not treasure the laudable values of one's
> own culture, it is indeed a disgrace to one's nation and
> oneself, even more so than the despicable gesture of the girl. I
> have learnt that I will become less vulnerable to racial
> discrimination if I treasure the valuable things of my own
> culture. Of course, I should also face the darker sides of my
> own culture. The better outcome is a hybrid of the best of the
> Oriental as well as the Occidental. The colonial period has long
> passed. But the remnants of British invasion: colonization of
> the mind is even more far-reaching and disturbing. (diary, first
> week)

Niki's comments evoke Ryan's admonition that conflict may arise 'when there is significant divergence between the local values and those linked to a global culture' or 'in situations where there is an apparent contradiction between an individual's own sense of identity and an identity externally specified for that individual' (Ryan, 2006: 32). Throughout much of the sojourn, Niki was engaged in an intensely personal struggle as she resisted the 'colonization of the mind', while simultaneously opening herself up to other worldviews and values.

Like Ada, Niki was mistaken for a Japanese. In the first week of her stay, she wrote about the incident in her diary using a matter of fact tone:

```
In the evening, we went to my host mum's sister's house to have
a family gathering. When I first arrived, they were very warm
and cordial in welcoming me. They did have considerable hospi-
tality. The host asked me if I was Japanese. I wondered why
people often mistook Chinese for Japanese. 'No', I said,
'actually, I come from Hong Kong'. That was how I told him.
```

Later at the same social event, another guest mistook her for a Mainland Chinese: 'My host mum's brother asked if I was the only child in my own family back in Hong Kong because of the one-child policy in China. The interesting thing is, he did not know there is a slight difference between Hong Kong and Mainland China' (diary, first week). Again, her reaction was more muted than some of her fellow sojourners. It is important to note, however, that both of these incidents involved relatives of her host family, not her hosts. Would these negative encounters impact on her relationship with her hosts and others in the community?

Similar to the other women, lack of recognition of her preferred identity and the realization that she was visibly different from most locals made her more attuned to her ethnic/racial identity: 'Being in England deepens my awareness of being a Chinese. There is an undeniable difference' (survey, beginning of second week). A week later, she revealed that she had become more sensitive to cultural differences in beliefs and practices. While not embracing all of these new behaviours, she did not openly reject people who were different: 'I'm now more aware of my Chinese identity. I don't like dyed hair and piercings in me. I can make friends with people with these but I guess I will never do this myself' (survey, beginning of third week).

Niki was proud of her achievements at this point in the sojourn and felt that she was becoming more open-minded and sociable: 'I'm developing new social skills and strategies. I become more open to people from different walks of life, ages and genders' (survey, beginning of third week). Her flexibility and openness to difference, an essential characteristic of 'the intercultural speaker' (Byram, 1997, 2003), set her apart from the women whose stories were told in Chapters 5 and 6.

8.2.5 Coping with homesickness: cultivating the host–sojourner relationship

Niki had been anxious about getting lost when she first arrived; however, by the beginning of the third week she had become more self-confident, especially after overcoming a brief bout of homesickness: 'I've become more eager to explore around, which I dared not do at the beginning since I was afraid of getting lost. Sometimes, I prefer to explore by myself since this will force me to be self-dependent' (survey, beginning of third week).

In the first week, Niki had also been worried about 'offending her host family' but gradually, after spending a lot of time with them, she became more relaxed and felt at home. Similar to Elsa, she found that communication with her hosts had become more natural: 'I've developed a friendly and comfortable relationship with my host family. I enjoy chatting with them…We normally watch TV or movies together or talk about the pets. I understand most of what they say. I can pick up more spoken English more than before' (survey, beginning of fourth week). According to Lave and Wenger (1991), it is through this process of mutual engagement with 'experts' in the community that newcomers, like Niki, build up new understandings and broaden themselves. Would Niki's exposure to new CoP lead to further personal and linguistic expansion?

8.2.6   Language, identity, and belonging

That same week Niki set 'complete mastery over English' as a personal goal but admitted that, like Cori and Ada, she still found it 'clumsy' to converse in the language with her peers. At this stage, her attitude toward English was quite different from Elsa's:

```
Personally, I have mixed feelings towards the English Only
Policy, and the English language. As an English major, I have an
inner compulsion to learn the language as well as possible. I
also understand that the English Policy is for our own benefit.
On the other hand, if we had to use English all the time among
ourselves, I felt quite clumsy. Sometimes I had to brain-rack
myself for the exact word whereas Cantonese simply came to me
naturally. I found Cantonese more handy and convenient in terms
of self-expression and communication purpose. (diary, third
week)
```

Like Ada and Cori, Niki missed her mother tongue and found speaking English 'like wearing clothes that did not fit her size'. She still felt much more comfortable using her first language. Would she persevere with English?

```
During the middle of the trip, I felt more at ease with using
English. I automatically used English to converse with my SES
buddies without being conscious of it… I would prefer to speak
in Cantonese back in Hong Kong with my classmates because during
these days, I missed Cantonese quite a lot. Although I chatted
with my classmates in English spontaneously, speaking English is
like wearing clothes that does not fit my size. Cantonese is
```

> like clothes that are tailored for me. I fit in perfectly and
> seamlessly. I feel good in it. It also feels like a right-handed
> person has to use his left hand only, with his right hand
> completely healthy. I guess the reason for my feeling is very
> much related to my competence. I can master my mother tongue
> perfectly whereas this is not the case for English. That's why I
> feel more confident and natural in Cantonese. (diary, third
> week)

Her feelings about her mother tongue were tightly bound with her identity. When she used it, she felt a 'sense of belonging' and, when homesick, these feelings intensified. Similar to Ada and Cori, she considered Cantonese to be lodged 'deep inside her bones'. Her first language served as a symbol of her affiliation with her cultural group, and this evoked strong emotions. Immersion in the host speech community, surrounded by native speakers of English, served as a significant identity trigger, raising her awareness of the connection between language, culture, and identity. In her diary, she explained:

> Though depressing, I think one's mother tongue is a hindrance to
> our learning a second language... I still find it a very good idea
> to forget that we know Chinese when learning English. However, I
> should not forget I am Chinese, no matter when and where I am.
> Speaking in a second language is a very effective way to
> integrate into another culture. If the English language is in my
> tongue, then Cantonese is deep inside my bone. My mother tongue
> is more than a language to me. It is associated with my
> childhood memories, my family. Most importantly, it assures me
> with a sense of belonging. (third week)

Later in the same week, Niki again wrote about the potential advantages of being bilingual and bicultural as well as the merits of 'achieving a global perspective'. Her comments are in line with Kramsch's observation that, 'the global spread of English challenges learners of English to develop both a global and a local voice' (Kramsch, 1999b: 131). While Niki wished to broaden herself, she emphasized that her ethnic identity could never be altered; like her mother tongue, it was 'deep inside her bones', providing her with a 'sense of belonging':

> All in all, the English Policy made me reflect on my cultural
> identity and my mother tongue. The advantage of bilingualism is
> that one can stride across different cultures and achieve a
> global perspective. It opens up horizons, possibilities as well
> as opportunities. As far as I am concerned, the most important
> thing is to get the best out of different cultures without
> forgetting one's ethnicity. I guess knowing one's position and
> identity gives one a sense of orientation in a foreign place.

```
You can change your lifestyle, your language, and even the way
you look. But you can never change your ethnicity. It is deep
inside your bones. (diary, third week)
```

Niki's comments were in accord with Kim's belief that, 'we can incorporate into our psyches new cultural elements without 'throwing away' or 'being disloyal to' our original cultural groups' (Kim, 2001: 233). This sounds simple but, as Niki's discourse revealed throughout the sojourn, this process of personal expansion may evoke an intense internal struggle, replete with conflict and contradictions (Kramsch, 1999b; Ryan, 2006).

Similar to Cori, the experience of living in another culture and linguistic environment had made her conscious of how little she knew about her cultural roots: 'I realize that I am not that familiar with Hong Kong and Chinese culture as I had thought. I realized when asked about Chinese history, I am at a loss for an answer' (survey, beginning of fourth week). Her awakening supports the INT (Identity Negotiation Theory) (Ting-Toomey, 2005) and Bakhtin's (1986) contention that contact with other cultures raises awareness of both Self and Other.

8.2.7   A linguistic breakthrough and 'sense of belonging'

At the beginning of the last week, I noticed a change in Niki's attitude toward the language policy as well as her perception of her English language skills. She had become much more comfortable in her new environment and more positive about her language skills. This impacted on her willingness to use her L2, even with her peers. Similar to many of her peers, she used the collective 'we' to express her views about the policy:

```
The 'English only' policy is well received   After 4 weeks we
become more at ease and comfortable with the language.  I think
it is definitely a constructive idea as it facilitates total
immersion in English.  We don't have much time here and we can't
afford to waste the opportunity to use English and we are all
doing it for ourselves. It is definitely an excellent idea.
(survey, beginning of fifth week)
```

Niki had longed to enhance her language skills and was convinced that she had achieved this goal: 'My spoken English has improved discernibly since I chat with my host family member every day. It's probably due to the total immersion in an English-speaking environment that I did achieve a linguistic breakthrough' (survey, beginning of fifth week). Through sustained participation in sociocultural practices in the host community, Niki gradually became more comfortable living in English. She also began to notice the 'communicative intentions' and 'specific perspectives' that are embedded in these practices (Bourdieu, 1991; Vygotsky, 1987).

In contrast with Ada and Cori, Niki devoted much of her time to building a close relationship with her hosts and, significantly, felt that the effort was reciprocal. Her host mother served as an informant in her ethnographic research project and also chatted freely with her in the evenings. As a result, like Elsa, Niki felt that she had developed 'a sense of belonging' in her homestay:

```
My relationship with my host family becomes closer as time
passes. In fact, my greatest accomplishment is that I've been
able to establish rapport with them… I really enjoy chatting
with my host mom and her family members. She is very generous
with her time and willing to offer me a hand. She was my chief
informant for my ethnographic research… Apart from lessons and
excursions, I spent most of my time with my hosts before I go to
bed. Sometimes my host mom express her opinion on politics, the
movies or the TV soap operas. My host mom is a very sympathetic
person. I realized it when we watched a very sad and tragic
movie. When the innocent boy was shot to death, she cried at the
end. It is a movie on racism. This makes me feel more attached
to her because she has a kind heart. Every now and then my host
dad will do the karaoke. He becomes very happy and chatty.  We
all have a good laugh. By joining them, we communicate better
with each other. (survey, beginning of fifth week)
```

Lave and Wenger have argued that 'legitimate peripherality is a complex notion, implicated in social structures involving relations of power. As a place in which one moves toward more-intensive participation, peripherality is an empowering position' (Lave and Wenger, 1991: 36). Niki took full advantage of her positioning in her homestay placement and, like Elsa, was a 'willing-to-learn guest'. As a consequence, over time she enhanced both her intercultural and linguistic skills.

Niki also found her hosts to be gracious and respectful; this helped her to feel secure and develop a sense of belonging in the homestay. In stark contrast with Ada and Cori, who experienced 'a lack of mutuality', she believed that her hosts' interest in her and her culture was sincere:

```
The homestay experience is a unique and precious chance to
communicate with people from another culture and it gives me
daily practice in English.  Just as we want to know more about
the English culture, my host family members want to know more
about our culture too. (survey, beginning of fifth week)
```

Niki and Elsa both experienced 'mutuality and engagement' (Wenger, 1998) in their homestays. Were their hosts genuinely more receptive and supportive, or did these young women make more of an effort to engage?

8.2.8   Personal expansion and identity reconstruction

By the end of the sojourn, Niki was very pleased with her accomplishments and her 'personal expansion' as reflected in her last sojourn survey: 'I'll always remember this experience. When I look back in the future, I will be proud of myself because I've tried new things. It has widened my horizon… This is one of the happiest moments in my life.' She felt differently about herself and her place in the world: 'To a large extent, I feel I've changed. I've become more confident and culturally sensitive. An independent student with a cosmopolitan outlook.' Her last comment reflected her pride in her new, expanded global identity.

Like Elsa and the women in the previous chapter, she had become more accepting of her culture in the face of perceived racism: 'I've learnt to shrug off some unpleasant experience like racial discrimination. I've also learnt to treasure my Chinese identity more via some unpleasant racist experience' (survey, beginning of fifth week).

8.3   Post-sojourn

Back in Hong Kong, Niki thought about the impact of the sojourn on her life. Similar to Elsa, she opted to be interviewed in English even though her earlier interviews had been in her mother tongue.

She expressed support for the 'English only' policy, commenting that it had been 'very constructive', motivating her and her fellow sojourners to enhance their language skills: 'We proved to ourselves that we were quite competent in communicating with each other. We were able to express our emotions and discuss some very intimate matters with each other in English.' This contrasted significantly with her views in the first half of the sojourn. She had persevered with the language, and, in her own words, had experienced a 'linguistic breakthrough'. Drawing on the support of her host family and peers, she had broken down some psychological barriers. She had become more comfortable using English in informal, social settings with both her peers and hosts. By the end of the sojourn, she was less concerned about making mistakes in the language. This was a significant step forward for her: 'I now think it's okay to make grammatical mistakes. L2 speakers may be self-conscious when they make grammatical mistakes but it's quite inevitable and natural. You shouldn't be intimidated and should continue to use the language. It's very important. It's okay to make mistakes' (interview).

Niki had also become more courageous when interacting across cultures and less fearful of rejection. Unlike Ada and Cori, she had learned many idiomatic expressions, reflecting a growing investment in the enhancement of her social discourse skills and interpersonal relationships across cultures. Similar to Elsa, frequent face-to-face contact and successful communication with her host family and other locals had boosted her self-confidence. These largely positive experiences had, in turn, made her more open to people from other cultures. In her interview Niki said:

> I've become more confident to use English and more willing to accept people from other nations. My English improved. I picked up some English expressions, especially some phrasal verbs and idioms. For example, 'to wind somebody up' means to annoy somebody. I think these expressions were very useful to me.

Another significant change was her perception of English. After living and functioning in the target speech community for five weeks, Niki no longer viewed the language merely as a tool for academic success; she had begun to think of it as a 'living language'.

> I think I'm now more willing to use English to communicate with others. I think it's very important to master the language even more so than before the trip. Before the sojourn, I thought English for me was somehow restricted to academic or classroom settings. But after the trip, I think English is a living language. People are using it all the time. My views changed because we had to live in English and communicate with others in English so we had more chances to speak in English. And for practical purposes, we had to use English, not just to pass exams or do papers. That's why my attitude changed. (interview)

In stark contrast with Ada and Cori, Niki felt that she had had ample opportunity to use English and interact with people outside the SES group. She had initiated conversations across cultures and reaped the benefits: 'We had many chances to speak in English and communicate with people from other cultural backgrounds and this enhanced my self-confidence' (interview). While some of her peers saw only 'obstacles and rejections' in their environment, Niki saw linguistic affordances and made an effort to take advantage of them.

Although she had developed a warm relationship with her hosts and felt accepted by them 'as a friend', she was acutely aware that she was visibly different from most locals she encountered in the small towns of Warwickshire, including her host family. Niki's race became problematized in her eyes, through her interaction with Others. In an interview, she explained:

> I think I adapted quite well into the family life of my host family. They didn't treat me as a stranger. They just treated me as a friend. At the end of the trip I still felt a bit like a foreigner because I'm still Chinese. The way I look is very different. People were not necessarily unkind to me. In fact, most were very kind to me but they just feel, I don't mean my

```
host  family,  most  people  in  England  they  just  treat  us  as
Chinese.
```

Throughout the sojourn, she had tried to be positive and accept differences; this degree of openness had eased her intercultural adjustment. In her interview, she revealed that she had made a conscious effort to accept differences and push past an ethnocentric mindset:

```
Going to a foreign country and living there for a certain period
of time will open up your horizon. No matter which country, it
makes you more open to other cultures and new things. Sometimes
you have to adapt to things that you don't understand. I think
it's very good for personal development and personal growth…I
just accepted the lifestyle in England because it's the way they
live. If you come to the place of others, you have to adopt
their lifestyle. A fruitful way to adjust is to avoid ethno-
centrism. Just accept new things in a new culture as far as
possible. Tolerance is important.
```

This positive orientation and eagerness to try new things naturally enhanced her relationships across cultures. While Ada and Cori had not developed a close bond with their hosts, Niki's sojourn had unfolded quite differently. In her eyes, her host family had been very welcoming and she had fond memories of the time she had spent with them: 'I miss the UK quite a bit, especially Kenilworth and my host family. I miss the people there. They are very friendly, especially my host family; they are very kind and nice. They accepted me as I am' (interview).

Niki's openness to other cultures also impacted on her perception of her identity. Dialogic relations and encounters with Others made her realize the importance of developing a deeper understanding of her own culture and cultural roots in order to become a successful intercultural communicator:

```
The trip made me realize that I wasn't really familiar with my
home culture. When they asked me about it, I just told them some
very superficial stuff. To improve my intercultural communi-
cation skills, I have to know more about my own culture before I
learn about another culture or adapt to it. (interview)
```

Her words are in line with the recommendations of Byram and Zarate (1997a) and other interculturalists.

As well as accepting her Chinese ethnicity, this emergent 'intercultural speaker' (Alred and Byram, 2002) was open to other cultures: 'I still feel myself as a Chinese but I also think there are some good things in western culture that the Chinese should adopt. I think it's good to get the best of the two cultures.' Exposure to

Others, coupled with 'outsideness' presented Niki with the opportunity for 'highly productive hybridity' (Bakhtin, 1981, 1986). From this perspective, Niki aimed to integrate the best values, practices, and approaches of several cultures. In the last half of the sojourn, elements of 'thirdspace' (Bhabha, 1994; Kramsch, 1999a; Soja, 1996) had begun to emerge in both her oral and written narratives.

In the post-sojourn survey, Niki's advice to the next group of sojourners offered further insight into her maturity and the positive mindset that had helped see her through difficulties in England:

```
Always focus on the bright side, even when unpleasant things
happen and try to talk to someone you can trust when facing
problems or feeling upset. It's natural to become more sensitive
and vulnerable in a foreign place. Conversely, a listening ear
to other group mates will make a lot of difference. Time is
everything.
```

Back on home soil, Niki began to consider her future, including the possibility of becoming an English teacher after undertaking further studies abroad. This was a significant development. Prior to the sojourn, she had been very vague about her career path. In her interview, she outlined her new goals:

```
I'm thinking of studying English in an English-speaking country
because if you're immersed in a language, in an English-speaking
environment, you're forced to speak it and live in it. This
helps improve your English a lot. Academically, I think I will
pursue the linguistics area. For a professional goal, I've been
thinking of teaching English in a secondary school or helping
second language speakers to master the English language.
```

After graduation, she opted to pursue postgraduate studies in literature in Hong Kong.

8.4   Niki's journey in review

Similar to Cori, before the sojourn, Niki had experienced feelings of cultural marginality (J. Bennett, 1993) and had struggled to define herself in the 'hybrid' environment of Hong Kong. While she aspired to acquire a global identity through English (Arnett, 2002; Ryan, 2006), like Ada, she believed that she possessed 'a core, central' Chinese self that could not be changed. She lacked confidence in her oral skills in English but, like Elsa, she created opportunities to practise the language at home. Most relaxed in her L1, she primarily regarded English as a 'useful tool for public discourse' and was not as close to the language as Elsa. Like her peers, Niki was very aware of the 'symbolic and material resources' that she could acquire through the language (Bourdieu, 1991).

Her transition to English life was far from smooth, however. Initially, she experienced 'pangs of inferiority' and had difficulty following the discourse of locals (Dörnyei, 2005; Pellegrino, 2005). Like Ada and Cori, she found it psychologically challenging to function in an L2 (Byram, 2003; Dörnyei, 2005). Drawing on the socio-emotional support of her hosts and peers, she persevered with her goal to become a 'competent, bilingual person who strides across the Eastern and Western cultures and adopts the best of the two'. Displaying a higher level of investment in English and relationship-building across cultures, she paid attention to the discourse of locals and made an effort to learn colloquial language. Like Elsa, she took advantage of linguistic affordances (Gibson, 1979; van Lier, 2000, 2004) and developed a close connection with her hosts, gaining more exposure to social discourse in new CoP (Lave and Wenger, 1991). Her self-esteem and self-efficacy grew during her stay; that is, she gradually became more confident of her ability to communicate successfully in English across cultures. Over time, she began to view English as 'a living language' rather than just a tool for professional advancement As her perception changed, her investment deepened, similar to what Norton and Toohey (2002) discovered in their investigations of other L2 learners. While Niki experienced 'identity misalignments' (Ting-Toomey, 1999, 2005) and incidents she perceived as racist, she did not let negative encounters hold her back for long. More resilient and accepting of differences than Ada and Cori, she developed a deeper awareness and appreciation of both Chinese and English cultures.

9 Dialectical, situated L2 learning

As I worked with the cases that were presented in Chapters 5 to 8, I discovered how diverse and complex these young women's individual journeys actually were. Weaving together data from various sources deepened my understanding of the challenges they faced and the choices they made as they crossed languages and cultures. This reiterative process sensitized me to the ways in which their linguistic practices were shaped by the constraints of their sociocultural, sociopolitical context. The longitudinal nature of my study also heightened my awareness of how contradictory, relational, and dynamic their identities were as each woman's sense of self shifted over historical time and space.

Simply put, no single theory fully accounts for the internal and external factors that impact on the language and cultural learning and identity reconstruction of L2 learners/sojourners. While sociocultural, environmental elements played a significant role in the ways in which the young women's journeys unfolded, I could not ignore internal (individual, social psychological) factors that influenced the choices they made and the ways in which they responded to difficulties. Some took advantage of linguistic affordances in their environment, others did not. Some resisted their positioning in new sociocultural settings (Lave and Wenger, 1991; Pavlenko and Piller, 2001), others embraced the opportunity to experiment with new expressions and 'ways of being' (Bakhtin, 1986). While some opted to 'converge' and appropriate the discourse of their hosts, others resisted, leading to differential relational outcomes (Bourhis et al., 2007). Some of the women became more positive about themselves and their L2 use, others continued to feel insecure and were plagued with self-doubts. What can we learn from this? The L2 sojourn is far more complex and multifarious than most educators assume. To understand the situated learning of L2 speakers (whether in their home environment or abroad) we need to draw on multiple, interdisciplinary perspectives.

This ethnographic study of advanced language learners at home (in Hong Kong) and abroad (in England) afforded me the opportunity to test many of the theoretical notions that were discussed in Chapters 2 and 3. While some hypotheses were found to be too idealistic (e.g., overlooking the constraints of unequal power relations), I discovered that others resonated with the young women's experiences. In this chapter, I review and synthesize the findings (pre-sojourn, sojourn, and post-sojourn) and problematize these theoretical notions. In particular, I explore the links between language, culture, and identity (re)construction, the assumptions of the identity negotiation theory (INT), and the construct of communities of practice (CoP) in relation to stays abroad.

While some aspects of the women's journeys are specific to them, I believe their stories reach across ethnic, linguistic, and geographic lines. Many of their emotions, experiences, and actions may be representative of other L2 learners and border crossers. In this chapter, I provide a detailed review of the findings so that readers are better positioned to decide which elements may be linked to language learners/ sojourners in their particular situations and contexts.

9.1   Pre-sojourn

9.1.1   Identity formation and change

Before departing for England, the young women discussed the people and events that had helped to shape and reshape their identities. I discovered that their sense of self was deeply rooted in their personal histories and the social, political, historical, and linguistic realities of Hong Kong and the Motherland (Mainland China). As children and adolescents, they had largely accepted the input of their parents and extended families in shaping their cultural identity; in 1997, however, they were bombarded with mixed messages about the impact that the change of sovereignty would have on local society. Not surprisingly, this was difficult to ignore, and, for most, it triggered reflection on who they were and how they should relate to the Motherland, Britain, and the wider world. It also raised questions about their language choices, which were closely linked to their identities and the sociocultural context of their interactions.

Prior to the sojourn, it was impossible to ignore the relational, interdependent nature of their self-construals (Bakhtin, 1981, 1986; Hall, 2002; Meinhof and Galasiński, 2005) and their definition of 'ingroup' and 'outgroup' memberships (Ting-Toomey and Chung, 2005). I discovered that the young women generally preferred to be identified as 'Hong Kongers', emphasizing aspects of their culture and language that differed from that of Mainland Chinese. They talked at length about the unique hybrid nature of the region, with the influence of both Chinese and Western cultures. The former provided their ethnicity, traditions, and 'core values' and also affected their style of communication; Western cultures linked them to the 'modern' (outside) world, primarily through the international language of English. After the Handover, the women felt pressured to identify more closely with the Motherland. Still, none regarded blood ties with the larger Chinese ethnic group as binding, although some acknowledged that their attitude was changing due to positive face-to-face contact with Mainlanders. While they appreciated many aspects of Chinese culture, negative stereotypes of Mainlanders held them back from more fully embracing the Motherland.

Significantly, many of the women found themselves in turmoil as they tried to define their place in the world. Nearly all had felt 'divided' or 'rootless' at some point, in part due to the political uncertainty and hybridity of Hong Kong. Several had experienced or were experiencing what J. Bennett (1993) termed 'cultural marginality'. When in this state, they felt lost and insecure as if perched precariously on the edge of more than one culture and unsure where they fit in. This had led to some ambivalence about their cultural identity and a lack of attachment to Hong Kong and the larger ethnic group. The women's pre-sojourn stories provided compelling evidence that their self-construal was not fixed and static, supporting Norton and Toohey's depiction of identity as 'contradictory, dynamic and changing over historical time and space' (Norton and Toohey, 2002: 121).

When analyzing the pre-sojourn data, I also realized that the process of global-ization was impacting on their evolving sense of self. Several of the women revealed that they felt connected to the wider world through the use of English. While some wished to nurture their emerging 'global self', others felt conflicted about the values they associated with this international language. Their varied, conflicting responses are in line with Ryan's observation:

> [G]lobal English requires learners to assess the values linked to this global culture and how they as individuals relate to them. Is this global culture a 'subtractive' threat to existing cultural identities, or is it 'additive', in the sense that it offers opportunities to develop a social identity as a fully-fledged member of a global community? (Ryan, 2006: 31).

All of the women were influenced to varying degrees by social, psychological, economic, and historical factors as well as by contact with their own and other cultures. In essence, their identities were co-created in relationship to other people and events, as Collier explained: 'Who we are and how we are differs and emerges depending on who we are with, the cultural identities that are important to us and others, the context, the topic of conversation, and our interpretations and attributions' (Collier, 1999: 23). Throughout life, L2 learners may actually enact several cultural identities depending on the particular context and their reactions to it. Elsa and Niki, in particular, were receptive to developing both 'a global and a local voice' (Kramsch, 1999b). While all of the participants were from the same official ethnic group, spoke the same first language, had a similar proficiency level in English (advanced), and were raised in Hong Kong, there were variations in the nature, salience (strength of affiliation), and emotional significance of their self-construals.

In line with Heath and McLaughlin (1993), Rampton (1995), and Pennycook (2001), these findings caution us to adopt a nonessentialist stance and refrain from affixing rigid identity labels (e.g., ethnicity) and expectations on individuals.

9.1.2   Language, identity, and cultural socialization

9.1.2.1   Language, identity, and emotions

I also discovered that the women's views about the languages they spoke were directly linked to their sense of self and the sociocultural nature of their environment. Most of their family members did not speak English and those who did preferred to use Cantonese at home. Enveloping the young women with 'warmth', and 'a sense of belonging', their mother tongue affirmed their attachment to their family and community (Meinhof and Galasiński, 2005). It enabled them to express their innermost feelings ('true' selves) and emotions with those closest to them (e.g., relatives, friends from the same 'ingroup'). Not surprisingly, then, all of the women opted to be interviewed in their mother tongue prior to the sojourn. In the community, they also preferred to communicate with other Hong Kongers in Cantonese. Their first language served as an important identity marker (Zuengler, 1989), distinguishing them from Mainlanders who spoke Putonghua, the official language of Mainland China.

In Hong Kong the young women had easy access to English in academic settings and were most familiar with formal discourse. Their exposure to English in social contexts was partially restricted by sanctions against its use among Hong Kong Chinese in informal contexts. Not surprisingly, then, most of the women were somewhat detached from the language, largely viewing it as a pragmatic 'tool' (Csizér and Dörnyei, 2005). While most sensed a barrier between themselves and English, interestingly, some imagined themselves linked to the wider international community through this global language (Wenger, 1998; Kanno and Norton, 2003). For these women, their proficiency in English facilitated the potential emergence of a 'global self'.

9.1.2.2   Code mixing

My analysis of the pre-sojourn data also provided insight into the young women's attitudes towards code-mixing, a phenomenon that is widespread in many parts of the world where more than one language is spoken. Auer (2005), Meyers-Scotton (1993), and McKay (2005) observed that this resource can be used to display identities and group memberships in particular settings and contexts. In Hong Kong, where code-mixing is very common among young adults, it usually involves the insertion of isolated English lexical items into primarily Cantonese discourse (Li 1998; Luke 1998). The women in my study found that 'this habit' helped them to express their ideas more easily when communicating with each other. Interjecting English words into their Chinese discourse served as an identity marker and status symbol.

I also found their attitudes towards code-mixing to be context-dependent and variable, conjuring up strong, mixed emotions, similar to the findings of Li (1998) and Luke (1998). Some considered it a 'normal' mode of communication in their environment and felt 'proud' that they were able to mix some English words into their largely Cantonese discourse. At the same time, most were conflicted about 'this habit', lamenting that it disclosed a lack of proficiency in both languages and did not show respect to either.

9.1.2.3   The strategic nature of language choice

Significantly, I soon discovered that the women's language choices (e.g., use of Cantonese, English, code-mixing) were quite strategic, involving far more than simply ease of communication. Sociocultural (e.g., level of formality in the context, ethnicity of interlocutor), linguistic (e.g., the interlocutor's proficiency level in English), and psychological factors (e.g., attitude towards English, link between language choice and self-construal) figured prominently in their decision-making.

All of the women were sensitive to the potential ramifications of the 'overuse' of English in contexts where their interlocutors (e.g., other Hong Kong Chinese) might brand them as 'show-offs' and no longer view them as 'ingroup' members. I discovered that this made them somewhat reluctant to use the language with each other in situations where it was not absolutely required (e.g., informal settings outside of class). In fact, most were uncomfortable with the use of English by Hong Kongers in informal situations. As they were English majors, this discovery underscores the strength of the social sanctions at play in their home environment. Further, it provided compelling evidence of the strategic use of language to show one's affiliation with a particular group (e.g., Ochs, 2001; Zuengler, 1988, 1989). One might expect language learners in other foreign language settings to be influenced by similar pressures and constraints.

The women's level of confidence, their fluency in English, and their self-efficacy (belief in their ability to perform successfully) also impacted on their language learning and use (Csizér and Dörnyei, 2005; Dörnyei, 2005). Those who were less proficient or confident in their oral skills were more anxious and reluctant to speak English with someone who was more fluent. They also tended to have a more restricted view of the language and its role in their lives. These findings may be linked to the 'willingness to communicate' (WTC) construct, which has been extensively researched by Peter MacIntyre and his associates (e.g., MacIntyre, Baker, Clément, and Donovan, 2003, Clément et al., 2007). They also found that anxiety and a lack of self-confidence can negatively impact on a learner's 'readiness to enter into discourse at a particular time with a specific person or persons, using a L2' (MacIntyre et al., 1998: 547).

Another interesting discovery was that the young women were also very tactical in their use of code-mixing. When deciding whether or not to engage in this practice, some took into account such factors as the attributes and preferences of their interlocutor (e.g., cultural identity, proficiency level in both languages, attitude towards English/Cantonese) and the sociocultural context of the exchange. They cautioned that code-mixers would be 'outgrouped' by their peers if they used 'too many' English words when the mother tongue could easily be used instead. Their candid revelations highlighted the highly sensitive, socio-political nature of this practice.

9.1.2.4   Motives and investment in English

All of the women recognized the 'linguistic capital' of English (Bourdieu, 1991), convinced that fluency in the language was essential to gain access to 'symbolic and material resources' in their community (e.g., higher status, a more lucrative job). Prior to the sojourn, they were primarily motivated to enhance their English for reasons that were closely linked to their academic success and plans for future employment (e.g., to become English language teachers, journalists). In Gardner and Lambert's (1972) terms, they displayed an instrumental motivation prior to the sojourn, reflecting targeted, pragmatic purposes for learning the language. Elsa and Niki hoped to reduce the barrier they felt between themselves and English and make it more a part of their life. Both wished to nurture a global identity that would give them 'a sense of belonging to a worldwide culture' (Arnett, 2002). They already appeared to have a higher degree of investment in the language than many of their peers and made much more of an effort to practise it outside of class.

9.1.3   Relationship between language, identity, and culture

The women's candid revelations highlight the complex, sometimes contradictory, relationship between language, identity, and culture. They also challenge the structuralist notion of identity as 'fixed, static, and one-dimensional'. In particular, their storied experiences draw attention to the interdependent nature of the self and provide evidence that identity is 'multiple, changing, and a site of struggle' (e.g., Norton, 2000; Weedon, 1987). This raises our awareness of the need to view learners as 'social beings' who are 'embodied, semiotic and emotional persons who identify themselves, resist identifications, and act on their social worlds' (Norton and Toohey, 2002: 123). We must be mindful of the multifarious, sometimes contradictory, ways in which one's sense of self can affect language choice and use in a particular sociocultural context. It is also imperative that we recognize the impact that globalization may have on a learner's identity and motivation to learn a language.

The pre-sojourn findings pinpointed a range of factors (e.g., individual, sociocultural, psychological, historical, political) that can impact on a learner's willingness to communicate (WTC) in the target language (Clément et al., 2007) and degree of investment in L2 learning (Norton, 2000). Self-perceptions of one's language proficiency and ability to perform (self-efficacy) (Dörnyei, 2005) and the degree of access to linguistic resources may support or hinder an individual's willingness to use an L2 in a particular sociocultural setting. A learner's vision of membership to an imagined global community may also impact on her motivation to take a more active role in learning an international language.

9.1.4   Perceptions of sojourn language policy

For the five-week sojourn in England, there would be an 'English only policy' in place to encourage full immersion in that context. By the eve of departure, all of the women seemed determined to use the language to make the most of their stay. Even so, some expressed reservations about their ability to 'stick to English', believing that they lacked sufficient vocabulary to express their ideas on a daily basis. Several also thought it would initially seem 'weird' or 'awkward' to converse in English with their peers outside of a classroom situation. Their comments raised awareness of the sensitivity of language choice and the importance of thoroughly discussing such issues prior to departure.

9.1.5   Pre-sojourn aspirations, expectations, and anxieties

An examination of the women's pre-sojourn aspirations revealed that many of their ideas about what could be accomplished in a five-week stay were rather unrealistic (e.g., to 'attain a beautiful British accent'). Many had also set a rather long list of goals and had not prioritized them. I discovered later that some had clung to rather romantic, outdated images of England and English people in spite of the pre-sojourn preparation. These findings are significant as previous research on sojourners established a link between unrealistic expectations and sojourn outcomes, as noted by Ting-Toomey and Chung: 'individuals with realistic expectations are better prepared psychologically to deal with actual adaptation problems than are individuals with unrealistic expectations... Negative expectations tend to produce the opposite effect' (Ting-Toomey and Chung, 2005: 119).

All of the women wished to improve their English-language skills (e.g., become more fluent) and widen their horizons. Some also set goals that were socio-emotional in nature (Ward et al., 2001) (e.g., to make friends from other cultures). These women aimed to enhance their cultural sensitivity and intercultural communication skills as they established relationships across cultures. In the process, they hoped to undergo personal change.

While excited about the impending sojourn, I observed that most of the women were, understandably, anxious about living with strangers from another culture. Some voiced concern about their safety, their ability to adjust to cultural differences, the 'standard' of their English, meeting new people, interacting with 'native speakers', and their lack of cultural awareness and sensitivity. Many of their comments revealed a low tolerance for ambiguity, a lack of independence, and negative self-images. I also observed that some had a more elevated level of stress than their peers.

In Pellegrino's investigation of SA students in Russia, she discovered that

> positive attitudes toward oneself aid learners' L2 development by helping them feel secure, while negative attitudes threaten learners' sense of status, create doubt in their ability to control their environment and maintain their safety, and cause them to question the validity of their efforts to communicate in the L2 (Pellegrino's, 2005: 88).

I wondered how the low self-esteem and self-efficacy of some of my students would impact on their intercultural adjustment and use of English during the sojourn. Would they be able to achieve their goals?

9.2   The sojourn

9.2.1   Culture shock

On arrival in England all of the women experienced a 'honeymoon period'; for most, however, this euphoria was short-lived as they began to feel like 'fish out of water' (Ward et al., 2001). In this stressful transition period, they experienced symptoms of culture shock, a common phenomenon among border crossers. Hall explained the source of this malaise:

> Culture shock is a feeling of disorientation and discouragement due to the build-up of unmet expectations. The hundreds of expectations we have (most without even knowing we have them) about how people should act and how we should go about daily activities are often violated in many small and perhaps a few big ways. This creates an increasing sense of frustration that is often difficult to pinpoint to any one thing…when we are in a new culture we are forced by differences in language and behaviours to maintain a heightened state of awareness. This need for greater awareness often promotes a mental exhaustion… (Hall, 2005: 272–3).

In this liminal or transitory state, 'the individual's identity appears to be stripped of all protection' and 'previously familiar cues and scripts are suddenly inoperable' (Ting-Toomey and Chung, 2005: 117). This can lead to frustration and overwhelming fatigue as the young women's diaries attest. Doubts about their ability to cope may have led to a 'self-fulfilling prophecy' for the sojourners who struggled most in this new cultural setting. Some of their expectations about English people and life had been quite idealistic despite the intensive pre-sojourn preparation. In line with Ward et al.'s (2001) predictions, I believe that the incongruity of their expectations and reality may have been partially responsible for their malaise.

What is significant is that all of the women experienced some distress when their 'familiar cultural safety net' was no longer there. As Kim warned, sojourners are apt to encounter 'many moments of self-doubt and self-inquiry – a kind of existential despair that grows out of the restless inner spirit that seeks the known and the constant when familiar relationships and routines are broken' (Kim, 2001: 227). Some of the women were plagued by psychosomatic problems (e.g., stomach aches, nightmares) and, at times, were overcome with depression, homesickness, and drastic mood swings. Ada, in particular, felt insecure, emotionally vulnerable, and 'out of place' in her new surroundings, and sensed a significant cultural distance between herself and her hosts (Ward et al., 2001). It is important to note that she had exhibited a very high level of stress before the sojourn and had been concerned about her lack of independence and ability to adapt to a new culture.

Further, all of the women found that their race was problematized as they became 'members of a visible minority' in England. This new, unfamiliar positioning was especially unsettling for those who were venturing outside Asia for the first time. As predicted by the INT, feelings of insecurity (e.g., as 'young, defenceless, female foreigners') led to a fear of outgroups (e.g., 'those white people'). It also brought about a heightened awareness and appreciation of their Chinese roots (Ting-Toomey, 2005; Ward et al., 2001), a development that I explore further in Section 9.2.8.

The women were also preoccupied with the psychological pressure that engulfed them as they struggled to function in an L2 on a daily basis (Byram, 2003; Dörnyei, 2005). Some felt compelled to serve as a 'cultural ambassador' for their homeland and this added pressure to perform well. To 'survive', Ada and Cori limited their contact across cultures and made more use of their L1 and code-mixing when interacting with their peers. In terms of the communication accommodation theory (CAT), they were less willing to 'converge' and become full-fledged members in their homestays (Bourhis et al., 2007). Suffering from culture shock, they were generally more resistant to the host culture and language throughout their stay.

9.2.2   Critical incidents, sociopragmatic failures, and perceived racism

All of the sojourners were sometimes confused about the norms of interaction (e.g., discourse markers of politeness) in the host culture, and in the first few weeks were ill at ease in informal social situations involving locals. Unsure how to initiate and sustain conversations, Ada and Cori, in particular, found it difficult to develop rapport with their host family members and others in the community (e.g., employ situation-appropriate discourse markers). While this had been an important element in their pre-sojourn preparation, they found it challenging to translate what they had learned into practice.

As predicted by Bakhtin (1986), the young women encountered difficulty with new speech genres in the host culture, when they were exposed to different 'ways of speaking, knowing, and understanding'. Elsa, for example, did not understand the social norms of discourse at play in the informal gathering that she attended in her first week in England. She did not have the cultural or linguistic background necessary to decipher the chitchat of locals and, in this unfamiliar sociocultural setting, was unsure how to enter conversations and sustain them. This event also raised questions about host receptivity and inequality, which are addressed in Section 9.2.5.

All of the women experienced sociopragmatic failures (Thomas, 1995); drawing on ethnocentric tendencies, their first inclination was to perceive their interlocutors to be rude or racist (Ward et al., 2001). Over time, however, there were differences in how the women responded to unsatisfactory encounters. Those who experienced more adaptive stress and displayed a rigid personality were less willing to 'converge' (Bourhis et al., 2007). These individuals were less inclined to abandon 'already prepared viewpoints and positions' (Bakhtin, 1986) and tended to retain a judgmental stance throughout much of their stay. They also became less enthusiastic about building relationships with locals through the mediational means of their L2. Ada's and Cori's unpleasant experiences and reactions to them reinforced their negative stereotypes of the host community.

By contrast, Elsa and Niki were gradually able to step back and reflect on possible reasons for critical incidents across cultures and made better use of their pre-sojourn preparation (e.g., instruction in sociopragmatics). They started to consider how their own behaviour (e.g., communication style, absence of discourse markers of politeness) might have contributed to poor outcomes. Realizing that their interlocutors may not have been deliberately trying to annoy or insult them, they pressed on with further dialogue across cultures. While Cori considered the impact of her actions in intercultural encounters early in the sojourn, she was unable to sustain this level of introspection; as a consequence, like Ada, she became increasingly disillusioned with the host culture.

9.2.3   Identity misalignments and lack of mutuality

A troubling finding was that Ada's and Cori's hosts failed to recognize the young women's preferred identities, and they sometimes mislabelled them as Japanese or Mainlanders. This was very upsetting to these young women and, not surprisingly, had a negative impact on their attitudes toward the host culture, their desire to spend time with their hosts and other locals, and their willingness to use English (Clément et al., 2007). These young women viewed themselves as 'foreigners' or 'outsiders' throughout their stay and often felt misunderstood by their hosts, who failed to grasp their insecurities. Ting-Toomey warned that 'without collaborative effort, the hosts and the new arrivals may end up with great frustrations, miscommunications, and identity misalignments' (Ting-Toomey, 2005: 221). This appeared to be a key factor in Ada's and Cori's stories. While Elsa and Niki were also mislabelled by locals, significantly, their host family members validated their preferred identities and the host–sojourner relationship flourished. This, no doubt, contributed to different perceptions of the sojourn among the women.

9.2.4   Coping strategies and intercultural adjustment

All of the sojourners suffered symptoms of culture shock and threats to their identity; however, the malaise that Elsa and Niki experienced did not last long and they bounced back more quickly. What can account for their more successful transition to English life?

These women were more adept at managing their adaptive stress. Recalling their pre-sojourn preparation, they recognized that culture shock was a normal part of the adjustment process. Early on, they developed the habit of reflecting on their mood swings and problematic encounters in the host environment. They expressed their emotions through writing (e.g., diary) or confided in others (e.g., their hosts, SES friends) and throughout the sojourn took an active role in the weekly debriefing sessions. The socio-emotional support they derived from those around them helped to alleviate their stress and put their experiences in perspective. This kept them on course for further explorations and personal expansion.

Similar to many of their peers, early in the sojourn Elsa and Niki attributed unsatisfactory intercultural encounters to racism and rudeness. Instead of clinging to their peers and rejecting Others out of hand, however, these women chose a different path. As they became more at ease in their environment, they concentrated on building connections with people in the host community and attempted to understand unfamiliar behaviours, resisting the temptation to make snap judgments. In essence, they cultivated a more 'ethnorelative mindset' (M. Bennett, 1993; Ting-Toomey and Chung, 2005) and this facilitated their transition to English life. Elsa, in particular, tried to view the world from her host mother's perspective and displayed empathy in her homestay situation.

Elsa and Niki also employed a wider range of strategies to strengthen bonds across cultures and feel a part of the community (e.g., self-disclosure, appropriation/ bending of Others' voices, convergence) (Bakhtin, 1981, 1986; Bourhis et al., 2007). Both women made a concerted effort to adjust their communication styles to better 'fit in' and make their hosts feel at ease. They considered relationship-building a responsibility of both parties and did not sit on the sidelines and wait for their hosts to make the first move. According to the CAT, these language convergence strategies are thought to lead to 'harmonious relational outcomes' and a broadening of one's identity (Bourhis et al., 2007). This proved to be the case for Elsa and Niki.

These women also displayed more interest in the world around them (e.g., watched local news) rather than focusing on what was happening in Hong Kong. While they were making connections across cultures, some of their peers spent hours in the computer room checking on news from back home. In essence, Elsa and Niki heeded Kim's advice: 'we facilitate our own successful adaptation by going beyond our ethnic community and reaching out for opportunities to participate in the interpersonal and mass communication processes of the host milieu' (Kim's, 2001: 229). Elsa and Niki also made better use of their ethnographic skills training, paying far more attention to linguistic and cultural details in the host environment than many of their peers. Significantly, their diary entries and our debriefing sessions revealed that they went beyond noticing surface-level features as they gained more exposure to new CoP.

Variations in personality dispositions could also partially account for differences in the women's intercultural adjustment and sojourn experiences. Overall, Elsa and Niki tended to be more open (receptive to cultural differences), flexible, empathetic, positive, and resilient (e.g., rebounding more quickly after critical incidents) than many of their fellow sojourners. This degree of openness requires 'a formation in our basic and stable psychological orientation that is less self-centred and judgmental and more altruistic and accepting of those who are alien to us' (Kim, 2001: 231).

While some of their peers resisted anything new, Elsa and Niki were more willing to try everything from Yorkshire pudding to a more direct style of communication, as long as it did not conflict with their core values. They were much more sensitive to culture-appropriate styles of communication and willing to 'converge' to enhance their social relationships across cultures (Bourhis et al., 2007). These aspiring 'intercultural speakers' recognized that they were on the periphery of new CoP (Lave and Wenger, 1991) and were visibly different from most locals, but, by the end of their stay, they did not feel quite as much like 'outsiders' as Ada and Cori. What is important to note is that Elsa's and Niki's adjustment to English life was more successful due to a complex mix of both internal and external factors.

9.2.5   The host–sojourner relationship

During the sojourn, Elsa and Niki were more amenable to acting as 'willing-to-learn' guests (Ting-Toomey, 2005) or 'apprentices' in new CoP (Lave and Wenger, 1991). They appeared to have a much stronger desire to enhance their social skills in English and become immersed in their new environment. From the onset, they found their host families to be welcoming, supportive, and willing to self-disclose. When difficulties inevitably arose, they drew on socio-emotional support from their host families, peers, and our debriefing sessions. As they experienced more 'mutuality and engagement' in the host culture (Wenger, 1998), not surprisingly, they developed a more favourable impression of it than those who did not feel welcomed or understood. This finding supported Ting-Toomey's hypothesis that 'the more help the newcomers receive during the initial cultural adaptation stages, the more positive are their perceptions of their new environment' (Ting-Toomey's, 2005: 221). This is not as straightforward as it appears, however. Were their hosts more supportive or were the other student sojourners simply more resistant? Were Ada and Cori less invested in building relationships across cultures or did they find their new environment too daunting?

9.2.6   Investment in language and cultural learning

In their writings, Bakhtin (1981, 1986) and Bouris et al. (2007) raised the possibility that individuals (e.g., sojourners) might reshape their expressions and communication styles due to exposure to Others (e.g., locals in the host community). In Elsa's and Niki's discourse, I did find some evidence that they had begun to appropriate the voices of their hosts and experiment with new 'ways of being' (Bakhtin, 1986). In particular, they tried out a more direct style of communication, new discourse markers of politeness, and colloquialisms. Why did these women engage in the act of 'ventriloquation' and 'convergence' more frequently than some of their peers?

Elsa and Niki exhibited a stronger desire to expand their knowledge of the host language and culture and develop 'a sense of belonging' in new CoP (Corder and Meyerhoff, 2007). They spent much more time conversing with their host family members in relaxed social settings and, consequently, gained more exposure to informal discourse in English. They also developed a more favourable impression of the host culture and their own ability to communicate successfully across cultures. A positive cycle was set in motion. I believe that their willingness to experiment with novel forms of expression was directly linked to their desire to make social connections across cultures, a deeper level of investment in enhancing their social English and intercultural communication skills, a growing self-confidence, and a more open mindset.

By contrast, throughout much of the sojourn, Ada and Cori seemed to feel that becoming closer to the English language and culture posed a threat to their cultural identity and L1; they both expressed the fear that they were losing their Cantonese even though they had only been in England for a few weeks and knew they would soon be returning to Hong Kong. Their anxieties and a lack of self-confidence curtailed their participation in the host culture and, subsequently, their investment in language and cultural learning. When investigating the self-presentation of L2 sojourners in Russia, Pellegrino (2005) also found that similar factors negatively impacted on outcomes of stays abroad.

9.2.7   Agency, positioning, and linguistic affordances

One of the most interesting findings related to the women's perceptions of their linguistic environment. Near the end of the sojourn, Ada and Cori complained that they had not had enough opportunity to use English outside the SES group; Elsa and Niki held the opposite viewpoint. What can account for these disparate positions?

Situated in the same linguistic and cultural environment, with both invitations and constraints, these L2 learners ('social actors') viewed their surroundings quite differently. In accord with Gibson (1979) and van Lier's (2000, 2004) predictions, those who were more open and receptive to the world around them (Niki and Elsa) took more advantage of linguistic affordances and, subsequently, played a more active role in their language and cultural learning. By contrast, those who primarily saw obstacles and rejections (Ada and Cori) withdrew and assumed a more passive, and sometimes resistant, role. This, in turn, reduced opportunities for linguistic and cultural enhancement. This finding cautions us to be mindful of a language learner's response to her environment. It also highlights the need for ongoing support throughout the sojourn to encourage more involvement in the host environment. It is naïve to assume that all participants will enhance their language and cultural learning simply by being in the field.

While agency (the ability to understand and control one's own action) is clearly a significant factor in determining what unfolds on stays abroad, it must be understood within 'the bounded structures' of society and self (Bourdieu, 1991). Although the language policy was very successful for the group as a whole, low host receptivity, perceptions of racism, cultural distance, and the 'outsider' status held some back from full immersion in English. It is important to acknowledge that power relations and structures within a CoP (e.g., homestay) may limit entry and participation (Barton and Tusting, 2005; Bourdieu, 1991) and, ultimately, curtail a sojourner's exposure to and use of social English. As Kinginger observed in her study of L2 sojourners, not all L2 learners have the same access to the 'social networks' that afford opportunities for language development in the host culture: 'Access to language is shaped not only by learners' own intentions, but also by those of the others with whom they interact – people who may view learners as embodiments of identities shaped by gender, race, and social class' (Kinginger, 2004: 221).

Not all hosts are sensitive to the needs of their 'guests'. Some may actively encourage full participation in family activities, others may not. The reality is that sojourners experience differential opportunities to engage in social practices in their homestay and the wider community. This then impacts on their exposure to the L2 and their language and cultural enhancement. Moving toward full membership in the homestay not only involves a significant amount of effort on the part of L2 sojourners ('newcomers'/'nonnative speakers') but the willingness of the hosts ('experts'/'native speakers') to share their resources with them (Bourdieu, 1991;

Pavlenko and Lantolf, 2000; Wenger, 1998, 2005). What are the implications of this?

We cannot assume that sojourners will dramatically enhance their L2 and inter-cultural communicative competence simply by being present in the host speech community. They may encounter significant barriers that curtail their participation; without adequate access and support, they may be sidelined and feel 'disempowered'. At the same time, it would also be an oversimplification to attribute all impediments to language learning to the sociocultural environment. The dispositions, motives, attitudes, and actions of learners themselves play a role in determining outcomes. The situated learning of L2 sojourners is far more complex than what is often conveyed in the literature on SA.

9.2.8   Awareness and appreciation of Self and Other

In an unfamiliar cultural environment, all of the sojourners developed more awareness of Self and Other (Bakhtin, 1981, 1986), including a deeper appreciation of their Chinese heritage and language. There were, however, some striking differences in their reactions to this awakening. Much of Ada's and Cori's discourse in both their oral and written narratives remained focused on 'us' vs. 'them' scenarios. They were less successful at pushing past ethnocentric tendencies and, under threat, clung more tightly to their Chinese ethnicity, as predicted by the INT (Ting-Toomey, 1999, 2005). These young women seemed to feel that their cultural identity and value system would be compromised if they drew closer to the host culture and language. In response, they resisted new 'ways of being', limiting their contact with their hosts.

By the end of their stay, Elsa and Niki seemed to better understand that the love and appreciation of one culture did not have to come at the expense of another. In other words, more fully embracing their 'Chineseness' did not mean that they had to reject English norms of behaviour or values that appealed to them. They were generally 'willing to learn guests' (Ting-Toomey, 2005) and more open to personal expansion than many of their peers. They seized chances to engage in conversations in English with people outside the SES and put more energy into cultivating relation-ships with their hosts. Through sustained participation in socioculturally organized practices in the host environment (Vygotsky, 1978, 1987), they became more aware of other 'ways of being' (Bakhtin, 1986) and gradually more accepting of cultural differences.

These women ventured further into 'thirdspace' (Bhabha, 1994; Kramsch, 1993, 1999a), or what Bakhtin (1981) described as 'cultural–semiotic spaces' on the bounda-ries of the Self and the Other. By the end of their stay, they displayed a stronger desire to make connections across cultures, open themselves up to new ideas and worldviews, and experiment with novel forms of expression and behaviours – as long as they did not conflict with their core values. They travelled further down the road to intercultural personhood, 'a new, alternative identity that is broader, more inclusive, more intercultural' (Kim, 2001: 232–3). In sum, different trajectories among the women further highlight the diversity of the sojourn experience and the impact that differing levels of investment, agency, and host receptivity can have on language and cultural learning and one's sense of self.

9.2.9   Mutual identity expansion

In intercultural encounters, Bakhtin theorized that, 'a struggle occurs that results in mutual change and enrichment' (Bakhtin, 1986: 142). He was convinced that exposure to another culture provides *both* interlocutors with the opportunity for personal expansion and identity transformation. The women's stories provided ample evidence of 'struggles' and personal expansion, to varying degrees; however, it is not clear that their interlocutors (i.e. hosts) were changed in the process.

Elsa's and Niki's hosts seemed to be genuinely interested in Hong Kong culture and the personal life of their 'guests.' In these homestays, warm host–sojourner bonds were established. It would seem reasonable to assume that these hosts were positively impacted by the hosting experience and perhaps broadened in some ways. As Ada and Cori did not experience the same degree of mutuality and spent less of their free time in their homestay, it is less likely that their hosts were 'enriched' by the experience. In fact, since their 'guest' appeared to be more difficult to please and somewhat distant, it may have reinforced any negative stereotypes of Hong Kongers or Chinese that they might have harboured prior to the sojourn. Without interviewing the hosts and observing interaction in the homestays this can only be speculative.

Some hosts may welcome international students into their homes to expose themselves (and their children) to other cultures and worldviews. These individuals may be receptive to personal expansion, whereas other hosts may be far less open to interculturality. Moreover, while some may recognize the efforts their 'guests' are making to communicate their thoughts and feelings in an L2, others may be less sensitive to this. They may also fail to understand the difficulties the sojourners are facing as they confront elements of culture shock in a new environment, far from home. Hosts who are members of the ethnic majority may not realize that their 'guests', who are visibly different, may feel threatened and insecure in their new surroundings. To make matters worse, the hosts may be 'mindless' about the preferred identities of their guests, alienating them further (Ting-Toomey, 1999, 2005). Consequently, Bakhtin's (1986) notion of 'mutual expansion' is rather idealistic, not paying enough heed to such issues as power, status ('expert' host vs. 'apprentice/newcomer'; fluent speaker vs. L2 learner), investment, and agency (e.g., behaviour of hosts/sojourners).

9.2.10   Perceived outcomes of sojourn

As the departure date approached, the women reflected on what they had gained from spending five weeks in the host speech community. Most identified the following outcomes: enhanced personal growth, self-confidence, and maturity; a higher degree of independence; a broader worldview; more awareness and acceptance of cultural differences; enhanced intercultural communication/social skills; and a greater appreciation of their own culture and identity. I also observed that Elsa and Niki had enhanced their sociopragmatic awareness during their stay: they had become much more connected to English than the other women and had developed closer bonds across cultures.

Of the four women, Elsa and Niki were the most satisfied with their progress. In the field, they revised their goals in light of the opportunities and constrains their environment afforded them (e.g., access to CoP, time available). With determination, they stayed focused on aspects that mattered to them; as a consequence, their self-confidence grew, and these women maximized their short stay abroad. Despite their more turbulent adjustment, Ada and Cori also believed that they had benefited from the sojourn. Overall, however, they strayed further from some of the goals they had set prior to the sojourn. For example, Cori had aimed to learn 'British slang or idioms', but without sufficient contact with her hosts failed to do so.

Interestingly, several of the women assessed their language gains in terms of traditional academic measures (e.g., reduction in grammatical errors), which were more appropriate for formal language lessons than informal situated learning. Not surprisingly, this led to some disappointments. Nonetheless, I discovered that most believed that they had become more fluent and comfortable talking with native speakers and each other in informal situations. As they had used English in daily life, they had developed a broader view of the language and no longer regarded it simply as a tool for academic purposes (Dörnyei, 2005). Most had become more accepting of the use of English by Hong Kongers as long as the aim of the interlocutors was to 'practise' the language.

9.3   Post-sojourn

9.3.1   Language of communication

Back in Hong Kong, Ada and Cori chose to be interviewed in their mother tongue; they were still not at ease expressing their emotions in English, especially with another Hong Konger. Their L1 gave them a strong 'sense of belonging'; it was closely linked to their cultural identity, which had been under threat in England. By contrast, Elsa and Niki elected to talk about their experiences in English, even though, like the other women, their pre-sojourn interviews had been in Cantonese. What might account for their different choices?

Elsa and Niki had become more comfortable expressing their thoughts and feelings in English and were less concerned about making mistakes. They were more invested in the language on a personal level and had become more accepting of its use by Hong Kongers in situations where it was not required. As predicted by Norton and Toohey (2002), their sense of themselves and their desire to use their L2 had increased as its 'cultural capital' had grown in their eyes.

9.3.2   Re-entry culture shock

Although Cori and Niki's love of Hong Kong had deepened, Ada was somewhat dissatisfied even though she felt more secure in her home environment. She was surprised to discover that she was seeing the city through a different lens, a common phenomenon on re-entry (Citron, 1996; Ward et al., 2001). While happy to be back in the warm embrace of her family and close friends, Elsa was also overtaken by a sense of letdown and dissatisfaction with her home environment. She and Niki, in particular, missed their host families and the freedom they enjoyed in England. Back in a Chinese context, Elsa displayed a heightened awareness of different cultural frames of reference. She experienced temporary identity disjunction (e.g., feelings of 'in-betweeness' (Yoshikawa, 1987)) and did not feel 'fully accepted' by either culture. Her disequilibrium was short-lived, however, as she soon became immersed in familiar routines.

9.3.3   Identity reconstruction

Bakhtinian (1981, 1984, 1986) theories about the dialogic formation of the Self and the role of the Other in the process of identity reconstruction, in general, resonated with the experiences of the students, both in their home environment and in the host speech community. Following Bakhtin's (1986) prediction, they came to more fully comprehend themselves and their own culture when in contact with another (e.g., the host culture, Mainlanders). Crossing cultures heightened their awareness of their cultural identity, race, and ethnicity. It is important to note, however, that they did not always react in the same way due to a complex range of internal (e.g., personality attributes, degree of investment in personal expansion) and external (e.g., host receptivity, access to new CoP) factors.

When reflecting on the impact of the sojourn, Ada and Cori revealed that they had become more aware and accepting of their Chinese roots in a foreign environment. They had noticed differences between themselves and their hosts and, consequently, had become more aware of the uniqueness of their own culture (Bakhtin, 1981, 1984; Ting-Toomey and Chung, 2005; Ward et al., 2001). In general, they had not found their host environment welcoming, and their preferred identity had not been validated. Feeling insecure and threatened by difference, they clung more tightly to their 'Chineseness' and their Hong Konger identity.

Elsa's and Niki's re-entry also served as a significant identity trigger, raising their awareness of their personal expansion during the sojourn. Both women had moved closer to a broader, more international, intercultural persona (Arnett, 2002; Kramsch, 1999b). Along with a deeper appreciation of Chinese culture, they were able to cite specific aspects of English culture that they appreciated. They also expressed the desire for further personal expansion.

9.3.4   Different trajectories

When I reviewed the sojourn data of the four young women, I was struck by differences in their intercultural adjustment, attention to linguistic and cultural details, depth of reflection and self-analysis, and ability to stay focused on their goals. While all of them had expressed the desire to interact with locals and establish relationships across cultures, there were significant variations in their sojourn experiences and outcomes. What can we learn from this?

First, we cannot assume that every sojourner will wish to become a 'full-fledged member' of the host culture (Lave and Wenger, 1991) through the act of convergence (Bourhis et al., 2007). Not all sojourners will be willing or interested in opening themselves up to identity expansion (Bakhtin, 1986). These findings are in accord with Pavlenko and Lantolf's observation that 'the individual may feel comfortable being who he or she is and may not wish to "become" a native of another language and culture. Thus, negotiation of new meanings and construction of new subjectivities may be irrelevant to her/his personal agenda' (Pavlenko and Lantolf, 2000: 170). In other words, once in an alien environment, a sojourner may take the decision to preserve his or her identity and resist or reject being positioned as an 'apprentice' (Lave and Wenger, 1991). As well as environmental conditions, agency may play a crucial role in determining sojourn outcomes.

Sitting on the sidelines, however, does not have to be an inevitable outcome. If adequate preparation and ongoing support and encouragement are provided during the sojourn, adaptive stress may be reduced. Sojourners may then be better equipped to overcome inevitable obstacles and setbacks more quickly. They may gradually become more self-confident, positive about themselves and their journey, and receptive to change – on their own terms. Chapter 10 offers some practical suggestions to facilitate this.

9.3.5   Internal and external factors

It is important not to underestimate the effect that individual, personality factors (e.g., tolerance for ambiguity, degree of rigidity, ethnocentrism, resilience) (Dörnyei, 2005; Pellegrino, 2005) and depth of investment (Norton, 2000) can have on the situated learning of L2 sojourners. In this study I found that the young women who made a concerted effort to overcome their fears of interacting with locals ('native speakers' of English) gained more first-hand exposure to the host language; when encounters were positive, their self-confidence and self-efficacy grew. As a consequence, they became more willing to take risks and ventured further in the host culture. Generally more resilient and open to differences, they employed a wider range of coping mechanisms that helped them to rebound when intercultural events (e.g., service encounters, conversations) did not go as well as they had hoped. A positive cycle was created by a complex intermingling of sociocultural factors (e.g., host receptivity, quality and degree of exposure to new CoP), personality attributes (e.g., ability to overcome psychological barriers, reflexivity, high acceptance of ambiguous situations, flexibility, a more 'ethnorelative' positive mindset), and a deepening level of investment in their L2 and cultural learning.

Both hosts and sojourners play pivotal roles in determining outcomes of stays abroad. While most host families in my study appeared to make a genuine effort to provide a welcoming, safe haven for their guests, some failed to understand their newcomers' anxieties and need to have their preferred identities validated and respected. The hosts may not have fully grasped the powerful role and position that they had in that context (e.g., native speakers of the language used in the community, life-long residents and 'experts' in the host environment). This suggests that more attention should be paid to the preparation of host families to make stays more enjoyable, satisfying, and worthwhile for all involved. This issue is discussed further in Chapter 10.

9.3.6   Lasting impact of the sojourn

Most of the women viewed their stay in England as a valuable and life-changing experience. Living with a family in the host speech community enabled them to experience the culture firsthand and opened up new possibilities for their lives. It expanded their view of English, to varying degrees, and sparked an interest in future forays into the English-speaking world. Interestingly, even the women who had had a more difficult adjustment expressed regret about not spending more time with their hosts. Back on home soil, free of the pressures of living in an unfamiliar culture, Ada and Cori were able to take a more objective look at their behaviour. They seemed to recognize that their choices may have been partially responsible for a weak connection with their host family members. This suggests that, given more time, they might have been able to develop a closer relationship with them. It is also possible that they would never have fully engaged with their hosts no matter how long the sojourn.

Elsa's and Niki's stories provide more compelling evidence of the potential benefits of even a five-week stay in the host speech community, with the proviso that appropriate support is in place before, during, and after the sojourn. Firsthand exposure to the host culture (with socio-emotional support from hosts, peers, and teachers) had a major impact on the young women's perceptions of their L2 and the development of their intercultural communicative competence (Byram, 1997; Byram and Feng, 2005). It also stimulated personal growth, boosted their self-esteem and self-efficacy, and inspired further identity reconstruction. What then, can we learn from their more successful border crossings?

Significant differences between their experiences and those of Ada and Cori alert us to the important role that the sociocultural context (e.g., degree of 'mutuality' and access in homestay placements, quality and quantity of intercultural contact in CoP) can play on stays abroad. The findings also caution us not to ignore individual differences in the language and cultural learning of L2 sojourners or border crossers (e.g., personality traits, degree of investment, agency, desire for personal expansion, self-efficacy, self-esteem). For too long, educators have naïvely assumed that language and cultural learning will occur simply by placing students in the host speech community, but this is clearly not the case. Successful outcomes require a substantial amount of time, effort, and expertise on the part of SA planners and a significant investment on the part of the learners themselves.

9.4   The situated learning of L2 sojourners in review

What became apparent when reviewing the key findings is the complexity of the situated learning of L2 sojourners. In order to understand what was happening during the young women's stay in England, I found myself drawing on theoretical perspectives from a variety of disciplines (e.g. applied linguistics, social psychology, intercultural communication, speech communication). In the process, I was able to test many of the hypotheses that were discussed in Chapters 2 and 3.

During the sojourn, the young women struggled to cope with an unfamiliar environment and different norms of behaviour (e.g., discourse, routines) in new CoP. I discovered that there were considerable differences in the amount of time they chose to spend with their hosts and the quality of these interactions. While some sojourners found their host families receptive and supportive, others did not. As a consequence, host–sojourner relationships did not always flourish. I also found that the women exhibited different levels of investment in the enhancement of their English and intercultural communication skills as the weeks unfolded. What lessons can we draw from this?

Some L2 sojourners or border crossers may focus their energy on becoming more intercultural and proficient in the host language; they may be more willing to 'converge' to develop harmonious intercultural relationships. As a consequence, they may undergo more identity reconstruction. Others, for various reasons (e.g., limited access to CoP, power structures), may not be positioned as favourably in the new environment. In response, they may withdraw from the host culture and not take advantage of linguistic affordances. Those with a more rigid personality and low tolerance for ambiguity may be less willing to explore their new surroundings and interact across cultures. A wide range of multifarious internal and external factors determine the outcomes of stays abroad.

While five weeks in the host speech community is not long, my study has shown that it does have the potential to provide L2 speakers with the opportunity to become more aware of Self and Other, offer exposure to the host language and culture in a variety of informal settings, and stimulate personal expansion, especially in those who are receptive to change. What is clear from the case studies, however, is the importance of providing adequate, well-planned pre-sojourn preparation and on-going socio-emotional support during the sojourn. The findings also point to the need for better preparation of hosts, who may be well intentioned but 'mindless' about their guests' insecurities and need to have their preferred identities recognized and endorsed.

While this ethnographic study centred on the experiences of Chinese university students who travelled from their home environment to England and back again, their stories have implications for others who cross cultures. One can easily imagine that other border crossers (e.g., business people, long-term sojourners, short-term sojourners who visit other countries) may experience similar challenges and triumphs as they navigate in new CoP in unfamiliar cultural settings.

The concluding chapter focuses on ways in which my discoveries and theoretical understandings can serve as an impetus for change in existing SA research and practices.

10   Towards a critical praxis in study abroad

Drawing on my ethnography of the L2 sojourn, Chapter 9 examined the complex connections between discourse, language learning/use, and identity reconstruction, bearing in mind sociocultural, political, and historical contexts. How might these new understandings inform the design and delivery of study abroad (SA) programmes? How can SA educators and L2 sojourners be empowered to effect change in existing practices? What action might we take to harness the transformative potential of sojourns/border crossings?

As advocated by Pennycook (2001), Guilherme (2002), Norton and Toohey (2004), and other critical theorists, I aim to go beyond a practice/theory dichotomy to address the dialectical and multifaceted nature of language and cultural learning. Adopting critical pedagogy as the educational framework, this chapter seeks to engage readers in the process of praxis – a continual, reflexive interplay between knowledge, research, and action, which, ideally, leads to transformation. As explained by Carr and Kemmis, critical praxis is a mode of practice in which 'the "enlightenment" of actors comes to bear directly in their transformed social action. This requires an integration of theory and practice as reflective and practical moments in a dialectical process of reflection, enlightenment and political struggle carried out by groups for the purpose of their own emancipation' (Carr and Kemmis, 1986: 144).

Premised upon a democratic critical education (Freire, 1970), this chapter is rooted in the desire to evoke innovation and change in current SA practices, from the preparation phase to re-entry. In particular, it aims to:

- raise awareness about limitations and power imbalances in current SA practices;
- articulate a stance towards intervention that aims at engaging participants (SA educators and L2 learners) in reflection and praxis;

- identify ways to empower participants to develop their own voice and become active, positive 'agents' who can imagine different positionings and take action to achieve their goals;
- propose ways to involve L2 learners in the decision-making process and make SA curricula more relevant and 'learner-centred';
- identify ways to prepare L2 learners and other border crossers to deal with linguistic, cultural, and racial differences when crossing cultures;
- suggest approaches that can enhance the language and cultural learning and identity reconstruction of L2 sojourners and other border crossers.

These ideas cannot be reduced to mere techniques, neither should they be viewed as prescriptions for SA practice. Rather, in this chapter, I offer suggestions as framing ideas for critical praxis, bearing in mind the need to constantly question one's assumptions. Through concrete examples and dialogue, I promote the notion that every educator and L2 learner/sojourner has the potential to become a 'critical agent of change' and 'transformative intellectual' (Freire, 1970; Giroux, 1988). As such, this chapter is targeted at SA professionals (e.g., L2 educators/interculturalists/ programme designers) who are committed to making a difference.

To fully maximize stays abroad, I argue that foreign-language students benefit from comprehensive pre-sojourn preparation and on-going support, encouragement, and programmed experiential learning during the sojourn. Adequate debriefing after they return to their home country is also an essential, yet often overlooked, element. I also highlight the advantages of guided reflection to help sojourners make sense of their personal journeys of discovery of Self and Other and take steps, however tentative, towards intercultural personhood (Kim, 2001, 2006).

As homestay accommodation (the placement of sojourners with private families) is prevalent on short-term sojourns, I offer suggestions for the selection, preparation, and support of hosts. Building on the idealistic notion of 'mutuality and engagement' (Bakhtin, 1986; Lave and Wenger, 1991; Ting-Toomey, 1999, 2005), I hope the ideas I put forward will lead to a more rewarding homestay experience for both sojourners and hosts.

As there are significant variations in SA programmes (e.g., duration, goals, curricula, format, location, accommodations, activities, and travel), my ideas are intended to promote reflection on a range of possibilities. Adjustments would need to be made to meet the evolving needs and constraints of individual programmes, participants, and institutions. Ultimately, my aim is to stimulate informed thinking and inspire innovation in the design and delivery of SA programmes. With this in mind, I also advance suggestions for future investigations of the SA experience and border crossings.

10.1   Pre-sojourn

10.1.1   The preparation of L2 sojourners

10.1.1.1 Intercultural learning

At present, many SA programmes provide a few hours of orientation prior to departure, focusing on logistics (e.g., travel arrangements, advice for packing) and a brief introduction to the host culture. Not only is this woefully inadequate, the students are typically positioned as 'passive vessels', with little or no input into their own preparation. It is imperative that students have a stake in the shape and focus of their own pre-sojourn preparation. Their areas of interest and concern must be elicited to provide direction for the content and flow of this phase of the SA programme. Facilitators should also provide the opportunity for the students to discuss and negotiate aspects of the sojourn.

The findings of my study underscore the importance of carefully planned preparation for the cognitive, affective, and behavioural dimensions of intercultural adjustment. To be meaningful, this phase must address the challenges (e.g., identity 'threats', sociopragmatic differences, language barriers) that L2 sojourners are apt to face in an unfamiliar sociocultural context, taking into account the specific concerns and aspirations of the participants.

Learning at this stage should build on the students' existing knowledge and previous intercultural contact and travel experience (if any). A well-designed intercultural communications course or series of workshops can provide students with a frame of reference for making sense of their new environment and help them develop strategies to ease their transition to a new culture. In particular, this phase should address their pre-departure assumptions and reactions to issues that often emerge when crossing cultures (e.g., differences in communication styles, cultural values, and behaviour; culture shock; racial awareness; identity change). An awareness of the natural ebbs and flows of adjustment (including symptoms of culture shock and re-entry) and potential coping strategies should be an integral part of the orientation (Citron, 1996; Kinsella, Smith-Simonet, and Tuma, 2002; Thebodo and Marx, 2005). During this phase, experiential learning activities (e.g., role plays, simulations) can provide students with the opportunity to experience the challenges of communicating across cultures before they cross borders. This can bolster their self-confidence, reduce their anxieties, and, hopefully, enhance their willingness to communicate (WTC) (Clément et al. 2007) in their L2 and take an active role in the host culture.

If the group will be visiting the same host community, culture-specific information (e.g., customs, etiquette) should feature in the pre-departure phase, bearing in mind the aims and format of the sojourn. At minimum, the participants should acquire a basic understanding of the geography, history, and religion(s) of the host country as well as the linguistic and sociopolitical context. Since unrealistic expectations can lead to disappointments and disillusionment on stays abroad, it is important to ensure that current, accurate information is reviewed. To stimulate student interest and involvement, small groups could gather information about specific aspects of the host culture (e.g., surf the web, visit cultural centres/trade offices, do library research) and report back to the larger group. (See Box 10.1 for a sample of guiding questions; consult Dowell and Mirsky (2003) for additional suggestions to engage students in their pre-sojourn preparation). These student-led information sessions should motivate the participants to learn more about the host culture prior to departure, deepen their involvement in the planning process, and encourage them to assume some ownership of their own learning.

10.1.1.2 Linguistic/sociopragmatic development

In the pre-departure phase, it is also important to address language-related issues. For example, if there is to be a language policy for the sojourn, the socio-political and emotional implications must be critically examined. The rationale for the policy must be clearly identified (e.g., to encourage full immersion in the host culture) and explained to students. Most importantly, they must be given ample opportunity to express their views and concerns; adjustments can then be made, accordingly. Language choice is a deeply personal and sensitive matter, and a language policy should not be imposed on students. In the programme described in this book, the policy was discussed in small groups, and students were encouraged to express their views about it in surveys and interviews prior to the sojourn. Students from previous groups also discussed their reactions to the policy with new groups. All of this was necessary for the students to take ownership of the policy and be better prepared psychologically to 'switch channels' and function in English on a daily basis, not just across cultures but with their peers.

Familiarity with a range of learning strategies can help the participants to maximize their language and cultural learning during their stay abroad (e.g., see materials developed by Cohen, Paige, Shively, Emert, and Hoff, 2005, and Paige, Cohen, Kappler, Chi, and Lassegard, 2003, 2006). Prior to the sojourn, some exposure to the informal, social discourse (e.g., idiomatic expressions, colloquialisms) of the host language would be useful, especially in foreign language contexts where language courses concentrate on academic, formal discourse. An awareness of socio-pragmatics-related issues could help students become more attuned to differing norms of politeness and communication styles in the host speech community (LoCastro, 2003; Thomas, 1995) and facilitate relationship-building across cultures. This is especially important for advanced foreign-language learners, as their hosts are apt to expect more culturally appropriate behaviour/discourse from them. Armed with knowledge about 'politeness norms' in the host culture, students can then decide for themselves whether or not to appropriate these communicative behaviours ('converge') while abroad. At minimum, this preparation can raise their awareness of potential reactions if they choose to 'maintain' or 'diverge' from the host culture norms (Bourhis et al., 2007). This may lessen perceptions of racism in situations where their behaviour has broken local norms.

Students who participate in the SA programme that is featured in this book, are exposed to critical incidents, cases (longer, problem-based narratives), and discourse

Box 10.1   Researching the host country

If possible, visit a cultural/trade centre or request information (e.g., maps, brochures) from the official tourist board of the host country. When you surf the web, keep track of useful websites to share with others. Identify useful books and other materials as you search for <u>current</u> answers to the following questions:

1. What languages are spoken?
2. What are the main religions?
3. What type of government does the country have? What party is in power? Who is the leader?
4. What kinds of jobs do people do? What is the economy based on?
5. What are the official holidays? Will you be in the host country when there is a special festival or event?
6. What do people do in their leisure time? What are the most popular pastimes?
7. When are daily meals usually served? Identify some foods that are common at each meal.
8. What is the currency? What is the exchange rate?
9. What is the cost of living? How does this compare with where you live?
10. What are the common forms of transportation? How much do they cost?
11. You will have a free weekend in the middle of your stay. Where might you go? Would you travel alone or in a small group? What mode of transportation would you use to get there? How much time will it take to get there? What would you see/ do at your destination? What entrance fees would you need to pay? Where would you stay (e.g., a youth hostel)? Develop an itinerary. Search the internet for current information and use the following to prepare your budget:

Transportation to destination	£ _____
Transportation at destination	£ _____
Lodging	£ _____
Food	£ _____
Entertainment (e.g., entrance fees)	£ _____
Personal expenses	£ _____
Total estimated budget	£ _____

Share your findings in small groups/with the class. What information did you not find that you would like to know?

completion tests (DCTs) that draw on the intercultural experiences of previous SES students in England. (See Boxes 10.2 and 10.3, respectively, for sample DCT questions (requests and apologies) and a critical incident that is designed to promote pre-sojourn reflection). Working through these reality-based scenarios, first individually and then in groups, compels students to consider how they might react in similar situations. This affords them the opportunity to confront problems and raise questions in the safety of the classroom before entering the field. Their written responses on the DCTs also provide direction for the sociopragmatic component of the pre-sojourn programme, which is an integral part of their preparation for the homestay experience.

Box 10.2   Discourse completion exercise

Directions: Imagine you are participating in a five-week sojourn in England with 14 of your classmates. Each one of you is living in a homestay in Kenilworth, a small town. Please read each situation and write down what you would say.

1. It's 11:30 pm and your host family has already gone to bed. After having a snack you decide to have a shower. In the morning your host mum tells you that you woke everyone up because of the noise you made in the bathroom. What do you say?

   ____

   ____

2. On the bus to the University, you're sitting beside a middle-aged woman who has just finished reading the free newspaper that is provided by the bus company. All of the other copies are gone and you'd really like to read it. What do you say to the woman?

   ____

   ____

3. Soon after arriving in Kenilworth, you and five of your friends decide that it would be fun to visit each other's houses to see what they're like. Early in the afternoon the six of you arrive at your homestay unannounced. Your host mum sees all of you in the hall and looks shocked. You realize that she's not pleased. What do you say?

   ____

   ____

4. You're having Sunday dinner with your friend's host family. The roast beef is delicious and you'd really like some more. What would you say?

   ____

   ____

Box 10.3   Critical incident

When Ma Lei first learned that she would join 14 of her classmates on a trip to England she was overjoyed. She had never travelled outside Hong Kong before and was keen to experience a different way of life. She also wished to improve her English but was a bit anxious about living in a homestay for five weeks. When she arrived she was relieved that her host family was very welcoming and kind. In the first few days she was tired but very happy as everything around her was new and exciting. By the second week, however, she began to miss her favourite foods and phoned home everyday just to hear her mother's voice. The stores in the small town where she was staying closed early and the buses did not always arrive on time. Everything was so much more efficient in Hong Kong! She sometimes found it hard to catch what her hosts were saying and became very discouraged about her English level. She was exhausted trying to express herself in the language every day and usually escaped to her room right after dinner. When her hosts invited her to go on outings she declined. Ma Lei began to have stomach aches and did not sleep well at night. Her friends seemed to be having a good time and she didn't want to trouble them so she did not tell them about her difficulties. In the group debriefing sessions she remained silent as she listened to others talk about their adventures. After class she decided to go to the student health centre for relief. She told the doctor that she had an upset stomach, headaches, and was having trouble sleeping. The doctor gave her some aspirin but the problems did not go away. Whenever she saw a plane in the sky she wished that she was on her way back to Hong Kong. How would she ever get through the next few weeks?

Questions for thought and discussion:

1. What are the main issues facing Ma Lei? Explain what is happening to her.
2. Why did she not find relief after visiting the clinic?
3. What might Ma Lei do to make the most of the remaining weeks of the sojourn?
4. What would you do if you were in her shoes? Why?
5. What might Ma Lei have done to prevent this situation from becoming so severe?
6. Have you ever been in a situation similar to Ma Lei? Please describe it. How did you cope?
7. What did you learn from this critical incident that you might apply to your own experiences in new situations?

10.1.1.3 Input from previous sojourners

Previous sojourners can be a wonderful resource, provided they have developed an ethnorelative mindset and taken an active role in the host culture. With enthusiasm and a positive tone, they can offer practical advice that is relevant to their peers. For example, they might discuss strategies that they used to build relationships with their hosts. They can encourage the setting of realistic goals and inspire newcomers to take steps to influence the ways in which their own sojourn unfolds. In the SES, students who have made the trip to England share their photos and experiences with those in the new group. In particular, they offer advice about homestay life and help allay the fears of those who have not yet ventured outside their own cultural environment.

10.1.1.4 Cultural self-awareness

Building up knowledge of the host culture is not enough. Prior to a sojourn, it is important for participants to reflect on their own culture and culturally conditioned behaviour and thinking (Byram, 1997, 2003; Ting-Toomey and Chung, 2005). As Shusterman explained, 'since the concepts of Self and Other are interdependent, I think it could also be conversely argued that a knowledge of oneself is necessary for understanding the other' (Shusterman, 1998: 107). By reflecting on their identities and language use prior to a sojourn, participants will be in a better position to consider the potential impact of their attitudes, perceptions, and communication styles on intercultural encounters. Writing their own cultural identity narrative, for example, can heighten their awareness of particular dimensions of their language and cultural socialization that might affect their interactions with others.

It is also helpful to raise awareness of the fluid nature of identity and the possibility that sojourners may experience identity reconstruction when they cross cultures, especially if they are open to new 'ways of being'. Prior to the sojourn, the participants should be encouraged to reflect on their attitudes towards their own culture and the host culture. This can bring to light stereotypes or outdated, romantic images they hold of their future hosts. These revelations can provide valuable information for programme planners and highlight issues that should be addressed prior to departure.

10.1.1.5 Ethnographic groundwork

In 'year abroad' programmes, an ethnographic approach to language and cultural learning has long been used to help student sojourners become better prepared for life in the host speech community (e.g., Roberts, 1997, 2003; Roberts et al., 2001). I have also found that carefully sequenced, systematic ethnographic training can be effective in helping short-term sojourners become more focused and engaged in the host culture (Jackson, 2006a, b). In the pre-departure phase, students can be introduced to the methods and issues of ethnographic exploration: ethics, participant observation, the recording of detailed field notes, interviewing techniques (including the facilitation of informal ethnographic conversations), and the use of visuals (e.g., digital photographs, graphics). Through weekly tasks they can hone the skills necessary to undertake a small-scale ethnographic project in their home environment. With adequate support and preparation, even the most reticent student can develop enough confidence to explore a cultural scene and gradually move from description to interpretation and analysis. (See Box 10.4 for the ethnographic project proposal form.)

Box 10.4   Preliminary ethnographic project proposal form

I appreciate that the topic of your project may change during the semester. Nonetheless, it is important that you identify a plan of action now. Please complete this form as fully as possible and submit it by the due date in order to receive feedback/approval for your ethnographic project.

Name ____   Date ____________

Proposed theme/topic (Identify your broad area of interest)

____

____

____

Specific aspects you would like to explore (Identify what you would like to learn more about)

____

____

____

Rationale for selection of theme/topic (Explain why you are interested in this subject)

____

____

____

Research questions (List specific questions you would like to explore)

____

____

____

Relevant places for participant observation (Identify the cultural scene)

____

____

____

Possible informants (Provide a brief profile)

____

____

____

Criteria for the selection of your informants (Explain why they would be 'good' informants)

____

____

____

<table>
<tr><td>

Methodological implications (How do you intend to go about collecting data? Do you foresee any problems or particular issues you may have to deal with? (e.g., access to cultural site) How might you deal with these problems?)

____

____

____

Additional comments about your proposed study

____

____

____

</td></tr>
</table>

In the SES the students conducted projects on a variety of culture-related topics (e.g., code-switching in a Chinese family, the transition of a Mainland student to Hong Kong, the life of a Filipino domestic helper). (See Box 10.5 for abstracts of two of the 'home ethnography' projects.) 'Making the familiar strange' heightened their awareness of aspects of their home culture and helped them to become more observant and independent, providing essential groundwork for their fieldwork in England. In many cases, these novice researchers developed empathy and appreciation of another 'way of being' (Bakhtin, 1986).

10.1.1.6 Preparation for homestay life

While some students may live in a campus residence or in private accommodation during their stay abroad, homestays have the potential to provide a rich, supportive linguistic and cultural environment. If this mode of accommodation is chosen, preparation for homestay life should be included in the pre-departure phase. To facilitate their placement with appropriate hosts, before the sojourn the students could complete a profile form that provides insight into their interests, hobbies, personality, and preferences (e.g., to live with a family with small children). Ideally, students should be given the names, addresses, and profiles of their hosts (e.g., number and age of children in the house, if any) prior to departure so they can contact them before the trip, if they wish. If the students will be travelling in a group, they may also be given a map indicating where all of their fellow sojourners will be based, along with their contact information. This can reduce anxiety, especially for those who have never travelled before.

To help sojourners make the most of their homestay situation, the following topics and issues should be addressed: ways to break the ice (e.g., sharing photos of family with hosts), roles and responsibilities, expectations, and sociopragmatic norms in the host culture (LoCastro, 2003; Thomas, 1995). The students should be advised to contact the homestay coordinator if difficulties arise in the homestay. Knowing that

Box 10.5   Abstracts of pre-sojourn small-scale 'home ethnography' projects

Code-mixing in a Chinese family: a code of convenience and confidence
Code-mixing is a common phenomenon in Hong Kong. It is not difficult to hear people around utter English words amidst their Cantonese speech. In this project, I looked into code-mixing in a Chinese family to get insights into possible reasons for such flourishing speaking behaviour in Hong Kong and how they are related to the Hong Kong community specifically. I was especially interested in my informants' motivation/intention of code-mixing, as well as their respective feelings about their own and others' code-mixing. Ethnographic data was collected through participant observation of code-mixed conversations, some informal chats with my participants on this topic and several formal interviews conducted on an individual basis. The interview transcripts and field notes were reviewed to reveal their emic perspective and my personal interpretation (etic perspective). I found out that code-mixing is produced under Hong Kong's mixed culture. Its effective usage can become the quintessence for communication. Yet, there are both pros and cons about code-mixing. Sometimes, it is, interestingly, an art of vocal mimicry with the goal of accomplishing self-recognition and getting others' admiration. These ideas generate my conclusion that code-mixing is indeed a code of convenience and confidence in Hong Kong. (Elsa)

Video gaming: a special sociocultural practice among young people
Video gaming has become a controversial issue in Hong Kong society and most often is related to many teenage problems like violence and poor academy. This rather strong stereotype is imposed on this interest and its negative effects are significantly stressed in society. This research is carried out with the aim of investigating how video gaming works among several young people in Hong Kong and therefore explores how it shapes their social and cultural life. Both positive and negative effects of video gaming are discussed in this paper so that readers can have a more complete picture of such interest. This research is written on the basis of analysis made from participant observation, informal conversation, and interviews with two male university students and one female secondary school student in Hong Kong. Materials from the internet are also incorporated into the analysis of the cultural scene. The reasons why young people play video games were explored and it was found that video gaming had more good than bad effects on the three participants. The discussion of findings revealed that a broadened and enriched sociocultural life was the most significant benefit gained by the participants through video gaming. Negative effects, like withdrawal from society and the frequent use of violence, as emphasized by mass media, were not found in the participants. The overall findings give the impression that video gaming may not be as unhealthy as people may believe. (Fion)

support will be available can further reduce anxiety. This can prevent small problems from becoming major issues and, when necessary, students can be moved to another homestay situation if warranted.

10.1.1.7 Goal-setting

After adequate information has been provided about the sojourn and host culture, the participants should be encouraged to set and prioritize realistic goals and objectives for their stay. Discussion could centre on potential gains in a range of domains (e.g., personal, linguistic, intercultural, and academic). It is helpful to raise awareness of the need to periodically revisit their goals and objectives while abroad. This can help them keep on track and make adjustments, if necessary, in order to maximize their time in the host environment. This pre-departure orientation can encourage students to reflect on how the sojourn fits into their long-range personal, academic, and professional plans. Goal-setting is important, as I discovered that many of my students had not prioritized their goals and had set language objectives that were more appropriate for formal language lessons than informal learning in the host community. Some had also had very high, unrealistic expectations about what could be accomplished in a short stay (e.g., acquiring a British accent).

10.1.2 Selection, preparation, and support of host families

For homestay placements to work well, hosts should be well matched with the sojourners and keen to share their culture/home with them. As my study revealed, one cannot assume that host–sojourner relationships will flourish; however, steps can be taken to improve the odds. For example, the homestay coordinator in the host institution could facilitate an orientation/sharing session prior to the arrival of the sojourners. This would give programme administrators the opportunity to clarify their expectations and, just as importantly, provide a venue for hosts to raise questions and discuss issues and concerns.

This orientation session could include an overview of the SA programme (e.g., a detailed schedule), background information on the sojourners and their home country, insight into the dangers of stereotyping, and a list of common symptoms of culture shock. Roles and responsibilities of hosts and sojourners could be clarified, emphasizing the need for hosts to explain/negotiate 'family rules' early on to avoid misunderstandings. Discussion could then centre on practical strategies to help the newcomers adjust and more fully participate in their host family's life and culture. The homestay coordinator could use this opportunity to explain the importance of recognizing the preferred identities of the newcomers and stress the benefits for both hosts and sojourners to share their cultures. The session would give new and seasoned host families the opportunity to meet and share hosting experiences; they could then contact each other during the sojourn for support, as needed. It would also be advisable for the homestay coordinator to touch base with the hosts periodically. Surveys could also be used to gather information/suggestions from the hosts to provide input into the format/content of the orientation sessions and also lead to improvements in the overall hosting experience. At the end of each sojourn, students should also be given the opportunity to provide feedback about their homestay experience and offer suggestions for improvements.

10.2   The sojourn

10.2.1   Reflection and self-analysis

Reflection, dialogue, and self-analysis should be core elements of any SA experience. There are a number of ways this can be fostered while students are immersed in the host culture. As long as adequate guidelines and encouragement are provided, I have found that diary-writing can be very cathartic and otherwise beneficial for students. It can deepen their language and intercultural learning as they revisit their lived experiences. Through the act of writing and reflecting on their stories, sojourners can become more aware of their 'being in the world' (Bakhtin, 1986) and their responses to encounters across cultures. As Ochs and Capps explained: 'we come to know ourselves as we use narrative to apprehend experiences and navigate relationships with others' (Ochs and Capps, 1996: 20–1). This reflection can prompt sojourners to be more 'mindful' in future intercultural encounters. (See Box 10.6 for Guidelines for diary-writing.)

Students may be encouraged to review their diaries periodically and revisit past critical incidents. With some distance from the emotional impact of the events, they may reconsider what led to the miscommunication across cultures (e.g., the absence of discourse markers of politeness that are the norm in that context). This process has the potential to stimulate further learning and personal expansion. It can also help sojourners appreciate the growth they have already experienced in their new linguistic and cultural environment. They can then revisit the goals they set prior to the sojourn and revise them based on their progress and their knowledge of limitations and opportunities in the field (e.g., access to new CoP).

10.2.2   On-site debriefing and socio-emotional support

While in the host speech community, student sojourners need sufficient socio-emotional support to facilitate exploration and independence in the new environment. Regular debriefings, when handled well, can open up some discursive space and help participants make sense of their new environment. These group sessions can also foster personal growth and self-confidence and empower the participants to take a more active role in the host culture. Sojourners can share experiences and raise questions about confusing or troubling intercultural encounters. These group discussions can also heighten their awareness about interesting aspects of the host culture that otherwise might have gone unnoticed. For example, in the Monday morning debriefing sessions that my students participated in, a wide range of cultural features that had caught their attention were raised (e.g., idiomatic expressions, activities of the elderly, eating habits, greetings for bus drivers).

In the debriefing sessions, issues of race, ethnicity, positioning, and identity misalignments may surface and, if handled in a professional, sensitive manner, may lessen the number of critical incidents and encourage more exposure to the host environment. The views expressed in frank, open discussions can alert the facilitator about aspects of the sojourn (e.g., insecurity issues) that merit further attention. (See Box 10.7 for the field notes of the first debriefing session.)

Box 10.6   Guidelines for sojourn diary

During the sojourn you will be required to keep a reflective diary to record your reactions to experiences that you find interesting, puzzling, irritating, or otherwise significant. Entries about fears or expectations, rewarding or frustrating experiences or events, cultural observations, the language policy, your own cultural adjustment and/or any other thoughts and feelings you encounter during the sojourn will all be useful. You could also provide insight into your ethnographic data collection across cultures. Your entries will form a record of your language and cultural learning and your impressions of your new environment. Please provide enough details to contextualize your 'stories' and short narratives. Your diary should provide insight into what you are learning about yourself and your hosts/host culture while you negotiate the sojourn – and your life in England.

Keeping a personal log can help you remember the details of your experiences. Through the process of writing and reflecting you can deepen your understanding of events and your reactions to them. Your diary should be both descriptive *and* thoughtfully analytical (providing your interpretation and understanding of events). Your final entry should be a bit longer as it should provide evidence that you have reflected on your personal goals and your overall sojourn experience. You could respond to questions like the following: What has changed most significantly about your perception and attitudes towards the host culture since your arrival? Look back at your diary entries. Were you able to achieve the personal and academic goals that you set for yourself prior to the sojourn? Were you able to follow the 'English only' policy? Why or why not? What has been your proudest accomplishment? What do you wish you had done differently? What did you gain from the sojourn? What new experiences?

There should be a minimum of *three entries for each week* of the sojourn; each entry should be numbered and dated (e.g. Entry one; 29 May). Please number your pages. You could also use headings and sub-headings, if you like. Most entries should be approximately two double-spaced pages in length, although this may vary.

Box 10.7   Sojourn field notes

First debriefing session, Host institution in England
Monday, June 7, 10 a.m. (beginning of Week Two)

For our first debriefing session, the students sat in a semi-circle in a small classroom with our English host, a cultural studies specialist, and me. Our host invited them to ask questions and talk about their experiences in their first week in England. Elsa commented that people in Hong Kong work harder. Niki and Eva noted that many people participate in family gatherings and go out together in the park. Serena commented that it's nice that people greet strangers in the street. Then, much of the discussion centred on complaints and critical incidents. Cori talked about the problems she'd encountered on a solo trip to Coventry. First, she ran into difficulty when interacting with people at the bus station and did not find them very friendly. She then had problems in a coffee shop. She had been slow to order and the waitress told her to hurry and make up her mind. Cori commented that the woman was very rude and this would not have been acceptable in Hong Kong. Our host handled all of these complaints very well, listening patiently and offering his expressions of sympathy. 'I'm sorry this happened to you.'

Ada and Elsa revealed that they had been scared when returning home after dark. Elsa had felt threatened when men laughed at her as she ran past a pub late at night. On Sunday afternoon, several teenage boys had approached Lara and Elsa in Leamington and wanted to take a photo with them. They were not sure why and it had made them uneasy. Mira then recounted an incident involving the bus to the University. It had not pulled into the stop where she was waiting because she had not waved it down. When she told her host mother about it, the woman commented that 'it was a shame'. Mira interpreted this to mean that the woman felt embarrassed as this had affected her 'national pride'. Our host explained that this was likely not the case and that the woman was simply saying, 'sorry, that's too bad that you didn't know that you needed to flag down the bus and it went by'.

My impression of our first session is that many of the students are feeling insecure in their new environment. In this heightened state of alert they are feeling discriminated against when there are other possible explanations for what is happening. Our host handled all of their concerns in a quiet, respectful manner and the students seemed willing to express their views and ask questions. They also appeared more reassured at the end of the session. After he left, we discussed topics for their ethnographic projects and they seemed more settled.

For students who are reluctant to share their views in an open forum, short surveys with open-ended questions may be used to stimulate reflection and discussion on a variety of issues and concerns (e.g., intercultural adjustment, host–sojourner relationships, positioning in new CoP, personal goals, language development, cultural knowledge, intercultural communicative competence, attitudes toward the host culture and language).

In their diaries, several of the young women in my study wrote about the impact that the weekly surveys and debriefing sessions were having on their intercultural adjustment. These sharing sessions positively affected their willingness to persevere with English and build relationships across cultures. In particular, I have found that students who are very fearful or apprehensive in their new environment may draw strength from sessions of this nature provided the facilitator is a supportive listener, non-judgmental, and encouraging of open expression. Emphasizing the merits of a positive mindset, students can be encouraged to take stock of their progress, reflect on the goals they had set prior to the sojourn, and consider what they can realistically accomplish in the remainder of their stay. As well as full-group debriefing sessions, opportunities for individualized problem solving should be provided so that issues may be resolved before they become major obstacles to intercultural adjustment.

10.2.3   Coping strategies

While most of the students in my study followed the 'English only' policy during their stay in England, some struggled to live in the language and felt under psychological pressure to perform. A close examination of those who were more successful in using English throughout their stay revealed that they had successfully employed a wider range of coping strategies. They had cultivated closer relationships across cultures and were able to draw on socio-emotional support from a variety of sources (e.g., their host families, SES friends, our debriefing sessions). For sojourners who find it more difficult to cope in a new culture, short breaks from the pressures of using the host language (e.g., a relaxing meal with familiar food and close friends) may help them to get their language and cultural learning back on track. It is important for SA administrators to be sensitive to the pressures their students may be under as they experience the ups and downs of intercultural adjustment.

10.2.4   Programmed experiential learning

With adequate pre-sojourn preparation (see Section 10.1.1), sojourners may also carry out small-scale ethnographic projects in the host environment. Through meaningful, sustained contact in a cultural scene of their choice, sojourners can gain exposure to different worldviews and authentic communication styles and speech genres (e.g., humour). In the present study, many of the women explored some aspect of their homestay situation (e.g., pet-keeping, gardening) that caught their attention and, in the process, built closer ties with their hosts. Several of the students also ventured into the community to immerse themselves in a cultural scene (e.g., charity shop). (See Box 10.8 for abstracts of two of the sojourn ethnography projects.) With the support of regular research advising sessions, the young women were encouraged to assume ownership of their research and intercultural learning. Regular discussions about their research projects raised the group's awareness of a broader range of cultural aspects and helped create a supportive community of explorers.

In the process of carrying out their research, they learned to observe, listen, interpret, and analyse the behaviour and discourse of their 'informants'. Instead of limiting their use of the host language to service encounters or very brief conversations with their hosts, the projects provided them with a purpose for sustained interactions across cultures. In several cases, this extended their learning beyond the classroom and their homestays to the wider host speech community. When adequate support is provided, projects of this nature can help students deepen their meta-cognitive awareness of sociolinguistic differences and potentially enhance their linguistic and intercultural communicative competence.

Box 10.8   Abstracts of sojourn ethnography projects

People's mentors and friends: human animal interrelations in pet-keeping
This ethnographic study investigated the practice of pet-keeping in an English family in Kenilworth, England. It aimed to understand the human–domestic animal interrelations and the influences of pet-keeping on people's lives. In order to attain a full depiction of the cultural scene, a pet owner with years of pet-keeping experiences was interviewed and her daily interactions with her cats as well as the cultural setting were observed. Previous related studies were also referenced to provide further insights into this domain. The interview transcripts and observation field notes were analysed to identify the key issues and themes in the discourse. It was found that the cats in this research were recognized as other than animals by their owner. She considered them to be 'fellow people' and even her 'children'. The discoveries of the cats' various roles in the family also indicated the tremendous life-changing impact that pets may have on humans. (Zoe)

Home is where the sojourner is
Homestay is an important aspect in the SES five-week field trip programme in England. Aiming to maximize exposure to the English way of life, the CUHK English Department included a homestay for each student in the programme. This study looked into the homestay experience in relation to intercultural understanding, benefits, and challenges, mainly from the viewpoint of host families. Two host mothers were observed and interviewed to gain a deeper understanding of the hosting experience and their perceptions of life with overseas students in their homes. An interview with the host University's accommodation officer and questionnaires completed by SES students were included to help in the triangulation of interview data. The interview transcripts, surveys, and field notes were reviewed to examine how a homestay contributes to the understanding of different cultures for both the hosts and the students. Recurring themes included intercultural awareness, the use of language, host–student relationship bonding, and adjustment and conflict management. Information gleaned from both the hosts' and students' perspectives provided valuable messages for future SES students. It also suggested ways that institutions could enhance the homestay experience. (Eva)

Ethnography is not the only way to stimulate student involvement in the host culture. What is important is to recognize the merits of including an element of programmed experiential learning in SA programmes to take full advantage of the immersion context, no matter the length of the sojourn. Specific activities or projects can be tailored to the needs, abilities (e.g., proficiency level), and situations of the L2 sojourners, ensuring that adequate guidance and assistance are provided. Without these programmed opportunities we cannot assume that language and cultural learning will take place simply because the participants are residing in the host culture. Instead of engaging in dialogue with their hosts, they may use an 'avoidance strategy', limiting their exposure to the host culture.

10.2.5   Explorations in the field

To take full advantage of linguistic and cultural affordances in the host culture, sojourners must have adequate time to explore the world around them, interact with their hosts (and other locals), and reflect on what they have discovered about themselves and Others. If their days and weekends are filled with academic classes and excursions, exposure to informal authentic cultural scenes will be too limited for them to go beyond awareness of surface-level features of the host culture (e.g., differences in food, clothing, and architecture). It takes time to adjust and build relationships across cultures, and some sojourners will naturally need more time than others to break the ice and feel at ease.

In the SA programme described in this book, the students had most afternoons and Sundays free to spend time with their hosts, explore their new environment on their own or with friends, write in their diary, or gather data for their ethnographic project. For those who take advantage of linguistic and cultural affordances in the community, the sojourn can be a life-changing event.

10.2.6   Closure and preparation for re-entry

Adequate closure and preparation for re-entry should also be provided near the end of the sojourn, even after only a short stay in the host culture. Learner-centred, debriefing sessions can encourage sojourners to revisit their pre-sojourn goals and take stock of their language and cultural learning and personal expansion. They can also be prompted to reflect on their feelings about leaving their hosts and the host culture and their expectations about returning home. They may then consider ways that they might sustain their language and cultural growth and personal development once they are back on home soil. These sessions provide an excellent opportunity for the students to assess their learning during the sojourn and offer suggestions to improve the SA programme including the pre-sojourn preparation. (See Box 10.9 for a sample of questions that can be used to stimulate reflection on sojourn experiences.)

Box 10.9   Post-sojourn debriefing

Questions to stimulate thought and discussion: The sojourn and re-entry
(Individual reflection followed by small-group discussion and full-class debriefing)

1. Think back to the goals that you set for the sojourn. Which ones did you accomplish? Which ones were difficult to achieve? Did you change your goals once you were abroad? What did you accomplish or experience that you never expected to?

2. Before your trip, you described some of your concerns/worries. Did they happen? How did you cope?

3. What aspects of the sojourn did you find the most stressful, confusing, annoying, or irritating? Please list *5 aspects* and then rank them, with #1 being the most stressful aspect.

4. What strategies did you find most helpful to cope with the challenges you faced during the sojourn? Identify *5 strategies* and then rank them, with #1 being the most useful strategy (e.g., a strategy that you would strongly recommend for the next group of SES students).

5. During the sojourn, in what situations did you have the most difficulty using or understanding English? How did you feel about using the language with your classmates? Do you feel that your language and intercultural communication skills improved? If yes, how?

6. What are the lessons and skills that you've learned that you never want to forget? What did you discover about yourself?

7. How do you think you *changed* during the sojourn, if at all?

8. If you could do the sojourn all over again, what would you do differently? Why?

9. Have your sojourn experiences affected your future plans and goals? Do you now have any interest in studying/travelling/living abroad? Did the sojourn affect your views of English and your use of the language? Did it impact on your willingness to use the language and interact across cultures?

10. What advice would you give the next group to get ready for the sojourn? How should they prepare for the homestay experience and daily life in English?

10.3   Post-sojourn

10.3.1   Re-entry culture shock

Even after only a short stay abroad, sojourners may experience symptoms of reverse culture shock when they return home, especially if they have been very open to differences during the sojourn and changed in some ways (e.g., developed a broader worldview, a more intercultural persona, and a deeper investment in the host language). Initially, they may find their home environment unsatisfactory; they may miss their independence and life in their L2, as did some of my students. They may become somewhat frustrated when they again encounter social sanctions against the use of the language in informal situations. If the returnees can draw support from each other, they may create opportunities for their continued use of their L2 in social settings. They may discover contexts where they can use or gain exposure to their L2 that they had simply overlooked in the past (e.g., theatrical productions in international arts/film festivals). They may also keep in touch with friends (e.g., their hosts) they made abroad, providing another opportunity to use their L2 in meaningful ways outside the academic arena.

10.3.2   Extending the sojourn experience

To maximize the potential of stays abroad, efforts should be made to extend the language and cultural learning of sojourners when they are back on home soil. At minimum, the returnees could be encouraged to come together to reflect on their experiences and share their discoveries with others. This phase, unfortunately, is often neglected. Students slip back into familiar routines, and the impact of the sojourn quickly fades away. In this scenario, a valuable resource is wasted. This does not need to happen. Returnees may work collaboratively to prepare a presentation for subsequent groups. This activity gives them a chance to share their experiences and respond to questions. It can help them to consolidate their own learning and motivate others to take advantage of affordances in the host environment.

There are other ways to extend the learning of student sojourners after they return home. Debriefing sessions provide the opportunity for guided reflection, the analysis of sojourn experiences, and the setting of goals for further enhancement of their linguistic and intercultural communication skills. This phase can raise awareness of the participants' identity expansion and provide an outlet for them to discuss their new understandings of their place in the world and the role of language in representing their expanded self (multiple identities). In the SA programme described in this book, the students also take a credit-bearing report-writing course that is directly related to the sojourn. Over a 14-week period, they craft either a 30-page literature or ethnographic report drawing on their experiences in England. This serves to further consolidate their sojourn learning.

10.4   Implications for other border crossers

While my ethnographic case studies focused on the language and cultural learning of student sojourners, the findings have implications for others who cross cultures (e.g., business people, international aid workers). In particular, this research raised intriguing questions about the impact of sociocultural/environmental features (e.g., roles and relationships in CoP, host receptivity, quality and quantity of host-sojourner contact) and individual factors (e.g., personality traits, degree of investment, openness to differences, and identity expansion) on the intercultural adjustment and language and cultural enhancement of border crossers. Most importantly, the use of rich, qualitative data provided insight into what actually happens during stays abroad and dispelled the myth that all sojourners automatically benefit from mere exposure to the host speech community. Echoing the words of Dwyer, I believe that to be successful, SA programmes (of all lengths) require 'very careful educational planning, expert implementation, and significant resources' (Dwyer, 2004: 161). To maximize their potential, all phases of the experience merit attention: pre-sojourn, sojourn, and post-sojourn.

10.5   Suggestions for future studies

SA, when well planned and prepared for, can alter students' lives; however, much more research and reflection are needed to deepen our understanding of the conditions that maximize the development of intercultural communicative competence, sociopragmatic awareness, and intercultural personhood. Specifically, we need further studies that investigate the perspectives of short- and long-term student sojourners from other language groups and contexts. Making use of both qualitative and quantitative measures, researchers could explore the L2 and cultural learning and identity reconstruction of male and female sojourners of varying proficiency levels and ethnic backgrounds; the findings could provide deeper insight into the complex sociocultural, individual, and other factors that influence the sojourn experience (e.g., gender differences, length of sojourn, quality and quantity of host–sojourner interactions, degree of investment, housing situation, cultural distance, type of SA programme).

More research is needed to determine how variations in pre-departure, sojourn, and re-entry programming impact on the intercultural adjustment and development of intercultural communicative competence in participants. Comparative studies of sojourners in different SA programmes would also deepen our understanding of the impact of specific programme elements (e.g., duration, housing options, experiential learning). Outcomes-based assessment research could provide insight into how best to prepare students and support their sojourn learning. Longitudinal studies are also needed to examine the long-term impact of stays abroad on the linguistic, inter-cultural, and personal growth (e.g., identity expansion) of L2 students and other border crossers, including those who participate in the increasingly popular short-term sojourns.

As well as paying close attention to the voices of L2 sojourners and SA educators, we need more studies that investigate the perspectives of hosts. These individuals can play a significant role in the adjustment process and influence the language and cultural learning of their 'guests'. Few researchers, however, have focused on hosts' perceptions of their roles and responsibilities. Not enough is known about their understandings of the difficulties their 'guests' face when crossing cultures. We also need a deeper awareness of the strategies (if any) that hosts employ to enhance the host–sojourner relationship and ease the transition of their 'guests' to homestay life. What steps (if any) do they take to empower students to become more engaged and 'at home' in the host culture/community? What exposure do they offer to their CoP? The views of the hosts could then be triangulated with those of the sojourners to develop a more comprehensive picture of what actually happens in homestays. Ethnographic studies could also focus on hosts who interact with business people or other border crossers to better understand the impact of host nationals on the process of personal, linguistic, and cultural expansion in newcomers (and vice versa).

Further, we could benefit from more systematic studies of speech acts in the host culture (e.g., homestay environment) to better understand the types of social inter-actions L2 sojourners engage in, learner speech act behaviour, the nature of socio-pragmatic failures, and the negotiation strategies that hosts and sojourners use to repair and build relationships across cultures. While they might be intrusive, audio-recordings of host sojourner interactions in naturalistic settings (e.g., informal conversations at the dinner table) and stimulated-recall sessions with the interlocutors could deepen our understanding of factors affecting the homestay experience. This could supplement data obtained through participant observation, diaries, surveys, and interviews. Studies of this nature could provide valuable insight into the inter-language pragmatic development of sojourners with reference to specific speech acts (e.g., requests, refusals, apologies). The findings should lead to more effective, targeted pre-sojourn preparation (e.g., instruction in L2 pragmatics).

10.6   A final word

SA is expected to grow exponentially in the years to come, especially in terms of the number and variety of short-term sojourns. The responsibility of international educators is to promote the development of creative, well-designed programmes that support the language and cultural learning of sojourners and simultaneously empower their personal growth and identity expansion. How can this best be achieved? SA praxis, whereby educators continually engage in the dialectical process of action-reflection-transformative action, is one way forward. My ethnographic project, for example, informed my understandings of what can happen on stays abroad and (re)shaped my own SA practices. Interdisciplinary research that brings about critical thinking can stimulate reform and transform the very nature of what it means to study abroad. My hope is that this book will compel other SA educators to critically examine their own practices and work towards the creation of more emancipatory SA research and pedagogy to bring future sojourners closer to realizing their dreams.

References

Agar, M. (1996) *The Professional Stranger*. San Diego, CA: Academic Press.

Ahearn, L. M. (2001) Language and agency. *Annual Review of Anthropology* 30: 109–37.

Alred, G. and Byram, M. (2002) Becoming an intercultural mediator: a longitudinal study of residence abroad. *Journal of Multilingual and Multicultural Development* 23 (5): 339–52.

Alred, G., Byram, M., and Fleming, M. (eds) (2003) *Intercultural Experience and Education*. Clevedon: Multilingual Matters.

Alvesson, M. and Sköldberg, K. (2004) *Reflexive Methodology: New Vistas for Qualitative Research*. London: SAGE.

Arnett, J. J. (2002) The psychology of globalization. *American Psychologist* 57 (10): 774–83.

Auer, P. (2005) A postscript: code-switching and social identity. *Journal of Pragmatics* 37: 403–10.

Bailey, K. M. and Ochsner, R. (1983) A methodological review of the diary studies: windmill tilting or social science? In K. M. Bailey, M. Long, and S. Peck (eds) *Second Language Acquisition Studies* 188–98. Rowley, MA: Newbury House.

Bakhtin, M. M. (1981) *The Dialogic Imagination: Four Essays* (C. Emerson and M. Holquist, trans.). Austin, TX: University of Texas Press.

Bakhtin, M. M. (1984) *Problems of Dostoevsky's Poetics* (C. Emerson, ed. and trans.) Minneapolis, MN: University of Minnesota Press.

Bakhtin, M. M. (1986) *Speech Genres and Other Late Essays* (V. McGee, trans.) Austin, TX: University of Texas Press.

Barton, D. and Tusting, K. (2005) *Beyond Communities of Practice: Language, Power, and Social Context*. Cambridge: Cambridge University Press.

Baynham, M. (2006) Performing self, family, and community in Moroccan narratives of migration and settlement. In A. de Fina, D. Schiffrin, and M. Bamberg (eds.) *Discourse and Identity* 376–97. Cambridge: Cambridge University Press.

Baxter, L. A. (2004) Dialogues of relating. In R. Anderson, L. A. Baxter, and K. Cissna (eds) *Dialogue: Theorizing Difference in Communication Studies* 107–24. Thousand Oaks, CA: SAGE.

Bennett, J. M. (1993) Cultural marginality: identity issues in intercultural training. In M. Paige (ed.) *Education for the Intercultural Experience* 109–36. Yarmouth, ME: Intercultural Press.

Bennett, J. M. and Bennett, M. J. (2004) Developing intercultural sensitivity: an integrative approach to global and domestic diversity. In D. Landis, J. M.

Bennett, and M. J. Bennett (eds) *Handbook of Intercultural Training*. 3rd edn 147–65. Thousand Oaks, CA: SAGE.

Bennett, M. J. (1986) A developmental approach to training for intercultural sensitivity. *International Journal of Intercultural Relations* 10: 179–96.

Bennett, M. J. (1993) Towards ethnorelativism: a development model of intercultural sensitivity. In R. M. Paige (ed.) *Education for the Intercultural Experience* 21–71. Yarmouth, ME: Intercultural Press.

Bennett, M. J. (1998) Intercultural communication: a current perspective. In M. J. Bennett (ed.) *Basic Concepts of Intercultural Communication* 1–34. Yarmouth, ME: Intercultural Press.

Berry, J. W. (1997) Immigration, acculturation, and adaptation. *Applied Psychology: An International Journal* 46: 5–68.

Berwick, R. F. and Whalley, T. R. (2000) The experiential bases of culture learning: a case study of Canadian high schoolers in Japan. *International Journal of Intercultural Relations* 24 (3): 325–40.

Bhabha, H. (1994) *The Location of Culture*. London: Routledge.

Block, D. (2007) *Second Language Identities*. London: Continuum.

Bourdieu, P. (1977) The economics of linguistic exchanges. *Social Science Information* 16 (6): 645–68.

Bourdieu, P. (1979) The economics of linguistic exchanges. *Social Science Information,* 16: 645–68.

Bourdieu, P. (1982) Ce que parler veut dire: l'économie des échanges linguistiques. Paris: Librairie Arthème Fayard.

Bourdieu, P. (1986). The forms of capital. In J. G. Richardson (ed.) *Handbook for Theory and Research for the Sociology of Education* 241–58. New York: Greenwood Press.

Bourdieu, P. (1991) *Language and Symbolic Power*. Cambridge, MA: Harvard University Press.

Bourdieu, P., Chamboredon, J. C., and Passeron, J. C. (1991) *The Craft of Sociology: Epistemological Preliminaries*. Berlin: de Gruyter (first published in 1968).

Bourdieu, P. and Wacquant, L. J. D. (1992) *An Invitation to Reflexive Sociology*. Chicago: University of Chicago Press.

Bourhis, R. Y., el-Geledi, S., and Sachdev, I. (2007) Language, ethnicity, and intergroup relations. In A. Weatherall (ed.) *Language, Discourse, and Social Psychology* 15–50. Basingstoke, Hampshire: Palgrave Macmillan.

Brewer, J. (2000) *Ethnography*. Buckingham: Open University Press.

Brockington, J. L., Hoffa, W. W., and Martin, P. C. (eds.) (2005) *NAFSA's Guide to Education Abroad for Advisors and Administrators* 3rd edn. Washington, DC: NAFSA Association of International Educators.

Byram, M. (1997) *Teaching and Assessing Intercultural Communicative Competence*. Clevedon: Multilingual Matters.

Byram, M. (2003) On being 'bicultural' and 'intercultural' In G. Alred, M. Byram, and M. Fleming (eds.) *Intercultural Experience and Education* 50–66. Clevedon: Multilingual Matters.

Byram, M. and Feng, A. (2004) Culture and language learning: teaching, research and scholarship. *Language Teaching* 37: 149–68.

Byram, M. and Feng, A. (2005) Teaching and researching intercultural competence. In E. Hinkel (ed.) *Handbook of Research in Second Language Teaching and Learning* 911–30. Mahwah, NJ: Lawrence Erlbaum.

Byram, M. and Feng, A. (eds) (2006). *Living and Studying Abroad: Research and Practice.* Clevedon: Multilingual Matters.

Byram, M. and Zarate, G. (1997a) Defining and assessing intercultural competence: some principles and proposals for the European context. *Language Teaching* 29: 14–18.

Byram, M. and Zarate, G. (1997b) *Definitions, Objectives and Assessment of Socio-cultural Objectives.* Strasbourg: Council of Europe.

Canale, M. and Swain, M. (1980) Theoretical bases of communicative approaches to second language teaching and testing. *Applied Linguistics* 1 (1): 1–47.

Candlin, S. and Candlin, C. N. (2007) Nursing through time and space: some challenges to the construct of community of practice. In R. Ledima (ed.) *Hospital Communication: Training Complexities in Contemporary Healthcare Organizations* 198–216. London: Palgrave Macmillan.

Carr, W. and Kemmis, S. (1986) *Becoming Critical: Education, Knowledge and Action Research.* Geelong: Deakin University Press.

Carr, W. and Kemmis, S. (2005) Staying critical. *Educational Action Research* 13 (3): 347–57.

Carson, J. G. and Longhini, A. (2002) Focusing on learning styles and strategies: a diary study in an immersion setting. *Language Learning* 52: 401–38.

Chaiklin, S. (2003) The zone of proximal development in Vygotsky's analysis of learning and instruction. In A. Kozulin, B Gindis, V. S. Ageyev, and S. M. Miller (eds) *Vygotsky's Theory in Cultural Context* 39–63. Cambridge: Cambridge University Press.

Chan, A. H.-N. (2000) Consumption, popular culture, and cultural identity: Japan in post-colonial Hong Kong. *Studies in Popular Culture* 23 (1): 1–11.

Chieffo, L. and Griffiths, L. (2004) Large-scale assessment of student attitudes after a short-term study abroad program. *Frontiers: The Interdisciplinary Journal of Study Abroad* 10: 165–78.

Citron, J. (1996) *Short-term Study Abroad: Integration, Third Culture Formation and Re-entry.* Washington, DC: NAFSA: Association of International Educators.

Clément, R., Noels, K. A., and MacIntyre, P. D. (2007) Three variations of the social psychology of bilinguality: context effects in motivation, usage and identity. In A. Weatherall (ed.) *Language, Discourse, and Social Psychology* 51–77.

Basingstoke, Hampshire: Palgrave Macmillan.

Cohen, A. D., Paige, R. M., Shively, R. A., Emert, H. A., and Hoff, J. G. (2005) *Maximizing Study Abroad through Language and Culture Strategies: Research on Students, Study Abroad Program Professionals and Language Instructors.* Minneapolis, MN: Center for Advanced Research on Language Acquisition, University of Minnesota.

Coleman, J. A. (1997) State of the art article: residence abroad within language study. *Language Teaching* 30 (1): 1–20.

Coleman, J. A. (1998) Language learning and study abroad: the European perspective. *Frontiers: The Interdisciplinary Journal of Study Abroad* 4: 1–21.

Coleman, J. A. (2002) Translating research into disseminated good practice: the case of student residence abroad. In R. MacDonald and J. Wisdom (eds) *Academic and Educational Development: Research, Evaluation, and Changing Practice in Higher Education* 87–98. London: Kogan Page.

Coleman, J. A. (2006) Study abroad research: a new global overview. Paper presented at the joint conference of the American Association of Applied Linguistics/ Canadian Association of Applied Linguistics in Montreal, Canada, June 2006.

Coleman, J. A. (2007) *Study Abroad Research: Good Practices.* Clevedon: Multilingual Matters.

Collentine, J. A. and Freed, B. (2004) Learning context and its effects on second language acquisition. *Studies in Second Language Acquisition* 26: 153–71.

Collier, M. J. (1989) Cultural and intercultural communication competence: current approaches and directions for future research. *International Journal of Intercultural Relations* 13: 287–302.

Collier, M. J. (1999) Understanding cultural identities in intercultural communication: a ten-step inventory. In L. A. Samovar and R. E. Porter (eds) *Intercultural Communication* 16–33. Belmont, CA: Wadsworth.

Corder, S. and Meyerhoff, M. (2007) Communities of practice in the analysis of intercultural communication. In H. Kotthoff and H. Spencer-Oatey (eds) *Handbook of Applied Linguistics: Vol. 7 Intercultural Communication* 441–61. Berlin: Mouton de Gruyter.

Cortazzi, M. (2001) Narrative analysis in ethnography. In P. Atkinson, A. Coffey, S. Delamont, J. Lofland, and L. Lofland (eds) *Handbook of Ethnography* 384–94. Thousand Oaks, CA: SAGE.

Csizér, K. and Dörnyei, Z. (2005) The internal structure of language learning motivation and its relationship with language choice and learning effort. *The Modern Language Journal* 89 (1): 19–36.

Cushner, K. and Karim, A. U. (2004) Study abroad at the university level. In D. Landis, J. M. Bennett, and M. J. Bennett (eds) *Handbook of International Training* 289–308. Thousand Oaks, CA: SAGE.

Davis, T. M. (2003) *Atlas of Student Mobility.* New York: Institute of International Education.

Denscombe, M. (2003) *The Good Research Guide for Small-Scale Social Research Projects.* Philadelphia: Open University Press.

Denzin, N. and Lincoln, Y. (2003) *Collecting and Interpreting Qualitative Materials.* Thousand Oaks, CA: SAGE.

Dörnyei, Z. (2005) *The Psychology of the Language Learner: Individual Differences in Second Language Acquisition.* Mahwah, NJ: Lawrence Erlbaum.

Dowd, J., Zuengler, J., and Berkowitz, D. (1990) L2 social marking: research issues. *Applied Linguistic* 11: 16–29.

Dowell, M. M. and Mirsky, K. P. (2003) *Study Abroad: How to Get the Most out of your Experience.* Upper Saddle River, NJ: Pearson Education.

DuFon, M. A. and Churchill, E. (eds) (2006) *Language Learners in Study Abroad Contexts.* Clevedon: Multilingual Matters.

Dwyer, M. (2004) More is better: the impact of study abroad program duration. *Frontiers: The Interdisciplinary Journal of Study Abroad* 10: 151–63.

Eckert, P. and McConnell-Ginet, S. (1992) Think practically and look locally: language and gender as community-based practice. *Annual Review of Anthropology* 21: 461–90.

Edwards, J. (1994). *Multilingualism.* London: Routledge.

Emerson, C. (1997) *The First Hundred Years of Mikhail Bakhtin.* New York: G. K. Hall and Co.

Engeström, Y. (1999) Innovative learning in work teams: analyzing cycles of knowledge creation in practice. In Y. Engeström, R. Miettinen, and R.-L. Punamäki (eds) *Perspectives on Activity Theory* 375–404. Cambridge: Cambridge University Press.

Freed, B. (1995) *Second Language Acquisition in a Study Abroad Context.* Amsterdam: John Benjamins.

Freed, B. (1998) An overview of issues and research in language learning in a study abroad setting. *Frontiers: The International Journal of Study Abroad* 4: 1–18.

Freire, P. (1970) *Pedagogy of the Oppressed.* New York: Continuum.

Gallois, C., Ogay, T. and Giles, H. (2005) Communication accommodation theory. In W. B. Gudykunst (ed.) *Theorizing about Intercultural Communication* 121–48. Thousand Oaks, CA: SAGE.

Gardner, R. C. and Lambert, W. E. (1972) *Attitudes and motivation in second language learning.* Rowley, MA: Newbury House.

Gaw, K. F. (2000) Reverse culture shock in students returning from overseas. *International Journal of Intercultural Relations* 24 (1): 83–104.

Gibbs, G. (2002) *Qualitative Data Analysis Explorations with NVivo*. Buckingham: Open University Press.

Gibson, J. J. (1979) *The Ecological Approach to Visual Perception*. Boston: Houghton Mifflin.

Giroux, H. A. (1988) *Teachers as Intellectuals*. New York: Bergin and Garvey.

Giroux, H. A. (2002) *Border Crossings: Cultural Workers and the Politics of Education*. New York: Routledge.

Gudykunst, W. B. and Kim, Y. Y. (2003) *Communicating with Strangers: An Approach to Intercultural Communication*. New York: McGraw-Hill.

Guilherme, M. (2002) *Critical Citizens for an Intercultural World: Foreign Language Education as Cultural Politics*. Clevedon: Multilingual Matters.

Hall, B. J. (2005) *Among Cultures: The Challenge of Communication*. Belmont, CA: Thomson Wadsworth.

Hall, J. K. (2002) *Teaching and Researching Language and Culture*. London: Longman.

Hall, S. (1994) Cultural identity and diaspora. In P. Williams and L. Chrisman (eds) *Colonial Discourse and Post-Colonial Theory: A Reader* 392–403. New York: Columbia University Press.

Hall, S. (1996) Who needs identity? In S. Hall, S. and P. du Gay (eds) *Questions of Cultural Identity* 1–60. London: SAGE.

Hammersley, M. and Atkinson, P. (1995) *Ethnography: Principles in Practice*. London: Routledge.

Harker, R., Mahar, C. and Wilkes, C. (1990) *An Introduction to the Work of Pierre Bourdieu*. London: Macmillan.

Heath, S. B. and McLaughlin, M. W. (1993) Introduction. In S. B. Heath and M. W. McLaughlin (eds) *Identity and Inner-City Youth: Beyond Ethnicity and Gender* 1–12. New York: Teachers College Press, Columbia University.

Holquist, M. (2002) *Dialogism: Bakhtin and his World*. New York: Routledge.

Hornberger, N. (1994) Ethnography. *TESOL Quarterly* 28 (4): 688–90.

Huebner, T. (1998) Methodological considerations in data collection for language learning in a study abroad context. *Frontiers: The Interdisciplinary Journal of Study Abroad* 4: 1–17.

Hymes, D. (1972) On communicative competence. In J. B. Pride and J. Holmes (eds) *Sociolinguistics* 269–93. Harmondsworth: Penguin.

Ingulsrud, J. E., Kai, K., Kadowaki, S., Kurobane, S., and Shiobara, M. (2002) The assessment of cross-cultural experience: measuring awareness through critical text analysis. *International Journal of Intercultural Relations* 26: 473–91.

Isabelli-García, C. (2003) Development of oral communication skills abroad. *Frontiers: The Interdisciplinary Journal of Study Abroad* 9: 149–73.

Jackson, J. (2002a) In search of a place to call home: identities in transition in post-colonial Hong Kong. *English Today* 18 (2): 39–45.

Jackson, J. (2002b) Cultural identity and language choice: English majors in Hong Kong. In C. Lee and W. Littlewood (eds) *Culture, Communication and Language Pedagogy* 37–50. Hong Kong: Hong Kong Baptist University.

Jackson, J. (2005) Assessing intercultural learning through introspective accounts. *Frontiers: The Interdisciplinary Journal of Study Abroad* 11: 165–86.

Jackson, J. (2006a) Ethnographic preparation for short-term study and residence in the target culture. *International Journal of Intercultural Relations* 30 (1): 77–98.

Jackson, J. (2006b) Ethnographic pedagogy and evaluation in short-term study abroad. In M. Byram and A. Feng (eds) *Living and Studying Abroad: Research and Practice* 134–56. Clevedon: Multilingual Matters.

Jenkins, R. (1992) *Pierre Bourdieu.* London and New York: Routledge.

Joseph, J. E. (2004) *Language and Identity: National, Ethnic, Religious.* Basingstoke and New York: Palgrave Macmillan.

Kanno, Y. (2003) *Negotiating Bilingual and Bicultural Identities.* Mahwah, NJ: Lawrence Erlbaum.

Kanno, Y. and Norton, B. (2003) Imagined communities and educational possibilities: introduction. *Journal of Language, Identity, and Education* 2 (4): 241–49.

Kashima, E. S. and Loh, E. (2006) International students' acculturation: effects of international, conational, and local ties and need for closure. *International Journal of Intercultural Relations* 30: 471–85.

Kim, R. I. and Goldstein, S. B. (2005) Intercultural attitudes predict favorable study abroad expectations of U.S. college students. *Journal of Studies in International Education* 9 (3): 265–78.

Kim, Y. Y. (2001) *Becoming Intercultural: An Integrative Theory of Communication and Cross-cultural Adaptation.* Thousand Oaks, CA: SAGE.

Kim, Y. Y. (2002) Adapting to an unfamiliar culture: an interdisciplinary overview. In W. B. Gudykunst and B. Moody (eds) *Handbook of International and Intercultural Communication.* 2nd edn. 259–73. Thousand Oaks, CA: SAGE.

Kim, Y. Y. (2005) Adapting to a new culture: an integrative communication theory. In W. Gudykunst (ed.) *Theorizing about Intercultural Communication* 375–400. Thousand Oaks, CA: SAGE.

Kim, Y. Y. (2006) Intercultural personhood: an integration of eastern and western perspectives. In L. Samovar, R. Porter, and E. McDaniel (eds) *Intercultural Communication: A Reader.* 11th edn. 408–20. Belmont, CA: Wadsworth/Thomson Learning.

Kinginger, C. (2004) Alice doesn't live here anymore: foreign language learning and renegotiated identity. In A. Pavlenko and A. Blackledge (eds) *Negotiation of Identities in Multilingual Contexts* 219–42. Clevedon: Multilingual Matters.

Kinsella, J., Smith-Simonet, M., and Tuma, K. (2002) Orientation and reentry. In S. Spencer and K. Tuma (eds) *The Guide to Successful Short-term Programs*

Abroad 203–37. Washington, DC: NAFSA: Association of International Educators.

Knapp, M. L. (1999) Ethnographic contributions to evaluation research: the experimental schools program evaluation and some alternatives. In A. Bryman and R. Burgess (eds) *Qualitative Research. Vol. IV* 160–79. Thousand Oaks, CA: SAGE.

Kostogriz, A. (2005) Dialogical imagination of (inter)cultural spaces: rethinking the semiotic ecology of second language and literacy learning. In J. K. Hall, G. Vitanova, and L. Marchenkova (eds) *Dialogue with Bakhtin on Second and Foreign Language Learning* 189–210. Mahwah, NJ: Lawrence Erlbaum.

Kramsch, C. (1993) *Context and Culture in Language Teaching.* Oxford: Oxford University Press.

Kramsch, C. (1998) *Language and Culture.* Oxford: Oxford University Press.

Kramsch, C. (1999a) Thirdness: the intercultural stance. In T. Vestergaard (ed.) *Language, Culture, and Identity* 41–58. Aaalborg: Aalborg University Press.

Kramsch, C. (1999b) Global and local identities in the contact zone. In C. Gnutzmann (ed.), *Teaching and Learning English as a Global Language – Native and Non-native Perspectives* 131–46. Tübingen: Stauffenberg-Verlag.

Kramsch, C. (2000) Social discursive constructions of self in L2 learning. In J. P. Lantolf (ed.) *Sociocultural Theory and Second Language Learning* 133–54. Oxford: Oxford University Press.

Kress, G. (1989) *Linguistic Processes in Sociocultural Practice.* Oxford: Oxford University Press.

Landis, D., Bennett, J. M., and Bennett, M. J. (eds) (2004) *Handbook of Intercultural Training.* 2nd edn. Thousand Oaks, CA: SAGE.

Lantolf, J. P. (ed.) (2000) *Sociocultural Theory and Second Language Learning.* Oxford: Oxford University Press.

Lantolf, J. P. (2002) Sociocultural theory and second language acquisition. In R. Kaplan (ed.) *The Oxford Handbook of Applied Linguistics* 104–14. Oxford: Oxford University Press.

Lantolf, J. P. (2004) Sociocultural theory and second and foreign language learning: an overview of sociocultural theory. In K. van Esch and O. St. John (eds) *New Insights into Foreign Language Learning and Teaching* 13–34. Frankfurt am Main: Peter Lang.

Lantolf, J. P. (2005) Sociocultural and second language learning research: an exegesis. In E. Hinkel (ed.) *Handbook of Research in Second Language Teaching and Learning* 335–53. Mahwah, NJ: Lawrence Erlbaum.

Lantolf, J. P. and Thorne, S. L. (2006) *Sociocultural Theory and the Genesis of Second Language Development.* Oxford: Oxford University Press.

Lave, J. and Wenger, E. (1991) *Situated Learning: Legitimate Peripheral Participation.* Cambridge: Cambridge University Press.

Layder, D. (1997) *Modern Social Theory: Key Debates and New Directions.* London: UCL Press.

LeCompte, M. D. and Schensul, J. J. (1999) *Analyzing and Interpreting Ethnographic Data.* Walnut Creek, CA: AltaMira Press.

Li, D. C. S. (1997) Borrowed identity: signaling involvement with a Western name. *Journal of Pragmatics* 28: 489–513.

Li, D. C. S. (1998) The plight of the purist. In M. Pennington (ed.) *Language in Hong Kong at Century's End* 161–89. Hong Kong: Hong Kong University Press.

LoCastro, V. (2003) *An Introduction to Pragmatics: Social Action for Language Teachers.* Ann Arbor, MI: The University of Michigan Press.

Luke, K.-K. (1998) Why two languages might be better than one: motivations of language mixing in Hong Kong. In M. Pennington (ed.) *Language in Hong Kong at Century's End* 145–59. Hong Kong: Hong Kong University Press.

Lustig, M. W. and Koester, J. (2006) *Intercultural Competence: Interpersonal Communication across Cultures.* 5th edn. New York: Longman.

MacIntyre, P. D., Baker, S. C., Clément, R., and Donovan, L. A. (2003) Talking in order to learn: willingness to communicate and intensive language programs. *Canadian Modern Language Review* 59 (4): 537–64.

MacIntyre, P. D., Clément, R., Dörnyei, Z., and Noels, K. A. (1998) Conceptualizing willingness to communicate in a L2: a situated model of confidence and affiliation. *Modern Language Journal* 82: 545–62.

Marchenkova, L. (2005) Language, culture, and self: the Bakhtin-Vygotsky encounter. In J. K. Hall, G. Vitanova, and L. Marchenkova (eds) *Dialogue with Bakhtin on Second and Foreign Language Learning* 171–88. Mahwah, NJ: Lawrence.

Martin, J. N. and Harrell, T. (2004) Intercultural reentry of students and professionals. In D. Landis, J. M. Bennett, and M. J. Bennett (eds) *Handbook of Intercultural Training* 309–36. Thousand Oaks, CA: SAGE.

Martin-Jones, M. and Heller, M. (1996) Introduction to the special issues on education in multilingual settings: discourse, identities, and power, *Linguistics and Education* 8: 127–37.

McKay, S. L. (2005) Sociolinguistics and second language learning. In E. Hinkel (ed.) *Handbook of Research in Second Language Teaching and Learning* 281–99. Mahwah, NJ: Lawrence Erlbaum.

McNamara, T. (1997) Theorizing social identity: what do we mean by social identity? Competing frameworks, competing discourses. *TESOL Quarterly* 31 (3): 561–76.

Medina-López-Portillo, A. (2004) Intercultural learning assessment: the link between program duration and the development of intercultural sensitivity. *Frontiers: The Interdisciplinary Journal of Study Abroad* 10: 179–99.

Meinhof, U. H. and Galasiński, D. (2005) *The Language of Belonging*. Basingstoke: Palgrave Macmillan.

Mendelson, V. G. (2004) 'Hindsight is 20/20': student perceptions of language learning and the study abroad experience. *Frontiers: The Interdisciplinary Journal of Study Abroad* 10: 43–63.

Meyers-Scotton, C. (1993) *Social Motivation for Codeswtiching*. Oxford: Clarendon Press.

Meyers-Scotton, C. (2006) *Multiple Voices: An Introduction to Bilingualism*. Malden, MA: Blackwell.

Mitchell, R. and Myles, F. (2004) *Second Language Learning Theories*. London: Hodder Arnold.

Murphy-Lejeune, E. (2002) *Student Mobility and Narrative in Europe: The New Strangers*. Routledge: London.

Murphy-Lejeune, E. (2003) An experience of interculturality: student travellers abroad. In G. Alred, M. Byram, and M. Fleming (eds) *Intercultural Experience and Education* 101–13. Clevedon: Multilingual Matters.

Norton, B. (2000) *Identity and Language Learning: Gender, Ethnicity and Educational Change*. Harlow: Pearson Education.

Norton, B. and Toohey, K. (2001) Changing perspectives on good language learners. *TESOL Quarterly* 35 (2): 309–22.

Norton, B. and Toohey, K. (2002) Identity and language learning. In R. Kaplan (ed.) *The Oxford Handbook of Applied Linguistics* 115–23. Oxford: Oxford University Press.

Norton, B. and Toohey, K. (eds) (2004) *Critical Pedagogies and Language Learning*. Cambridge: Cambridge University Press.

Norton Pierce, B. (1995) Social identity, investment, and language learning. *TESOL Quarterly* 29 (1): 9–31.

Ochs, E. (ed.) (1991) Socialization through language and interaction: a theoretical introduction. *Issues in Applied Linguistics* 2 (2): 143–48.

Ochs, E. (1996) Linguistic resources for socializing humanity. In J. J. Gumperz and S. C. Levinson (eds) *Rethinking Linguistic Relativity* 407–37. Cambridge: Cambridge University Press.

Ochs, E. (2001) Constructing social identity: a language socialization perspective. *Research on Language and Social Interaction* 26: 287–306.

Ochs, E. and Capps, L. (1996) Narrating the self. *Annual Review of Anthropology* 25: 19–43.

OECD (Organisation for Economic Cooperation and Development) (2006) *Education at a Glance*. Paris: OECD Centre for Educational Research and Innovation. (Retrieved on 25 April 2008 from http://www.oecd.org/dataoecd /4/55/39313286.pdf)

Oguri, M. and Gudykunst, W. B. (2002) The influence of self construals and communication styles on sojourners' psychological and sociocultural adjustment. *International Journal of Intercultural Relations* 26: 577–93.

Paige, R. M. (1993) On the nature of intercultural experiences and intercultural education. In R. M. Paige (ed.) *Education for the Intercultural Experience* 1–19. Yarmouth, ME: Intercultural Press.

Paige, R. M., Cohen, A. D., Kappler, B., Chi, J. C., and Lassegard, J. P. (2003) *Maximizing Study Abroad: A Program Professionals' Guide to Strategies for Language and Culture Learning and Use.* Minneapolis, MN: Center for Advanced Research on Language Acquisition, University of Minnesota.

Paige, R. M., Cohen, A. D., Kappler, B., Chi, J. C., and Lassegard, J. P. (2006) *Maximizing Study Abroad: A Students' Guide to Strategies for Language and Culture Learning and Use.* Minneapolis, MN: Center for Advanced Research on Language Acquisition, University of Minnesota.

Parker, G. and Rouxeville, A. (eds) (1995) *'The Year Abroad': Preparation, Monitoring, Evaluation.* London: CILT.

Pavlenko, A. and Blackledge, A. (eds) (2004) *Negotiation of Identities in Multilingual Contexts.* Clevedon: Multilingual Matters.

Pavlenko, A. and Lantolf, J. P. (2000) Second language learning as participation and the (re)construction of selves. In J. Lantolf (ed.) *Sociocultural Theory and Second Language Learning* 155–77. Oxford: Oxford University Press.

Pavlenko, A. and Piller, I. (2001) New directions in the study of multilingualism, second language learning, and gender. In A. Pavlenko, A. Blackledge, I. Piller, and M. Teutsch-Dwyer (eds) *Multilingualism, Second Language Learning, and Gender* 17–52. Berlin: Mouton deGruyter.

Pellegrino, V. A. (1998) Student perspectives on language learning in a study abroad context. *Frontiers: The Interdisciplinary Journal of Study Abroad* 4: 91–120.

Pellegrino, V. A. (2005) *Study Abroad and Second Language Use: Constructing the Self.* Cambridge: Cambridge University Press.

Pennycook, A. (2001) *Critical Applied Linguistics.* Mahwah, NJ: Lawrence Erlbaum.

Rampton, B. (1995) *Crossing: Language and Ethnicity among Adolescents.* New York: Longman.

Reed-Danahay, D. (2005) *Locating Bourdieu.* Bloomington: Indiana University Press.

Reissman, C. K. (2002a) Analysis of personal narratives. In J. Gubrium and J. Holstein (eds) *Handbook of Interview Research: Context and Method* 695–710. Thousand Oaks, CA: SAGE.

Reissman, C. K. (2002b). Narrative analysis. In M. Huberman and M. Miles (eds) *The Qualitative Researcher's Companion* 217–270. Thousand Oaks, CA: SAGE.

Ricento, T. (2005) Considerations of identity in L2 learning. In E. Hinkel (ed.) *Handbook of Research in Second Language Teaching and Learning* 895–910.

Mahwah, NJ: Lawrence Erlbaum.

Richards, L. (2002) *NVivo: Using NVivo in Qualitative Research*. Melbourne: QSR International.

Roberts, C. (1997) The year abroad as an ethnographic experience. In M. Byram (ed.) *Face to Face: Learning Language-and-Culture through Visits and Exchanges* 62–76. London: CILT.

Roberts, C. (2003) Ethnography and cultural practice: ways of learning during residence abroad. In G. Alred, M. Byram, and M. Fleming (eds) *Intercultural Experience and Education* 114–30. Clevedon: Multilingual Matters.

Roberts, C., Byram, M., Barro, A., Jordan, S., and Street, B. V. (2001) *Language Learners as Ethnographers*. Clevedon: Multilingual Matters.

Ryan, S. (2006) Language learning motivation within the context of globalization: an L2 self within an imagined global community. *Critical Inquiry in Language Studies: An International Journal* 3 (1): 23–45.

Sampson, E. E. (1993) *Celebrating the Other: A Dialogic Account of Human Nature*. Boulder, CO: Westview Press.

Schensul, J. J., LeCompte, M. D., Hess, G. A., Nastasi, B. K., Berg, M. J., Williamson, L., Brecher, J., and Glasser, R. (1999) *Using Ethnographic Data: Interventions, Public Programming, and Public Policy*. Walnut Creek, CA: AltaMira Press.

Scollon, R. (2001) *Mediated Discourse: The Nexus of Practice*. London: Routledge.

Scollon, R. and Wong-Scollon, S. (2001) *Intercultural Communication: A Discourse Approach*. Oxford: Blackwell.

Sealey, A. and Carter, B. (2004) *Applied Linguistics as Social Science*. London: Continuum.

Segalowitz, N., Freed, B., Collentine, J., Lafford, B., Lazar, N., and Díaz-Campos, M. (2004) A comparison of Spanish second language acquisition in two different learning contexts: study abroad and the domestic classroom. *Frontiers: The Interdisciplinary Journal of Study Abroad* 10: 1–18.

Shusterman, R. (1998) Understanding the self's others. In C. Gupta and D. P. Chattopadhyaya (eds) *Cultural Otherness and Beyond* 107–14. Boston: Brill.

Smith, P. B., Bond, M. H., and Kağitçibaşi, Ç. (2006) *Understanding Social Psychology across Cultures: Living and Working a Changing World*. Thousand Oaks, CA: SAGE.

Soja, E. W. (1996) *Thirdspace: Journeys to Los Angeles and Other Real-and-Imagined Places*. Oxford: Blackwell.

Spencer-Oatey, H. (ed.) (2000) *Culturally Speaking: Managing Rapport in Talk across Cultures*. London: Continuum.

Stryker, S. (1994) Identity theory: its development, research base, and prospects. *Studies in Symbolic Interaction* 16: 9–20.

Sussman, N. M. (2002) Testing the cultural identity model of the cultural transition cycle: sojourners return home. *International Journal of Intercultural Relations* 26: 391–408.

Tajfel, H. (1981) *Human Groups and Social Categories.* Cambridge: Cambridge University Press.

Tajfel, H. (1982) Social psychology of intergroup relations. *Annual Review of Psychology* 33: 1–39.

Tajfel, H. and Turner, J. C. (1986) The social identity theory of intergroup behavior. In S. Worchel and W. Austin (eds) *Psychology of Intergroup Relations* 7–24. Chicago: Nelson-Hall.

Tan, P. K. W. (2001) Englishised names? An analysis of naming patterns among ethnic-Chinese Singaporeans. *English Today* 17 (1): 15 53.

Tan, P. K. W. (2004) Evolving naming patterns: anthropynomics within a theory of the dynamics of non-Anglo Englishes 23 (3): 367–84.

Thebodo, S. W. and Marx, L. E. (2005) Predeparture orientation and reentry programming. In J. L. Brockington, W. W. Hoffa, and P. C. Martin (eds) *NAFSA's Guide to Education Abroad for Advisors and Administrators* 293–312. Washington, DC: Association of International Educators.

Thomas, J. (1995). *Meaning in Interaction: An Introduction to Pragmatics.* London: Longman.

Thompson, J. B. (1991) Editor's introduction. In J. B. Thompson (ed.) *Language and Symbolic Power (Pierre Bourdieu)* 1–31. Cambridge, MA: Harvard University Press.

Ting-Toomey, S. (1993) Communicative resourcefulness: an identity negotiation perspective. In R. L. Wiseman and J. Koester (eds) *Intercultural Communication Competence* 72–111. Newbury Park, CA: Sage.

Ting-Toomey, S. (1999) *Communicating across Cultures.* New York: Guilford Press.

Ting-Toomey, S. (2005) Identity negotiation theory: crossing cultural boundaries. In W. B. Gudykunst (ed.) *Theorizing about Intercultural Communication* 211–34. Thousand Oaks, CA: SAGE.

Ting-Toomey, S. and Chung, L. C. (2005) *Understanding Intercultural Communication.* Los Angeles, CA: Roxbury Publishing Co.

Trubshaw, B. (2001) The metaphors and rituals of place and time – an introduction to liminality. Retrieved on 15 November 2006 from htto://www.indigogroup.co.uk/foamycustard/fc009.htm.

Turner, V. (1969) *The Ritual Process: Structure and Anti-Structure.* Chicago: Aldine.

van Ek, J. A. (1986) *Objectives for Foreign Language Learning.* Oxford: Pergamon.

van Lier, L. (1990) Ethnography, bandaid, bandwagon, or contraband? In C. Brumfit and R. Mitchell (eds) *Research in the Language Classroom (ELT Document 133)* 33–53. London: Modern English Publications in association with the British Council.

van Lier, L. (2000) From input to affordance: social-interactive learning from an ecological perspective. In J. P. Lantolf (ed.) *Sociocultural Theory and Second Language Learning* 245–59. Oxford: Oxford University Press.

van Lier, L. (2004) *The Ecology and Semiotics of Language Learning: A Sociocultural Perspective.* Boston: Kluwer Academic Publishers.

Vande Berg, M. (2004) Second language acquisition abroad. *Frontiers: The Interdisciplinary Journal of Study Abroad* 10: xii–xxii.

Vann, R. (1999) An empirical perspective on practice: operationalising Bourdieu's notion of linguistic habitus. In P. Lang (ed.) *Pierre Bourdieu: Language, Culture, and Education* 73–83. Berne: Peter Lang.

Vitanova, G. (2005) Authoring the self in a non-native language: a dialogic approach to agency and subjectivity. In J. K. Hall, G. Vitanova, and L. Marchenkova (eds) *Dialogue with Bakhtin on Second and Foreign Language Learning: New Perspectives* 149–69. Mahwah, NJ: Lawrence Erlbaum.

Vygotsky, L. S. (1978). Interaction between learning and development (M. Lopez-Morillas, trans.) In M. Cole, V. John-Steiner, S. Scribner, and E. Souberman (eds) *Mind in Society: The Development of Higher Psychological Processes* 79–91. Cambridge, MA: Harvard University Press.

Vygotsky, L. S. (1986) *Thought and Language.* Cambridge, MA: MIT Press.

Vygotsky, L. S. (1987) Thinking and speech (N. Minick, trans.). In R. W. Rieber and A. S. Carton (eds) *The Collected Works of L. S. Vygotsky: Vol. 1. Problems of General Psychology* 39–285. New York: Plenum Press (originally published 1934).

Ward, C., Bochner, S. and Furnham, A. (2001) *The Psychology of Culture Shock.* London: Routledge.

Weatherall, A., Watson, B. M., and Gallois, C. (eds) (2007) *Language, Discourse and Social Psychology.* London: Palgrave Macmillan.

Webb, J., Schirato, T., and Danaher, G. (2002) *Understanding Bourdieu.* London: SAGE.

Weedon, C. (1987) *Feminist Practice and Poststructuralist Theory.* Cambridge, MA: Blackwell.

Wenger, E. (1998) *Communities of Practice: Learning, Meaning, and Identity.* Cambridge: Cambridge University Press.

Wenger, E. (2005) *Communities of Practice: A Brief introduction.* Retrieved on 24 October from http://www.ewenger.com/theory/communities_of_practice_intro.html.

Wilson, J. (2001) Who needs social theory anyway? In N. Coupland, S. Sarangi, and C. N. Candlin (eds) *Sociolinguistics and Social Theory* 334–49. Kuala Lumpur: Pearson Ed.

Wiseman, R. L. (2002) Intercultural communication competence. In W. B. Gudykunst and B. Moody (eds) *Handbook of International and Intercultural*

Communication. 2nd edn. 207–24. Thousand Oaks, CA: SAGE.

Yang, R. P.-J., Noels, K. A., and Saumure, K. D. (2006) Multiple routes to cross-cultural adaptation for international students: mapping the paths between self-construals, English language confidence, and adjustment. *International Journal of Intercultural Relations* 30: 487–506.

Yoshikawa, M. (1987) The double-swing model of intercultural communication between the east and the west. In D. Lawrence Kincaid (ed.) *Communication Theory: Eastern and Western Perspectives* 319–29. San Diego: Academic Press.

Zuengler, J. (1988) Identity markers and L2 pronunciation. *Studies in Second Language Acquisition* 10: 33–49.

Zuengler, J. (1989) Identity and IL development and use. *Applied Linguistics* 10: 80–96.

Index

CPSIA information can be obtained
at www.ICGtesting.com
Printed in the USA
LVHW080728041218
598989LV00007B/88/P

9 781845 531423